"Jim Reese's new book is an illuminating social justice memoir focused on crime and the system built to contain it. Via deep reporting and his lived experience, Reese unravels a system shaped by fear, anger, retribution, and the irrational, with prospects for reform dependent on our better angels—empathy and education—and the struggle to confront the worst of our human nature."

—**Bill Conroy**, investigative journalist and author of *Dispatches from the House of Death*

"Jim Reese's *Coming to a Neighborhood near You* is an insightful and interesting memoir of his personal journey observing our criminal justice system. . . . [It will be] beneficial for those interested in criminal justice reform."

—**Richard R. Bennett**, emeritus professor of justice, Department of Justice, Law, and Criminology at American University

"Jim Reese has been touched by violent crime, has worked in various prisons to help inmates become better writers, and has spent a great deal of time thinking about what it means to be a criminal. What is the nature of evil? What is the nature of addiction? Although crime stories are a popular form of entertainment, there isn't much thoughtful engagement about crime and punishment in America. In *Coming to a Neighborhood near You* Reese challenges us to reconsider how we view crime. Well-paced, superbly researched, and full of excellent observations, this is a vital and necessary book—one that will spark new conversations for us all."

—**Patrick Hicks**, author of *The Commandant of Lubizec* and *Across the Lake*

PRAISE FOR *BONE CHALK* BY JIM REESE

"Reese's central concern is nothing less than the nature of evil and how best to deal with it. His schoolboy experience of citywide panic in Omaha during a wave of killings, and a few years later the murder of a friend, leave no room for naiveté or a Hollywood-style glamorization of crime. . . . Reese also knows that the difference between a man on the street and a man in a cell is most often no more than a bad decision. . . . This effort to change the lives of these men charges Reese's teaching. And it will charge readers of this book."

—*Cleveland Review of Books*

"From essay to essay, Reese bemusedly works to sort it out. . . . The narrative's true centerpiece is an essay reconciling his childhood fears growing up in Omaha with his hesitance to teach writing in prisons, something he's done for a dozen years regardless. There, he masterfully weaves his personal history with observations of the prison system both intimately (in the prisoners' writings, their tattoos, the strict regulations) and broadly (the troubled prison system, race and class divides). . . . The variety is the appeal, and Reese is skilled in many registers. . . . An eclectic, appealingly no-nonsense set of appreciations of the heartland."

—*Kirkus Reviews*

"The publication of this collection announces Jim Reese as a major writer on the Midwest in all its shades—lively and bright, somber and muted, violent and dark. Readers of all backgrounds will come away from his writings with a deeper understanding of the Midwest and of the human spirit itself."

—*Omaha World-Herald*

"This author has the ability to morph from *Green Acres* scenarios into situations more suitable to *Breaking Bad* without missing a beat. The reader will be transported from Fordyce, Nebraska, to San Quentin Prison with the turn of a page. . . . Reese finds universal truths in his work. Readers will discover that love of family, decency, honesty, and a sense of humor are not limited to any particular region of the country."

—*Lincoln Journal Star*

"A kind of operetta in prose, and it will stick with me for a good long while. I recommend it."

—**Ted Kooser**, winner of the Pulitzer Prize, thirteenth poet laureate of the United States

"Jim Reese's *Bone Chalk* is like a strong shot of rye, a piercing look from a stranger, or a stray bullet in the dark. There is a startling honesty that slams you against the wall by the throat and holds you there until you see the truth, a unique perspective into the world of true crime from a gifted writer."

—**Craig Johnson**, author of the Walt Longmire novels, basis for the Netflix drama *Longmire*

"In *Bone Chalk*, Reese transports his readers to the Great Plains with the narrative ease of someone chatting with a friend on the front porch. Sometimes tender and sometimes gripping, this memoir remains tethered to the soil and to the people with such a strong sense of place that the reader feels as though they had been there, walking beside the author, the whole time."

—**Allen Eskens**, best-selling author of *The Life We Bury* and *Nothing More Dangerous*

"*Bone Chalk* is the best kind of memoir, an expansive and bracing tour of a region and people both eminently familiar yet particular enough to feel like another universe. Fast, funny, dark, and surprisingly moving. Jim Reese is a brilliant tour guide of the plains."

—**Stephen Markley**, author of *Ohio*

COMING TO A NEIGHBORHOOD NEAR YOU

COMING TO A NEIGHBORHOOD NEAR YOU

The Repercussions of Crime and Punishment

JIM REESE

Potomac Books
An imprint of the University of Nebraska Press

Ted Kooser, "Splitting an Order," *Splitting an Order* (University of Nebraska Press, 2008). Used with permission.

Jim Reese, "Never Talk to Strangers," *Bone Chalk* (Stephen F. Austen State University Press, 2020). Used with permission.

Jim Reese, "Redefining Gonzo: Tattoos, Prisons, and My Friend Charles Bowden," *Journal of the Southwest* 65, no. 1 (Spring 2023): 107–47. Permission for reprint granted courtesy of the Charles Clyde Bowden Literary Trust.

∞

Library of Congress Control Number: 2025007073

Designed and set in Adobe Kis by L. Welch.

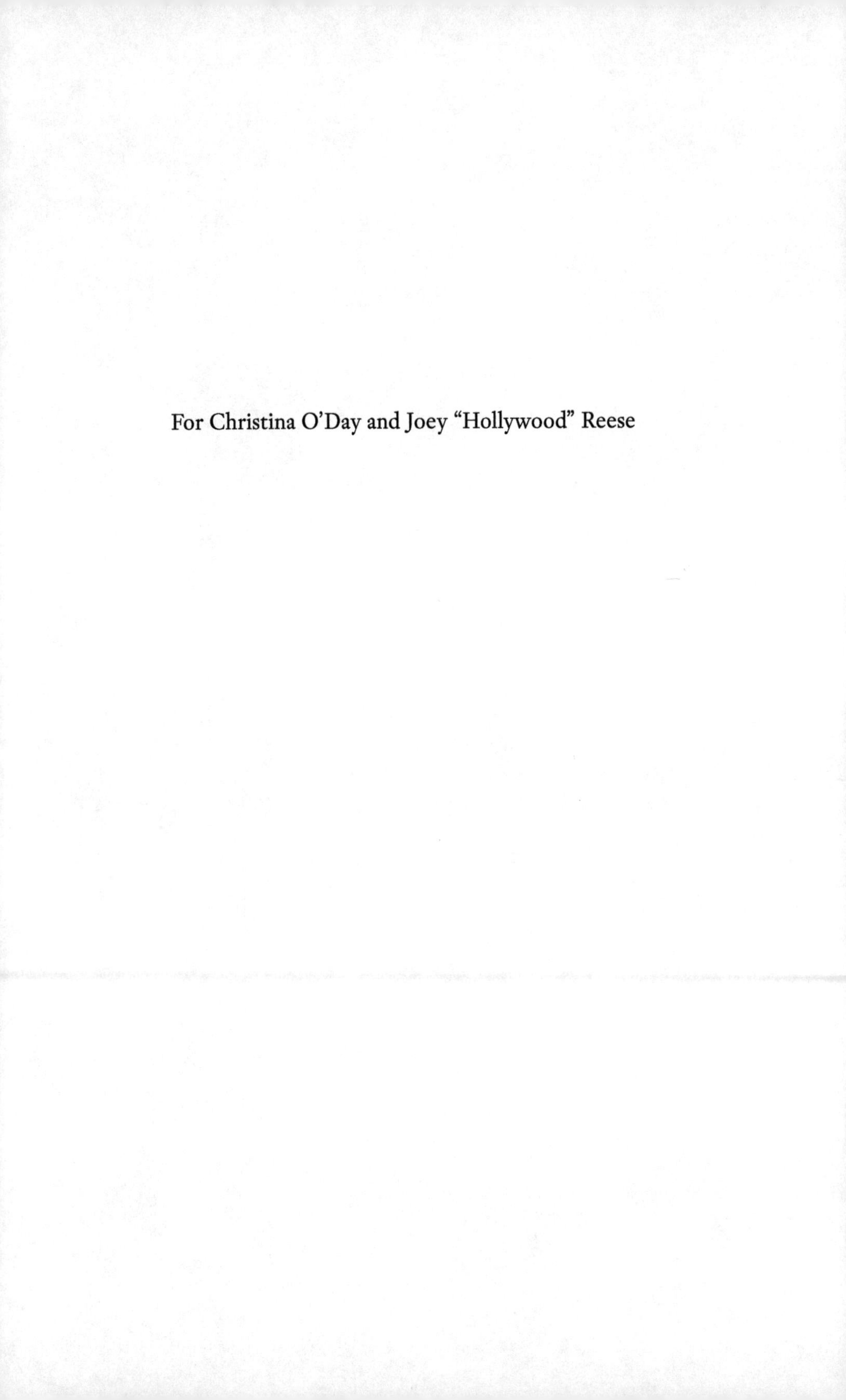

For Christina O'Day and Joey "Hollywood" Reese

These men are coming to a neighborhood near you. Do you want them educated or not?

WARDEN JORDAN R. HOLLINGSWORTH

You got to be right with yourself before you can be right with anybody else.

AUGUST WILSON

Contents

Author's Note

I tell stories. I may sound like a broken record when I construct them—especially to the people closest to me. I'm always formulating, listening for reactions, learning, exploring more ideas, talking over myself and others. I'm guilty and blame it all on my enthusiasm for living and what I call the "only child syndrome." I've always been afraid that I or the world will combust at any moment—that's why I talk. And, I suspect, why I write. With that said, my voice is not your voice. My recollections result from the way my memories jive in my head; they may not be exactly the way they replay in yours. Most importantly, the things that moved me to spend years researching and writing are about discovery, not display.

This is a true crime book. The information I gathered is from the most credible sources at my disposal. Facts about Christina O'Day's murder were collected from the Supreme Court of Nebraska and the Justia US Law website (https://law.justia.com/cases/nebraska/supreme-court/1992/283-1.html). For the purposes of this book, I have not used either of the killers' names in the text or in quoted material.

When referencing this crime, case, trial, and retrial, I relied on public record and current and archived articles from the *Omaha World-Herald*, *Lincoln Journal Star*, and Omaha news outlets. For the other sections of the book, I interviewed friends, scholars, editors, investigative journalists, members of professional law enforcement, advocates, criminalists, criminologists, and federal and state correctional staff. I also used the following sources: the Federal Bureau of Prisons (www.bop.gov/about/statistics/), the Prison Policy Initiative (prisonpolicy.org), and the *San Quentin News* (sanquentinnews.com).

COMING TO A NEIGHBORHOOD NEAR YOU

1
The Shadows We Carry

When I was eleven years old, I began to talk to a shadow—a presence. You might say I was talking to myself, but actually I was speaking subconsciously to what was haunting me.

American serial killer John Joubert kidnapped and killed two kids in the part of Omaha where I lived. Joubert volunteered as a Boy Scout troop leader and used his position to lure and torture young boys. I was the same age as the victims.

How could I see him so clearly with my eyes closed so tightly? To sleep, most nights I curled up in a fetal position and stared at my bedroom window shades.

John Joubert was the first real-life monster I feared.

Six years later, a friend of mine in high school, Christina O'Day, was raped and murdered by a classmate who had helped me with my math homework in middle school. Her killer became the second monster. When terror like this cuts so close to home, you become branded. Maybe *fear* and *monster* aren't the right words. Let me try to explain.

Thirty years later, I am up after most people go to bed. I am nocturnal. I am hypervigilant. All the fears I never knew how to speak about or articulate back then have manifested in behaviors that other people might find neurotic, or at least strange. I am very aware of evil. I check around corners and underneath beds, double-check bolt locks and alarms. I circle the interior of the house and check on the girls. It has become a natural act, a routine. There's not a three-hour window that goes by when I am not up, listening. I am ready for any intruder.

Terror is ingrained in me. Very early on, I came to understand my reality as full of potential threat, people as possibly menacing, myself and all of us as vulnerable. Heinous crime was not a nightly television show—it was as real as dusk. It lingered in sharp shadows, under neighborhood street lights, between dark suburban houses, in police sketches on milk cartons, in slow vans and cars with tinted windows, on missing persons posters tacked to public corkboards.

Am I really safe? Will I ever be? Will I ever stop fearing? Is there a killer inside me? *The killer in me is the killer in you.* My terror points both inward and outward. It isn't just the fear of others but the fear of myself. If I think of my loved ones and what I'd do if something happened to them, it scares me. I fear violent instincts—vengeance, retribution.

Crimes have altered the way I think and react to the world. When I was young, I felt like an outsider, a stranger, especially as an only child. I was someone who was never afraid to ask why. I am someone who has needed to ask how on earth some people do what they do. When I think of my parents' beige split-level house tucked among other almost identical homes and the murders that occurred in our city during my adolescence, I realize that I'll never stop inquiring.

As an undergraduate, I began my journey as a criminal justice major, but I changed my major because I couldn't stomach measuring blood splatter on walls. By happenstance, after I finished a PhD, and because of my editing and publishing credentials, I was asked to teach in a federal prison. My lingering curiosity about why criminals do what they do was no different from the curiosity that millions of other people possess. This paradox—that I feared criminals and the ways they shaped me and yet wanted to help them—doesn't escape me. What an ironic situation I found myself in. I soon embraced working with men, and later women, who had broken laws. I am a witness to their lives, to their humanity and inhumanity—their intelligence, ignorance, innocence, and manipulation.

Five years into the prison gig, feelings from the past resurfaced. Subconsciously, they were ever-present—brewing—most likely because I was around so many men who were under correctional supervision. My hyperawareness of crime and all of its repercussions was broadening. Inevitably, those not-so-distant memories of my adolescence began rearing their ugly heads.

In 2012 the U.S. Supreme Court ruled that juvenile killers can't receive life sentences without parole. I knew then that a retrial of Christina's case would happen. Christina's murder sprang unwanted back into my life, and I was no longer able to pretend that it was in the past and I had "gotten over it." The retrial came at a time when I checked my ego at the prison gate, when I wasn't bragging about working in prisons anymore, when I had begun questioning criminality and its aftermath. Through my work in prisons, I had discovered how big a monster our criminal justice system is, how many millions of people are incarcerated, and how many millions more are back out in society but under correctional supervision.

I am a secondary victim of a crime, but a victim nonetheless. There's a grief I will do my best to explain to you. A feeling of helplessness. The replaying—pressing the rewind button over and over—of a guilt I don't believe I should have to bear but can't get rid of.

Fyodor Dostoyevsky writes in *The Brothers Karamazov*, "Because everyone is guilty for everyone else. For all the 'wee ones,' because there are little children and big children. All people are 'wee ones.' And I'll go for all of them, because there must be someone who will go for all of them."

What's so bizarre is that I feel guilty for feeling grief about Christina's murder. I never labeled myself as a victim or felt victimized, because I wasn't the one who was murdered. I didn't feel like I had a right to these kinds of emotions. Confusion, sure. Anger, of course. But was it my fault? I never talked to any school counselors. I was sixteen. Talking to a counselor wasn't cool, especially in the late eighties. We did not talk about trauma the way we do now. A man, even a confused teenager, knew enough to suck it up and be quiet. If you talked to anyone, it was to yourself. And because of the way we handle crime in our society—the way we manage crime through "systems"—these issues never get dealt with the way they should.

X, although he is behind bars, has the strange luxury of never having to face his own guilt unless he truly wants to.[1] He can dance around it—deny it, then later admit he was there and "participated" in it. He's still trying to do easy time, while we, his multiple victims, do hard time as we try to wrap our heads around it, even though we shouldn't have to. Like most of Christina's friends, I wanted revenge.

For many years I ran from my feelings—pushed them away. I think about the teachers, the counselors, my fellow students, Christina's friends, and, of course, her family. I think of Beth Ann, the little girl whom Christina was babysitting and who lived through this horrific crime and still relives it more than she ever should have to. Beth Ann has suffered more than anyone.

We are all secondary victims. When a crime like Christina's murder occurs, there's a fear and paranoia—an awakening to atrocity among everyone whose life touched the victim's in any way. The stark white lightning of reality. This happened. And thirty years later, we are still reliving it. Somehow X has managed to get us—both primary and secondary victims—to take on his guilt, and yet consciously we all know, we even tell ourselves, that he and his accomplice are the only ones who could have prevented it. But it doesn't help to tell ourselves that we can't change anything. He has managed to occupy our minds and our lives. He has managed, through the very act of his heinous crimes, to transfer his guilt, distress, and undigested life materials to us.

||||

Where I come from—urban middle America, with apartment buildings, rows of split-level houses, manicured lawns, and shopping malls—"never talk to strangers" were four words that were drilled into us constantly because a lot of us were latchkey kids. We liked to believe that the neighbors looked out for us.

The most exciting feeling I had back then—after moving to Omaha at age seven in 1979—was waiting for my mom and dad to get home from work. I'd look out the first-floor, sliding-glass patio door, anticipating their arrival, and as soon as I saw my father's VW Bug or my mom's Datsun, I'd wave and hightail it to the middle of our apartment complex courtyard, where we played touch football almost every day. At around five o'clock we'd congregate, and someone's father would play quarterback for both teams. I got the nickname Jimmy Jo Jive. I have always been fast. I caught a lot of passes. I scored a lot of apartment complex touchdowns.

My parents had rules, and I followed them. There was absolutely no playing in the apartment parking lots. I was to stay away from the parked cars, the dumpsters, and the garages. I was told repeatedly never to cut through the parking lot on my bike to get somewhere faster. I had to ride through the complex on the designated sidewalks. One time some bullies in the complex took my bike and hid it behind a dumpster, knowing full well I couldn't venture out to get it. After they quit taunting me, got bored, and left, I ran to retrieve it. Of course my father saw me and grounded me. I tried to talk back, to tell my side of the story, but he would have none of it. I've never forgotten it. And now I understand his fears—how they constrain and constrict—for myself.

Around that time I fell at the bus stop and an icicle pierced my knee. The school bus driver hollered, "Either board or I'm leaving." He left and blood oozed as I limped back to the strip mall next to Country Club Village, the apartments where we lived. A guy came out of an office to help, tried without luck to reach my folks at work, and then took me to school. Mr. Shiver, my teacher, practically yanked my arm out of the socket for catching a ride from a complete stranger. "Someone you didn't even goddamn know!" That's when I knew my world had changed.

In 1981 we moved to the outskirts of Millard, a suburb of Omaha. Our backyard was at the end of the neighborhood, with cornfields, I-80, and dirt roads behind us. Giles Road, Ralston, Bellevue in one direction, Gretna and Elkhorn in the other. From our back porch the world appeared to go on for miles. Instead of apartment complex football, we had backyard ballgames. My friends and I rode our bikes on dirt trails in the fields and practiced wheelies on the streets. I still had to be close enough to hear my father's high-pitched whistle when the street lights came on. If I didn't, I was in trouble.

Safety didn't seem to be a concern. If a stranger appeared on our street, he was usually selling something. No one made it from Harrison Street all the way up Highland Boulevard to Chandler and pretended to be lost. We were where the sidewalk ended. Aside from trucker horns on I-80 behind us and the occasional kid on a YZ-80 burning tracks in dirt fields, there was a real sense of peace and normalcy. People turned on their porch lights at night. There were summer block parties. This was middle-class life; it was picturesque. My parents were climbing the corporate ladder of success.

Then, when I was eleven years old, the shadow of John Joubert was cast across my bright and luxurious life. Katherine Ramsland describes Joubert this way:

> During the 1980s, twenty-year-old John Joubert was convicted of the murders of two boys in Nebraska. He'd gotten his start in Maine at the age of thirteen when he'd stab other children with pencils, razors, and other implements and found that he enjoyed hurting others. He tried strangling a boy and then when he was 18, he killed an eleven-year-old. Then he fled the town. From a broken home, Joubert had been an angry child, and he discovered both solace and power in striking out at others and getting away with it. In Nebraska, he looked for victims while volunteering in a Boy Scout troop. For him, the torture and murder of young boys was a way to relieve sexual tension. But as with all predators, the experience did not ultimately satisfy, so he would soon plan another.[2]

I've been talking to you since I was eleven years old, Joubert. You got into my head then, and you never left.

None of us will forget the police crime sketch in the newspapers, the missing children's pictures on milk cartons, the gruesome cartoon profile of a man with his blue skullcap tight around his head, his flannel shirt. It was in our neck of the city that he committed murder, and we wanted our city back. One of his twelve-year-old victims was found in his undershorts, stabbed and with his throat slashed, on Giles Road, which ran behind my house. Court records would later report the gruesome details found on the body of one of the victims: "The full length and breadth of his chest and abdomen was covered with what looked like a representation of a large plant, including the stem and seven leaves. This figure appeared to have been rather carefully and deliberately carved into the skin and flesh with a sharp knife."[3]

Joubert was stationed at Offutt Air Force Base and worked as a radar technician. Suspicious activity was happening on Giles Road. The mutilated bodies of Danny Joe Eberle and Christopher Walden were found in Sarpy County. In the article "Inside the Chilling Crimes of John Joubert, the Eagle Scout Who Became a Serial Killer," author Marco Margaritoff writes, "When asked if he would kill again, Joubert stated quite plainly that he was grateful to have been caught as he undoubtedly would have. 'That's my big worry,' said Joubert. 'It's scaring me quite a bit, yes.' Charged with two counts of first-degree murder on Jan. 12, 1984, he pleaded not guilty before changing his mind."[4]

It didn't matter what our parents said to calm us—in spite of their consolations, we could sense their hate and their fear that this could happen in the Midwest, in the heartland. Malicious activity wasn't supposed to happen here. So we all reinvented worry and never again would talk to strangers, because every one of them was him. We looked over our shoulders and learned to run the second an unfamiliar car stopped and someone inside asked for directions. It was the paranoia of the eighties in Omaha.

These were the warzones of my home, which made us aware of our surroundings. And everyone began living faster and meaner.

This was when you, John, were living with your nightmares, perhaps calculating rapes, cuttings, and killings. Ashes, ashes, John. No. No. No.

1990: The Murder of Christina O'Day

Many of my fellow students participated in sports at Millard South High School. All my life I seemed to flock to roller rinks, asphalt, skateboard parks, and dance floors. Most of the time music was played loudly. Rhythm was key. Moves—god, we prayed to land them. And music was so much a part of us. I was writing my own songs, and on new music nights at The Swing (our favorite club), my band would play on the same floor we danced on. The Loopholes. Leafy Green Things. 13 Nightmares. Mousetrap. Cellophane Ceiling. Social Distortion. All bands who left a little bit of themselves reverberating off those cinderblock basement walls.

I think it's vital to understand the importance of dancing at this age. Really dancing. It seemed to come at a time when music and self-expression served not only as noise and a form of individualism but also as our pulse—the flow of our blue-black veins pumping blood. It was essential. It was addictive. It was ours.

Christina O'Day and I knew each other in high school. I can't pinpoint exactly when we became friends. I talked with her in the halls like I did with most friends. She was a year older than me, vibrant and mature. She never made me feel like an underclassman or shunned me for whatever clique I was trying to fit into. There were more than eighteen hundred students in our school. The Swing, ten miles away in the middle of Omaha, was far enough from our home turf that it felt exotic. Those of us who weren't afraid to dance ventured there. There were times when Christina and I drove there together. And I can tell you, it felt nice walking in together—paying our cover, going our separate ways, moving around with strangers, and then seeing one another on the dance floor. We looked out for each other as we met new people, discovered curiosities.

Christina had been babysitting overnight. Two perpetrators, one whom she had briefly dated, cut the phone line, broke in through a basement window, tied her up, slit her wrists, took turns raping her, and then left her to die. After it happened, after X and the other perpetrator's initial questioning by police and confession, X disappeared.

In our high school hallways, I remember some of the friends X used to hang with saying they knew where he was hiding. The gossip. The uneducated, immature comments from some people in our school were beyond disturbing. We wanted answers—revenge. We were tired of the bullies—the gangs of assholes who seemed to have no remorse or empathy for others. We listened closely. But the last thing some of us did was talk. Who could we tell our concerns to? We would never snitch, even though it was our friend who was murdered. These were the complications and the paranoia of being a teenager before social media, and this was how gossip—not Snapchat or Instagram—could make a heinous crime more evil. And what proof did we have? As teenagers we knew X had lurked around school, stalking her, and we had our suspicions immediately after her murder. For more than two weeks, X's headshot was constantly on rerun on the news—the high school and the whole city of Omaha were in an uproar. Can you imagine that now? For over two weeks he was missing—and he wasn't far away at all.

I can see the fluorescent lights overhead in the hallway. "Did you hear?"

"She's dead!"

"Blood on the ceiling. Blood everywhere."

"How would you know?"

"The neighbors said they heard the cops talking."

"You know he did it. You know he did it. They are looking for him."

"Orange body bag."

Just walking. Listening. The long cinder-block hallways. The bright lights overhead. Thinking, *What do we do?* Passing friends of his talking in corners, by lockers. Passing our friends in tears. Teachers trying to console students. Walls being erected everywhere. Invisible shields. Very quickly it seemed like we knew who the guilty parties were, and no one was saying anything about it. No one dared to. X was on the run.

The child Christina was babysitting was still alive twenty-six years later when the whole episode was replayed in the news. Joe Chiodo of WOWT wrote:

> X is one of two men who beat, raped and murdered Christina O'Day as she was babysitting. At the age of 8, Beth Ann listened as the brutal crime unfolded.
>
> Twenty-six years after the murder, a Supreme Court decision means one of O'Day's killers, then 16-year-old X, is in line for re-sentencing. That's based on new research showing at that age, a portion of a juvenile's brain is not fully developed.
>
> WOWT 6 News spoke exclusively with Christina's mother, Sheila O'Day, following the sentencing. "It's been hard to come to terms over the years—the anger, frustration, sorrow—but it's time to move on. I feel justice has been served," she said.
>
> "I wish I knew her. It's like your child left 26 years ago and you never saw them again. I believe she's at peace, but I still don't know her. I wish I could, I wish I could," Sheila O'Day told WOWT.

Beth Ann, now 34, returned from Georgia to attend the sentencing. She said it's a second chance at justice for O'Day.[5]

||||

The last time we were together, Christina, you were driving us to go dance. We weren't dating. You were a friend. At that age, for a guy to have a girl as a friend was unusual. But our common love of music and dance allowed a friendship to blossom. A rite of passage. I joke with you, say I know how much you like my company at the club because I am experienced, because I gave break dancing lessons in fifth grade in my garage for fifty cents. Hip Hop Don't Stop! I know I can dance. You laugh and smile, with those dimples and the way you look out the corner of your eye at me as you drive. We dance because we can—we aren't afraid to. Every ounce of me aches to be Kevin Bacon, and I dream of Hollywood endings.

We are driving on 108th Street. This I am certain about. I think. I question it all because in my memory we are in a maroon two-door hatchback, but on the news, in the footage of your car being pulled out of the river, the car is green. How much of our memory is certain?

I'm looking at you on our way to The Swing. We're wearing matching Z Cavaricci pants. Our shirts button to the neck. Our hair is long. As seriously as some people take football or A's on tests, we look forward to Friday and Saturday for our release. We are not afraid to let people see us move and shake. I am a permanent fixture at The Swing. I have held on to a skater flop. The band I play rhythm guitar and sing out of key in will soon headline a show there. It'll be a week after Social Distortion, the biggest band to play The Swing during our time, leaves a mess of smashed Jack Daniels bottles and porn magazines in its wake.

The Swing is a large cement room under a rent-to-own business off Blondo in Omaha. I know the doorman. The soundman will play my requests. It's where I get my first feel for marketing and showmanship. It's where I move from basement to performance. Maybe that's part of why I hold on to the memory. The last time we spent at least thirty minutes together was on our way there. I'm sure when we arrived we paid our cover and went our separate ways. I'm sure we laughed and danced and caught each other's smiles—the coolness of youth, trying hard to find identities within a large group of strangers. Was it the lust of others? Was it that we wanted to be loved for the first time? Or was it that we could just be ourselves?

New Order's "Blue Monday," The Cure's "Just Like Heaven," Dead or Alive's "You Spin Me Round (Like a Record)," OMD, *Kim Wilde's "Kids in America," M's "Pop Muzik"—the beginning of club techno's bombastic urge, while the metal and bad hair still lurked in our closets and grunge was on our horizon—all of this would consume my life, but not yours.*

This memory. It's dusk, early evening. Why are we leaving so early to go out? Answer: Appetite. Curfews. The urgency of being free from parental constraint, rules, real jobs that were coming at us whether we wanted them or not, our heavy and gorgeous lives. The sun is setting. I look over at you with what—admiration? Infatuation? I'm sure I'm feeling a bit stronger, more confident. I am sitting shotgun in a car with a beautiful person, not in the backseat on the hump. Perfume in the air. Too much Polo cologne. I am not drooling over you like I would some girls. I'm not trying to pretend to be anyone but myself—a helpless romantic, a ball of poetic nerves and pretty hair.

We are friends. Maybe it's the first time I realize a boy and girl can be friends. I don't believe you talk of your soon-to-be murderer as your ex-boyfriend, or even mention his name. I think I'd remember that. And if you had dated him briefly and moved on, there really would be no point in bringing him up. These high school flings. Brief snapshots of people we date. I guess we learn a little bit about ourselves and what we want in life from all our relationships. How to improve our flaws. How to know what to avoid.

What are the facts of your life?

I know very little outside this dance club and our casual conversations in school hallways. I've seen you getting in his low-riding Camaro. X stalking the parking lot after he dropped out. The two of you in the front seats—all wrong. The bullies, the cliques, the groups, the "gangs," the skaters and haters, the boxers, the drama club, the team, the . . .

We dance.

The way you smile. What is the word I'm looking for? Good? Your smile makes me feel good. Authentic. You are a year older and you make me feel a year older, too. Am I sure I'm not attracted to you? Or do I just know that friends are all we will ever be?

We sing along to our favorite songs.

For years I wondered if I had the authority to write this story. How someone takes your life—how we miss all the things we knew of you—and more. The future for so many that could have been different if this heinous act had never happened. This is a story about how your murder changed us. How we would never feel safe again. Your presence and eternal absence.

When I talk to people about you—my students in my Crime, Literature, and Film classes, my critical writing classes, my prison classes—I always say I am trying to give voice for you. This story—our story—needs to be talked about. How else do we understand what to do with evil in our lives? Crime is not an individual's problem—victims are multifarious. This story is not about display. It is about discovery. My desperate attempt to try to remember everything I can and tell it straight.

I can't remember what we said to each other. We are cruising. You driving, me surely trying to sing the song playing on the mix tape I brought along. Maybe it was one of our favorites at the time—maybe The Cure's "Just Like Heaven":

> *You*
> *Strange as angels . . .*
> *You're just like a dream*

Me looking over at you—a profile of your beautiful face, that smile, your right dimple, the sun in my eyes, a glow around your silhouette, your bear-claw bangs—the last spotlight.

What are we talking about?

You are smiling. You are singing, too. What do we say to each other when the song is over?

You are smiling.

Always smiling.

I look out the passenger window, turn back, and we are both gone.

No longer teenagers on our way.

This is where the memory stops.

||||

A year after Christina's murder, I found myself walking through my first metal detector. After a pat-down by police, two friends and I found our seats on hard benches in the courtroom. We were there to bail out a friend who had gotten drunk and beat up an innocent bystander—someone who probably looked at him wrong. This was a guy my friends really respected—and at the time, I guess I did, too. I went along with them. We listened to the same music. Told the same jokes. Wore identical brand-name clothing. Fought with each other and then made up because we had to hold onto this group—it was all we had.

Our friend standing in front of the judge was older. He had a fake ID and bought the beer. He had dropped out of school, but he had gone back, then quit going again and worked full-time in a fruit warehouse. When I think back on my friendships as a teenager, most of them were fleeting. And yet here we were—bailing him out, hoping it wouldn't be us who got busted the next time.

I once took his Ford Fairlane 500 without his permission, while he was making out with a girl. My best friend Todd and I drove that car fast through his neighborhood—or as fast as it would go. I whipped around a corner, and the lack of power steering along with my chicken-wing arms presented Todd and me with a dilemma. I drove the car up into the backyard of a stranger's house and it stalled. Unbeknownst to me, there was a choke—or some gadget I didn't know how to operate. By the time Todd could start the engine from the passenger seat and I could give it gas, the owner of the house had opened the driver's side door and yanked me out of the car. Todd stayed in the car and kept driving.

After a few minutes of pleading with the guy and lying every which way to Tuesday, I could hear the Ford Fairlane approaching. The homeowner looked startled. My "friend," the owner of the Fairlane, was now driving, with Todd still in the car. He was a big guy. He looked a lot older than his age. The car's shocks slumped on the side he drove on. He slammed on the brakes and demanded I get in the car—said my "brother" Todd had told him all about the accident. The homeowner didn't want to let go of my arm—until my large friend approached and reached for me. Then there was no tug of war. We got in the car as the homeowner stood there and watched. Inside the car, I remember my friend saying, "Reese, I'm gonna kick your ass!" And we all laughed. Because we could.

Throughout high school I found myself with these friends. For the most part, we skirted trouble, getting away with teenage mischief. Only once did the police bring me home for drinking and running from them. Actually, though, I wasn't drinking that particular night and I didn't run, but the others did and I was there. All the warning signs were posted that night—and so many others. I should have been arrested on multiple occasions. I'm not proud of that. But at the same time, I suspect most of my friends were breaking laws. As a senior, I saw less and less of my friend. He was working full-time, delivering fruits and vegetables around the city, and never came back to school. It was the choice he made. I sometimes wonder what he is doing now.

In the courtroom I felt ashamed when I saw him handcuffed, shirt torn from his Friday night brawl. I was not surprised, though. I was disgusted that I was forking over money for bond. But I was still in high school, I was ignorant, and I didn't think for myself. I was realizing, coming to understand, that the people I knew could be criminals.

He stood silently as they read his charge. Twice he looked over at us like a pathetic dog. They took him back into a jail cell, and the judge continued to read off the names of the accused. We couldn't leave until he was done. A sixty-year-old man hobbling on a cane was next. The front of his shirt was brown with dried blood. He was accused of child molestation. I wanted to throw up, but I couldn't, and I couldn't leave.

||||

It's over twenty years later and I'm in my daughter's room. I have learned to think for myself, to do unto others as I'd want done to me. I'll never forget that courtroom scene, seeing that man with his stained and ripped T-shirt. As I tuck my daughter into bed, I wonder if monsters with canes and bloody shirts will interrupt what should be her precious thoughts of this world we live in. I cannot follow her everywhere. I can only teach her what to look out for and tell her over and over again never to trust strangers.

Hit and Run

I converse with the past. I run with memories—flashbacks. I name them. I catch myself talking to myself. Loss, grief, and violence will make a person do that. I ask them to bear with me. I sometimes refer to myself by my own name—it's supposed to help—it's called *illeism*. Citing a 2017 article in the journal *Nature*, writer Samantha Enslen notes that "the scientists theorized that 'third-person self-talk leads people to think about the self similar to how they think about others,'" which "'provides them with the psychological distance needed to facilitate self control.'"[6]

Sometimes I ask the memories to speak back. Sometimes I ask them to show their faces. Sometimes I beg them to leave me the fuck alone.

||||

And you, Sixtieth Street Stranger, are one of them. This is what I remember, and I wish your memory would go away.

Walking down Sixtieth Street with Chad, smoking Camels, going nowhere. I remember you passing us on the sidewalk. We both did a double-take; you in your high heels and dress. Then you were darting across the street toward Elmwood Park between dimly lit street lights—your shadow, running; the click-click-click of your heels. Then—screech! Brakes. Thud. Bottle breaking. Tires spinning. Exhaust, smoke in the dark street. You lying motionless on the street, and me hearing the tires squealing away in the distance, growing fainter.

I ran to the first house I spotted with lights on. I frantically relayed the message, asked them to call the cops. "She's right there in the street!" I screamed and pointed in your direction. Chad and me again standing over you, checking your pulse, staring at your face—beautiful in the white street light. Sirens blaring.

I remember saying, "Maybe she's drunk. Why'd she run out like that?" Neighbors coming out of their houses, crowding the sidewalk. Cops showing up. I pointed out the broken wine bottle. The police officer kneeling down to inspect the bag the bottle was in. "It's corked. She never opened it. I believe she had plans for this evening."

||||

That police officer noticed a small detail that none of us caught. The unopened wine bottle didn't solve the hit and run, but it did suggest that the woman hadn't been drinking, as we suspected. These details added to the story. In spite of the shock of realizing how easily someone could just hit another person and keep driving, the blood on the concrete, and the loss of life, I was hooked. This was another reason I wanted to solve crimes. I had to figure out why criminals do what they do. Here again, after such a short time, was another dead woman. How could people disregard other human beings so easily? This one was accidental, of course. Christina's murder was premeditated. But in both instances the perpetrators refused to take responsibility for their actions—they showed no form of repentance.

Becoming a Criminal Justice Major

A year later, in 1991, when I went to college, I became a criminal justice major. My roommate was one, too. He and I had gone to high school together. Coincidence? In 1992 the psychological thriller *The Silence of the Lambs* would win the "Big Five" Academy Awards for best picture, best director, best writing, best actor, and best actress. The movie is a fictional portrayal of an amalgamation of serial killers. My friends and I have often quoted memorable lines from the flick: "It rubs the lotion on its skin. It does this whenever it's told." Or "Put the fucking dog in the basket!" It became so much a part of American pop culture at the time that the characters' monologues, as gruesome as they were, became jokes. We needed the laughter to compensate for the horrendous one-liners. It eased the fear that lingered long after the credits rolled.

We watched *Silence of the Lambs* time and time again and never forgot it. The criminals I imagined were always comparable to Hannibal Lecter or to the delinquent who raped and killed Christina, my friend, who I would never go dancing with and could never call on for advice again. Jodi Foster reminded me of Christina. They even looked similar. Jodi Foster was trying to save women from being mutilated and murdered. I knew it was a movie, but I was also naïve. The facts of my life and the fictions of film wove themselves into an internal dialogue, and the chatter seldom turned off.

No other movie has come as close to instilling the thrill, curiosity, and sheer fear that *Silence of the Lambs* stirred in me. It's a classic. The book, written by Thomas Harris, constructed the most frightening character I've ever read—an amalgamation of terror. "Thomas Harris did not base Hannibal Lecter on any one person," wrote Christopher Turner in "20 Things You Didn't Know about the Silence of the Lambs." "He was actually a general composite of all of the evil that he saw while doing research. 'There is no one, thank goodness, like him,' said FBI profiler John Douglas, the inspiration for Jack Crawford."[7]

Aside from the fact that it scares the bejesus out of us, what is it that made *Silence of the Lambs* such an iconic film, one that changed pop culture? In an article in *Vanity Fair*, Tracy Moore addresses the story's themes of class and the pursuit of the American dream, and its feminist merits. It was used as a recruitment tool to entice women to join the FBI, and some scenes were actually filmed on 547 acres within the Marine Corps base in Quantico, Virginia. Moore writes:

> Todd Boyd, a professor at USC's School of Cinematic Arts, teaches *Silence* as an exemplary retelling of the role that class plays in defining the American dream. Working-class Clarice Starling (Foster) has aspirations to do big things at the FBI and move to the middle class. Lecter (Hopkins) is the upper echelon, with his refined manners. And Jame Gumb, a.k.a. Buffalo Bill (Ted Levine) is a stand-in for white trash—living in a filthy dungeon where he skins women. (His kitchen was styled after the one owned by Ed Gein, a murderer and body snatcher who dug women up from their graves and skinned them.)
>
> The film consciously drapes itself in red, white, and blue—from the flag that covers the car in Lecter's storage space to the banners used to string up a murdered police officer. "The point was to make it look like these were all safe images that *weren't* so safe," Zea says. "This was about a guy who took the wrong path, and so all the things that represent security, and liberty, and the pursuit of happiness—here they had been aborted or twisted."[8]

My college friends, roommate, and I watched the movie multiple times. We studied it. I knew I had a special interest in it, perhaps because it might help me understand our childhood losses and fears and sense of vulnerability. My roommate, however, was stronger than I was—physically and maybe mentally too—and his disposition didn't allow for much internal inquiry. While I could talk this movie to death, he preferred to leave and go hang out with his girlfriend. We were getting older, growing away from high school, the close proximity of our neighborhoods, and our sense of home. Perhaps he was able to withstand Christina's death better than I was. At that age, we weren't able to recognize our differences. We would grow apart and speak very little of the crimes that occurred in our shared past. But they were present with us. We suppressed and were unable to articulate our feelings. My roommate would go on to become a police officer in another state, and that film lingered in our psyches.

Silence was released right after the infamous serial killers of the '70s and '80s and right before several horrific mass shootings and celebrity deaths that we still talk about today: Dahmer, Escobar, Simpson, Bowles, Bundy, Gacy, Ramirez, Selena, McVeigh, Shakur, Ramsey, Versace, Columbine. Moore continues:

> *The Silence of the Lambs* is the story of a woman succeeding in a man's world—of having to fend off advances, mask her emotions, placate her superiors, and minimize her femininity and sexuality to rise. Though the camera itself never objectifies Starling, it relentlessly tracks the leering head turns of the many men who do, so we feel her objectification to a claustrophobic degree. Needless to say, we root for Starling to succeed, but something curious happens when it comes to the murderers in her life: We applaud when Buffalo Bill is killed but laugh when Lecter escapes and is off to have a friend for dinner. They're both equally remorseless, vicious killers. "So why is it funny when one person does it, and when another does it, it's horrifying?" Boyd asks.[9]

Of course, it's a class issue. We excuse the upper class and fear and look down on the lower class. Money equates with power, and unfortunately, an accumulation of wealth allows some people to turn a blind eye to what's right and wrong. But I didn't know that then. When the movie came out, I was going to college and believed chasing paper was not only a rite of passage but the accomplishment of my goals and dreams. At nineteen years old, I was delusional enough to think that I was destined to be a rock star—that I was rising through bands, music, and showmanship—above my station, my neighborhood—into wealth, popularity, and superiority. That was just built into my person. It's what I truly believed. I had no idea how truly competitive the music business was, nor that wealth didn't necessarily mean money. Wealth might mean having the opportunity to play music as a career if you practiced hard enough.

Silence of the Lambs gets under our skin subconsciously and plays on what's still wrong with our culture. I'd like to believe that in the last thirty years we've come a long way in protecting women's rights—in treating women as equals—but then I remember our president, whom millions of women voted to elect and who was recorded saying, "I'm automatically attracted to beautiful—I just start kissing them. It's like a magnet. Just kiss. I don't even wait. And when you're a star, they let you do it. You can do anything. Grab 'em by the pussy."[10]

Some of our leaders still stand behind this man. And you have to ask yourself why. At the end of the day, this president's election and his abhorrent behavior—his role in the premeditated insurrection on the U.S. Capitol—are proof that with money, lies and deceit become normalized.

Corrupt politics is a class thing that's been eating the belly of our country for far too long. Money means power; the middle man—the lower-class citizen—*does* finish last; and crime, literature, and film are entertainment. We root for Lecter because he has credentials. Somewhere in his dreadful persona is a man with a brain and an indulgent brand that enables him to get away with murder. The U.S. flag and American ideals are present in the film—and corruption is, too. Class ideologies and prejudices prevail. Evil exists then and now because we allow it to.

Have you ever asked yourself why corporate America isn't held accountable? Why corrupt systems and organizations continue to run—business as usual? Why Purdue Pharma, Enron, Volkswagen, Wells Fargo, Boeing, and others are allowed to steal billions, with very few held accountable for their organizations' actions? Capitalism. Big Money, Inc. And that ugly, complicated truth seems to have come out of hiding and reared its cold and calculated head even more in recent years.

Another hard truth is that we root for Hannibal because this is a movie—it's make-believe—and hidden deep within ourselves is a fascination with corruption and chaos. We don't want to live it, but we like to watch it unfold. Yet our safe places are unsafe. We think corruption is make-believe because it's a movie, but it's real life.

When I told one of my daughters, then seventeen years old, that I was screening *Inside the Labyrinth: The Making of "The Silence of the Lambs"* for my Crime, Literature, and Film class, she replied, a little too excitedly, "You get to watch *that*?"

"I'm the professor. I get to teach it."

"Creepy," she said. And I wondered when and where she had watched it without me.

|||

I was a criminal justice major for only a year. I once had to report to an 8:00 a.m. criminalistics class taught by a retired cop who would lock the door if you were one minute late. I also had to measure blood splatter that semester, and that's when I decided that detective work wasn't what I'd imagined it to be. But I would dearly miss my Introduction to Criminal Justice class. At each class our professor would read aloud from an encyclopedia of cases—usually the most bizarre and shocking ones he could find. I'll never shake one case about a man who was caught inside (or underneath) a campground bathroom. He made a habit of crawling into the toilet and standing in the sewage, waiting for women to use the facilities. In 1987 the *Santa Maria Times* published this report:

MAN CAUGHT PEEKING IN OUTHOUSE

MORRO BAY (AP)—A man sitting on crates beneath a women's outhouse, waist-deep in muck and dressed in plastic, was arrested by rangers at Montana de Oro State Park, authorities said. "We've heard of a lot of yucky things like snakes and spiders being in there, but we've never heard of a human being down there," said state parks spokeswoman Susan Rocha. The man was wearing protective plastic clothing and surgical gloves as he sat on crates in the waste at the bottom of the outhouse at Spooner's Cove, 170 miles northwest of Los Angeles, authorities said. "This guy was like, waist deep," said Miss

> Rocha. Rangers hosed off the man and turned him over to the San Luis Obispo County Sheriff's Department. Donald H. Baker, of Santa Barbara, was booked at the county jail for investigation of loitering. Investigators said Baker had apparently been in the outhouse since before daybreak Sunday and was planning on staying all day. A man waiting outside the outhouse for his wife spotted Baker through a crack in the wall and called rangers, Miss Rocha said.[11]

When I changed my major to interdisciplinary studies and then finally to English and journalism, I still could never get enough of true crime. I tried to come to terms with Christina's murder and the influx of serial killers in the '90s. My knowledge of the country I lived in was coming into bloom during the Rodney King police beating and the infamous O. J. Simpson trial. My advisor taught a class about O.J. during the summer of 1995, and in it we learned how the trial split the country along racial lines.

We interrupt the NBA finals to bring you this LIVE special report . . . *Low speed pursuit—O.J.—white bronco . . . bloody glove—Brentwood—dream team—Marcia Clark—Christopher Darden—Mark Fuhrman—free O.J.—Nicole Brown Simpson—Ron Goldman—history of abuse—fry O.J.* Ninety-five million viewers glued to televisions across the United States as the bartender yells, "O.J. and anything for a buck!"

Most white Americans believed O.J. was guilty and most Black Americans thought he was innocent. O.J. had made it; he had captured the American dream. He had accumulated wealth and status, had moved above his station. He had left his neighborhood and gained wealth, popularity, and superiority. He seemed to have risen above racial inequality to achieve status and fame. Ask yourself, what have we learned from O. J. Simpson? Wealth and fame can distort our perception of what's right and wrong, and this demonstrates how a criminal like O.J. can be set free. O. J. Simpson had always cared about O. J. Simpson. Perhaps the case is more about class than race.

In the *New York Times Magazine* article "Why 'Transcending Race' Is a Lie," Greg Howard explains O.J.'s influence on our society in his discussion of the documentary *O. J.: Made in America*:

One of the most alarming anecdotes in the documentary comes from Robert Lipsyte, a former sportswriter for *The New York Times*. "He was telling me a story about being at a teammate's wedding with his wife and sitting at a table of mostly, as he said it, mostly Negroes," Lipsyte recounts. "And he overheard a white woman sitting at the next table saying, 'Look, there's O. J. sitting with all those niggers.' And I remember in my naïveté saying, 'That must have been terrible for you.' And he said, 'No, it was great. Don't you understand? She knew that I wasn't black. She saw me as O. J.'"

In a time of black revolution, Simpson was a counterrevolutionary; as blacks embraced black power and self-love, Simpson surrounded himself with white people. There were plenty of great black football players around his time, but Simpson was special: Not only did he play better than most, he also used his wit and charm in the service of making white people feel safe. In a period of nationwide change and unrest, he was "one of the good ones."

He played the role happily, and it brought him a level of fame as unprecedented as his eventual fall. "O. J.: Made in America" makes it very plain that Simpson almost certainly committed the murders and that he almost certainly was going to be acquitted from the beginning. The Los Angeles Police Department's collection of evidence from the crime scene was botched, as was the prosecution itself. The trial was held just two years after Rodney King's beating by L.A.P.D. officers, their acquittals and the ensuing riots. The two cases further divided the city along racial lines, laying bare the way that blacks and whites could occupy the same space yet live in separate worlds. When Simpson left the courthouse a free man, blacks across the country rejoiced, his white friends and fawners abandoned him and the universe around him crumbled.[12]

Flash Forward

Even after I'd completed three academic degrees, my fascination with crime remained. I had finished my requirements for a doctorate in English, published a book of poetry with a reputable press, and dabbled in editing and publishing. With my track record, I had the qualifications needed to work in a federal prison. Was this happenstance? A weird coincidence? The world moving full circle back to my original idea of pursuing criminal justice?

After I earned my doctorate from the University of Nebraska–Lincoln in 2006, I had searched for a job as an assistant professor near either my wife's parents or my own. My parents had left Omaha when my father took a job near Kansas City, Missouri. My wife's parents and some of her family farmed in Hartington, Nebraska. Our daughter Willow was just two years old, and we thought it would be great to live close to one of Willow's sets of grandparents. As luck would have it, I found a job at Mount Marty University, a small private university a half-hour north of Hartington, in Yankton, South Dakota. It had been nine years since we had been undergraduates in small-town America, but it seemed right—and the more hands on deck to help us with Willow, the better. We were young parents, and there just weren't and still aren't a lot of assistant professor jobs in creative writing anywhere in the nation—so this was a blessing. We wanted to raise our daughter near family, and all of ours was within a six-hour radius. It would be a culture change for me. Hartington, Nebraska, had a population of about 1,460 people—fewer than the number of students at my high school—but we were throwing the anchor in.

If you take U.S. 81 north of Hartington, go just over the Missouri River bridge, and merge onto Broadway, this is Yankton, South Dakota, an industrial river city—dirt's grime and chime. This was my half-hour commute to work. Census signs in town say the population is fifteen thousand, but if you factor in the Lewis and Clark Lake area, I'd say the population is around twenty thousand. Some reports state that during the summer months, more than a million people visit the area to fish, boat, and vacation at Lewis and Clark Lake.

Mount Marty University enrolls eleven hundred students and sits on the bluffs of the Missouri River. The eighty-acre campus includes the Benedictine Sisters of Sacred Heart Monastery, built by the Benedictine Sisters during the Great Depression. Yankton is also home to the Federal Prison Camp, Yankton (FPC Yankton), which is located right in the middle of town. It may be the only federal prison in the country with a public street that runs through it. There are no barbed wire fences—rather, a three-foot, cast-iron picket fence. House values went up when the Federal Bureau of Prisons took over the former Yankton College in 1988. In 2009 *Forbes* magazine ranked FPC Yankton as one of the top ten "cushiest" prisons in the nation.

||||

I was in my office—a brand new assistant professor in my second year, blazing new trails at the college—and the SOE (supervisor of education) from FPC Yankton was standing in the doorway explaining a new writing program, an interagency agreement with the National Endowment for the Arts. One of the main objectives of the new program was to produce a book of creative writing and art from inmates. I had been publishing books at small presses since I was an undergraduate. I knew the ins and outs of publishing. More importantly, I knew how to teach complete strangers how to write. I had degrees on the wall that said so.

Soon after an initial meeting with the SOE and an extensive federal background check, I was at the federal prison getting my fingerprints stamped on official documents and a photo taken for my contractor's badge. I was given a drug urinalysis and I was trained on procedure and protocol.

This was a minimum security prison. "No guards are present with me in the classroom? What if a student is disruptive?" I asked. "What if I think my life is in danger?"

"We don't call them guards; we refer to them as correctional officers."

Whatever, I thought. When I told friends I was doing this work, I was gratified by their reactions. It had made me feel exotic, adventurous. It felt cool to tell everyone I knew that I was working in a prison, but honestly, I was a little scared. I had a very rigid idea of who criminals were. I assumed some were just like X, who murdered Christina. I didn't understand the minimum security environment. I hadn't tried to comprehend the word *rehabilitation*, and I had no idea about the huge monster our criminal justice system had become. I was told there was a phone in the hall where I could call for assistance and that I could ask any of the staff on the floor for help. Right away I was informed that the incarcerated men were mostly nonviolent offenders and white-collar criminals, or that they had trickled down through the system to this minimum security unit because of good time (good behavior). No molesters. No murderers. No monsters. "Not that I know of," said the SOE.

Some big cities have billboards with a picture of a desolate highway and a slogan that reads something like "Do the Crime, End Up in South Dakota." Greyhound doesn't even run to Yankton, South Dakota, and the nearest urban areas are over an hour away. Students in my prison class have intentionally broken rules so that they would be transferred to a larger, higher-security prison to be closer to family.

I would often bring in reading material for the men. One day I brought in a month-old magazine to donate to the prison library. I showed it to the SOE, who approved it and filled out the necessary paperwork for the donation. I took the magazine to the library, got it stamped EDUCATION, but forgot one last step. A student in class said to me, "You might want to black out your address. Most of us are good people here, but you just never know." I was intimidated at first by the guy's comment, like anyone would be. He must have sensed my insecurity. He was trying to get inside my head. It worked.

Media accounts often portray our criminal justice system in a negative light, conveying sensationalized propaganda to instill fear and promote a tough-on-crime attitude. At first I was afraid to use the same drinking fountain as the men in the prison. Paranoia. Did I think I would catch a disease? I was afraid to bend over at the drinking fountain, to take my eyes off anyone who might be behind me. I didn't have any idea, really, what world I was walking into. One time a local asked me, "Why in the hell would you want to help prisoners? Seems like a waste of *my* tax money. Lock 'em up, forget about it." I didn't have a comeback. I knew, like any schoolteacher knows, the importance of education, but I had no idea how to effectively articulate what I was doing. I didn't have all my facts back then. I didn't know how to stand my ground.

I learned very quickly how many men were locked up for drugs—for addictions they couldn't shake. A lot of the men I worked with had made bad decisions, but they weren't murderers. What I never expected was that working with prisoners would bring me back to the emotions

I had suppressed for so many years—that sense of vulnerability, those conversations in my head that I had tried desperately to quiet. During my early years of working in prisons, I kept having this nagging feeling. I wondered if X, the guy who killed Christina, was ever getting out. The question would arise in my mind from time to time—as if through my work in prisons I had subliminally, or by some weird osmosis, become more in touch with criminals and should therefore have a better handle on my feelings toward X and his accomplice. I knew it didn't make much sense. It's like saying that because I know one person, I know them all. On one occasion I called a Nebraska prison where X was being held to ask about his prospects for parole. I learned that his prospects hadn't changed. He would be in prison for life, just like the person who committed these atrocious acts with him. I was relieved.

||||

When I first brought home the news that I'd be working in a prison, my wife was concerned. The pay was good. I reassured her that everything was going to be fine. Our contractor training through the National Endowment for the Arts included working with the William James Association Prison Arts Project, through which we visited the California state prisons and studied their arts in corrections programs. As I filled out waivers about my safety in preparation for my visit to San Quentin —"The CDCR [California Department of Corrections and Rehabilitation] will not negotiate for you in a hostage situation"— I was scared. But I was already invested.

As part of the training, I spent time working with murderers at San Quentin. After visiting one of the nation's most notorious prisons, as well as nearby New Folsom prison, I started to question whether the men I was meeting and working with should be in prison for the rest of their lives. They hadn't all committed calculated crimes like premeditated rape and murder. Some of them had been completely out of their minds. At least one of them had been in the wrong place at the wrong time and was an accomplice to murder.

||||

Critic David Doody reviewed some of my first poems in the *American Poetry Journal*, poems about training at San Quentin and my childhood. He wrote: "Such experiences make it hard to know why someone would place himself among the people who have been convicted of crimes like the one that took place in Reese's childhood neighborhood and have left him with a gnawing fear for his daughters' well-being. . . . Caught in the enigma of how humans can both love and hurt, Reese is torn between his constant drive to protect his daughters ('You want to ride your bike around the block-/by yourself') and his desire to help the sort of people whose actions have made the world a dangerous place in which his daughters need protecting."[13]

When I read the review, I realized that when strangers, rather than loved ones, start to question our intentions and well-being, we listen more. Why is that? This is a question I often ask inmates but seldom ask myself. In addition to receiving thoughtful reviews of my work, I have also had the great fortune to work with some gifted writers. Author Kent Meyers, for example, points out some things that are very important to me: "In entering the prison, you enter the most alien of all possible cultures and communities. And what do you find? People—people pretty much like yourself or your students, or even maybe your daughters. But—and this is so great as an idea if not as a fact of human nature—what you also discover is that the people outside the prison *could* be inside, and some of them maybe should be, or at least that the prisoners who seem so alien turn out to have come from families and communities and schools just like those you knew and know."[14]

After getting men in my classes to come to terms with their feelings and write from their hidden caves, after going back to San Quentin for five years and becoming a talking head for prison reform, I had a lot more facts—I could see that the war on drugs was a big mistake. I could rattle off statistics to anyone who questioned why education behind bars is so crucial to those who are imprisoned and to our society at large. I could see that even the most heinous of people I was working with—those who had committed murder—were people with feelings. I was tearing down walls—including a lot of my own preconceived notions about criminals—but I couldn't shake my anger at X. And there wasn't an ounce of me that wanted to. I wanted him to remain behind bars forever. We as humans are indecisive and unpredictable. We are of two minds, and when we are afraid or uncertain, we throw up walls. Is life merely a riddle of walls—prisons of our own making?

Flash Forward—2016—It's in the News Again

In 2012 the U.S. Supreme Court ruled that life without parole sentences for youthful offenders violated the Eighth Amendment and could be reexamined. It was an NPR moment: I was driving when I heard the news brief amid all the other stories of the day. I kept driving—the commentator's voice became white noise. All I could do was keep driving, watching the long white lines of the highway around every bend. This was it. I knew that one day X would be resentenced for his crime. At least his accomplice, who was eighteen at the time, would remain in prison forever.

In 2016 the newspaper and television accounts of Christina's murder were alive again. I had avoided social media and hadn't talked to many friends from high school for ages. Twenty-six years after this atrocious crime happened, these two headlines appeared in the *Omaha World-Herald*:

> She listened as baby sitter was murdered, and she wants killer to never walk free
>
> 'I won't get back the years of my life that I lost': Judge rules killer must spend at least 22 more years in prison for 1990 murder

I emailed my father. I couldn't remember the last time I'd spoken of Christina's murder with my family or friends. My father emailed back, "X doesn't look like he feels sorry for what he did. I'm not reading anything about rehabilitation or remorse." I agreed. By now X's brain had had a chance to fully develop. He'd had plenty of time to own his heinous sins. All of a sudden, that indescribable sickness in my gut emerged. In the *Omaha World-Herald*, Erin Grace wrote:

The commotion woke up Beth Ann, who then endured three hours of frozen fear until she heard someone leave around 5:30 a.m. She then drifted off to sleep and woke again when Chris's alarm clock went off at 6:30 a.m. Beth Ann slipped on some pants, crept outside her bedroom and peered inside her mother's room, where she saw blood on the pillowcases and sheets. Creeping downstairs, she saw Sunshine's feathers all over the floor and the home in disarray. She reached for the phone and dialed 911, but the line was dead. So Beth Ann opened the front door and ran to a neighbor's house. "I rang the doorbell five times, but nobody answered," she testified in 1990. "I went to the next house and rang the bell three times, but nobody came. I went to the third house and rang it once, and they were home. When he answered the door, I told him, 'I think my baby sitter's dead.'"[15]

||||

A lot of us at Millard South had been shaken by this crime. To say we had school spirit would be awkward. I'm not sure what we had left except a rock by the entrance of the school in memory of Christina. It was a rock we walked by quickly. I couldn't tell you what it said or what it looked like anymore. We gathered around it once when it was memorialized. It seemed so weird. I thought, *How can a rock signify someone's life? Pay tribute? Ever?*

Some of us moved after high school, putting distance between ourselves and our past. I made my way back for grad school in Omaha eight years later. One time I was sitting at a bar having drinks with someone I vaguely knew from high school, an aspiring writer like myself. I asked her if she could write about it. "No. I tried. What can you say? That we fucking hate the guy for what he did. What good does that do? Doesn't bring her back. What about you?" she asked. "I'm trying," I replied. "Surely there's something I can write to make some sense of it all."

The newspaper reported that more than seven hundred people attended her funeral. We had to sit in a hall by the church and watch it on a teleprompter. When it was over, I got up and walked past the stilled, zoned-out, and tear-stained faces of my classmates. I looked across the parking lot at the sea of mourners. I spotted some of the guys X hung out with before he dropped out. They were trying to act cool—smoking their cigarettes, flicking the ashes, glancing up at the church and away again. They were smiling. One of them pinched his cigarette, took a drag, and blew smoke rings. I knew they knew where X was hiding. This was after the police had questioned and released him and he had disappeared. She was brutally murdered, and they seemed to be worried about their image, about their little clique.

I left the funeral with one of my good friends. I wanted desperately to get revenge, to confront those who were blowing smoke rings. "All of this is wrong. Those fuckers. They know where he is. They know," I said.

I can't think of the words to describe the tension and sorrow we felt that day and in the weeks that followed. It was all so strange. Christina's death seemed to tamp down any immediate violence, but we were all frightened. Who could be next? And for what? Dating the wrong person? And then breaking up? It was clear that fighting truly achieved nothing. We all knew this. The fights we watched never solved anything. Blood on the ground, screams, bruises, and now murder. No one seemed to know how to react. We had never experienced these kinds of emotions. How did we know what to do? A year later, a lot of us went our separate ways—away from our once "safe" neighborhoods and from each other's lives.

Trauma

Ten years into teaching at the prison in Yankton, I began a program called Writing for Reentry at the men's and women's state prisons in Springfield and Pierre, South Dakota. It was similar to my class at the federal prison. On a particularly warm spring day in April, I was walking in the prison yard. Everyone was taking a little bit of extra time to enjoy letting the sun's rays warm their skin. We didn't need any jackets. Perennials and tufts of grass peeked out of the dirt, even in the prison yard. I was thinking about Christina's murder—how the act of murder spread into our school and neighborhood communities in waves, an ever-widening circle of grief, paranoia, loss, and fear. I was talking with the unit manager, Josh Klimek. I often picked his brain about my projects, asking questions about my writing and telling him what was on my mind.

"There's different trauma. You have different problems as someone who experiences trauma directly, firsthand," says Klimek, who won South Dakota's Santan-Canary Award, the state's highest honor in corrections.[16]

"Josh, people ask me, 'How good of friends were you with her?' But does it really matter? She was my friend. We went out, you know. We never dated, but we went to the same dance club. I mean, I can remember the last time we were together, and other times. It's all a bunch of flashbacks—snapshots. I think it must have been one of the last times we hung out and it was just her and me. It was one of those times I realized that I could be a guy and not want to date this girl. She was just a friend. She was attractive, but we were never attracted to each other—not that I was aware of. And that shows you a bit of our level of maturity—at sixteen and seventeen.

"You know, for adolescent guys that age, usually it's like, 'Oh, I want to date her.' Or you just hung around with other guys. It's traumatic, whether I was good friends with her or great friends with her.

"It was horrible what it did to everybody in our community, in our high school, which was a big high school. It affected everybody in different ways. Why am I still questioning my own emotions? It's like I become uncertain about them and think, *Well, if I don't have a right to feel these emotions, how can I feel other things?* Some days it feels like its own hellish merry-go-round. I feel like I should be tougher. Maybe I should be pretending it didn't happen. When I ask friends about it, they don't say anything. And I guess since we are here, in these prisons and doing this work, I do feel an obligation to society, to complete strangers, to address it. What the hell is the alternative? Christina is not here to speak for herself. Neither are other victims. But someone needs to."

I look up at Josh as he peers ahead through his sunglasses. He could be one of the best listeners I know. He's wicked smart. He's the guy I called when the heating element broke in our stove and started a small fire. I didn't need the fire trucks, but I needed assistance. He genuinely loves to help others. For once I feel like I'm understanding these feelings of mine. I'm learning more about crime and its repercussions, and I've finally found someone who understands the topic. I stare ahead and wait to see what he has to say. He grabs his sunglasses and moves them to the top of his head.

"There's the crime victim—the actual victim—and then there's secondary trauma," he says, "where you aren't the actual victim but you are tied to her, close to her, witnessing. There's different degrees for each one of those. The easiest way I can explain this is on a national level—for example, 9/11. The whole nation experienced at least some indirect trauma from that incident. It actually impacted the psychology of the nation. And then you have people in those situations who were first responders or family members of someone who died. They may get angry if a person expresses their own trauma. They may say, 'Well, you have no right to experience trauma because it wasn't your loved one, or you didn't respond, or you didn't have a direct connection to that situation.' So, it's interesting that you're expressing that kind of frustration. It's actually very common in prisons when you're dealing with trauma situations.

"Say, for example, you have a situation where a staff member is assaulted. There may be someone who's in a control room or working in a different unit that wasn't involved. They say they experienced trauma because of the incident, and somebody who's the victim says, 'You don't have any right to feel that trauma because I was the one who was assaulted.' Whatever the case is—your experience, your closure was not the same."[17]

Men move by us, cussing and joking. All these guys around us walking crooked lines on the sidewalk in the yard have no idea what we are talking about.

I say, "People will ask me, maybe because I'm a writer, maybe because I work in corrections, if I want to talk to him. I'm like, 'Why in the hell would I want to talk to him?' I wasn't friends with him. I hardly ever saw him. I remember him driving by the high school in his Camaro after he dropped out, and you could see he had that grudge, that attitude as if he had been dealt a shit hand and it was everyone else's fault. But man, he was smarter than me. At least when it came to math. He used to help me when we were in middle school, and he was decent about it. He tried to explain how to solve the problem."

Should he get some help? Sure. Does that make me squirm? Of course it does. Josh and I are both helping people who have committed murder. I'm sure others would be mortified to find out that we are showing them compassion. What we do probably makes others squirm. Maybe X can get help. I'm surely not going to give it to him—but that's okay. I'm split between my intellect and my emotions. I've carried a lot of hate for him and his accomplice, and I can have my feelings. That doesn't mean I can't believe that people can and should be rehabilitated. But I'm not making those rules. Nor should I be. Maybe X can help someone on the inside. I don't think he should be released, but I'm not the judge.

State v. X

At a California Lawyers for the Arts in Corrections conference in Los Angeles, I told the story about Christina's brutal murder. An advocate asked, "Why do you think he did it?"

"I'd heard that his father was in prison or had been locked up around the same time," I responded. "Was that motivation? Someone said he lived with his grandmother. Did the lack of parental supervision play into murder? Were there adverse childhood experiences? There was a rumor of drugs, although I didn't read any police reports that confirmed this. What we all know is that it was a crime of passion—a crime of control. He and Christina had dated."

It's grotesque, considering his education. He was smart. I can see him in our classroom. I want to reach out and shake him. Tell him, *Wake up, man! The path you are going down is all wrong.* I want to drive to that house where Christina was babysitting and get those girls out of there. We all do. But it's too late. Why do we, her friends, and all those who loved and cared for her want to change things, and why doesn't he?

Maybe the question isn't why X did it, but why I have such a strong desire to figure it out. With such a reckoning, perhaps I could explain it to myself, which in turn might diminish my feelings of despair. I have learned about adverse childhood experiences. I can see the repercussions when teenagers drop out of high school. I see it with this case and in the prisons I've visited and taught in throughout the country. In Nebraska, at the time when the murder was committed, you only needed to be sixteen to drop out of high school. X had dropped out. This might have been a result of adverse childhood experiences—or maybe it was just a bad decision. Author Mary Karr wrote, "Far as I can tell, a dysfunctional family is any family with more than one person in it."[18] But when does dysfunction turn into crime? I have heard men and women in my classes talk about extreme forms of neglect and abuse. I can't explain the murk in a teenager's mind that turns him into something bad—something evil—but we know it happens. X is a prime example.

One could see that X wasn't making things any easier for himself by dropping out of school. That should never have been an option for him. That this issue is still debated today in some states is wrong on so many levels. By now we should have a system of checks and balances that keeps adolescents in school until they are eighteen, and we should have a system that keeps them in line. Every year we do more and more assessment and standardized testing. Keeping kids in school should be just as important. But some teachers don't like to deal with troubled students. Maybe that's because they don't know how or where to begin.

In "Why Education Reduces Crime," writers Rui Costa, Stephen Machin, and Brian Bell state that "changes to compulsory school leaving laws that force some people to stay in school longer have been shown to boost education and reduce crime. . . . Crime rates peak at age 18, and keeping teenagers in school during this key period can help ensure that they never proceed down the wrong track."[19]

I think of a student in one of my prison classes, a repeat offender, who stated, "Dr. Reese, you don't understand; you weren't born a criminal." And immediately another student snapped back, "Man, what are you talking about? You weren't born a criminal, either."

While some of my memories are merely snapshots, the last time I hung out with Christina is vivid. Do I remember it because all this time I've held onto the notion that if I had asked more questions about her ex-boyfriend—her soon-to-be murderer—maybe I would have recognized and told her about the warning signs? Maybe then she could have been on the lookout. Maybe when he and his accomplice arrived at the house where she was babysitting, she would have spoken up and called the police. She could have taken extra precautions. Maybe she and Beth Ann wouldn't have been there at all. She could have said she didn't feel comfortable being alone in the house, and maybe the owner would never have left. Maybe all of this could have been prevented. Maybe asking myself these questions all these years later is a direct reflection on why I pry too much now. Why I can't let some things go. Why I seem to care too much. Why I try to solve more problems than I should, problems that aren't my business and that I don't have any control over anyway.

Caring too much may be the curse of some teachers. When I first started teaching in prisons, other educators and advocates urged me to never get too close to any inmate. They said that I should play a very narrow role and keep the art about the art. And maybe some teachers can do that, but I can't. Art is about the whole person. Teaching for me is much more than black words on white paper. Writing can transform a person for the better. But that takes discussion, careful listening, and creating an environment in which the classroom becomes a community.

There's a feeling in all of this that if I can just explain the reason for the murder to myself—*See, that's why this happened; that's why he did it*—I would come to understand that there wasn't a thing I could do to prevent it. And what I believe—what I know, the more I uncover about this crime—is that it was premeditated.

I asked a police officer friend of mine, Joe Erickson, why criminals do what they do. He said, "There are different kinds of criminals. Some simply do not learn, and continue to make mistakes. Some, however, feel they are above the law and are not able to feel things that most people can feel, like remorse."[20] It could be argued that X had feelings so strong that he obsessed over them—that he premeditated this murder in anger, jealousy, rage, and lust, and then acted out those feelings for hours.

I spent two years doing over two hundred hours of ride-alongs with Sergeant Javier Murguia in our small city. He was Yankton's Officer of the Year in 2017, and he had been a student at the university where I taught. Now he was a special agent at the South Dakota Division of Criminal Investigation. To truly understand crime and all of its effects, I needed to see it on the front end. Spending one night riding along with him wasn't enough. I vowed to spend at least two hundred hours acting as his shadow before I began to tell the bigger story.

I'm five feet nine and a half on a good day. Javier is a little shorter than I am. He's built. He played college soccer. He is fast and, more importantly, calm and collected. I stood next to him for two years, watching him keep his composure as grown men acted like immature teenagers and as grown women yelled racist slurs at him when they knew they were being arrested. He always maintained his professionalism. And on a number of occasions, I started shaking with anger and had to turn around and walk back to the police SUV. I could not keep my cool.

On slow nights I recorded a lot of interviews with him. When I asked him how he defined a heinous criminal, he said, "I believe the heinous criminals we hear about operate at a different level. It is difficult to really figure out what makes them tick. All humans are capable of and oftentimes do make mistakes. Most people recognize the errors they commit and show some form of remorse or regret. Then you have those that show no regret and have no remorse; there is an obvious disconnect going on there. Some believe it is mental illness while others prefer to say it is pure evil. I see it as something that cannot be ignored. It is as if the person does not know or has chosen to ignore the difference between right and wrong."[21] Maybe the reason I want to figure out why criminals do what they do is that it would allow me to gain some control over my feelings about Christina's murder—over the fear that a serial killer instilled in me in the 1980s.

||||

The facts of the case can be found in the transcript of the court proceedings for State v. X, the trial of the murder of Christina O'Day.[22] These are the facts that were presented during the trial, when the jury and judge decided his guilt. Sometimes the public makes decisions without facts, or feels we should have empathy for all criminals. Fair enough. I walk both sides of this fence. I have helped hundreds of criminals become better men. It's my job. However, I don't feel comfortable helping some of the men and women behind bars. There are lines I draw.

I believe that people should read the facts before making such decisions or rationalizing the idea that everyone should be set free. Evil exists. There are psychopaths and sociopaths living among us. WebMD includes this description of psychopaths and sociopaths:

> A key difference between a psychopath and a sociopath is whether he has a conscience, the little voice inside that lets us know when we're doing something wrong, says L. Michael Tompkins, EdD. He's a psychologist at the Sacramento County Mental Health Treatment Center.
>
> A psychopath doesn't have a conscience. If he lies to you so he can steal your money, he won't feel any moral qualms, though he may pretend to. He may observe others and then act the way they do so he's not "found out," Tompkins says.
>
> A sociopath typically has a conscience, but it's weak. They may know that taking your money is wrong, and they might feel some guilt or remorse, but that won't stop their behavior.
>
> Both lack empathy, the ability to stand in someone else's shoes and understand how they feel. But a psychopath has less regard for others, says Aaron Kipnis, PhD, author of *The Midas Complex*. Someone with this personality type sees others as objects he can use for his own benefit.[23]

The murder case's appeal transcript states that "although X was but 16, he was charged with violent adult crimes; he was an obvious threat to the public and, if convicted, could not easily be rehabilitated in the juvenile correctional system nor properly punished for the atrocities he would be adjudged to have committed."

It's haunting looking back. It's haunting looking forward. The lives of everyone who knew Christina changed forever—those who loved her, those who were friends with her, those who were merely acquaintances or classmates. We are grieving, lost, and confused. Perhaps you could call it a false regret, regret over something we know we couldn't have done any differently.

Christina O'Day's life was taken away forever. No life behind bars. No phone calls. No communication. No morning. No night. No visitors. No future. No commissary. No air. No breath.

||||

MAN LOSES APPEAL OF 90-YEAR PRISON SENTENCE IN 1990 KILLING

LINCOLN, Neb. (AP)—The Nebraska Supreme Court on Friday refused to overturn a 90-year prison term imposed during the mandatory resentencing of a man who was convicted in a 1990 Omaha killing when he was 16 years old.

X originally was convicted of first-degree murder and handed an automatic life sentence without parole for the slaying of Christina O'Day.

In 2012, the U.S. Supreme Court ruled that juvenile killers must not be sentenced to automatic life terms without parole, so X was resentenced in February. He then appealed his new 90-year sentence, arguing the district court abused its discretion by imposing an excessive term.

The Nebraska high court said in its ruling released Friday that the district judge considered all relevant sentencing factors and imposed a new sentence within the statutory limits and supported by the record.

"The (district) court acknowledged and gave credence to X's efforts to rehabilitate himself while in prison, but stated it also had 'to balance the nature of the offense and what was done to that young lady,'" the justices said.[24]

Public Facebook Posts after the Retrial

C. T.: He had a terrible temper, and it was on a fast trigger. He would just as soon kill you as look at you when you didn't do what he wanted.

K. W.: Shouldn't get another chance

J. F.: Most corrections officers dont have issues with older, more calm inmates but i guarantee that when he first came to L.C.C. he put fear in you guards . . . he put alot of work in . . . and dont forget him and his little butt buddy did terrible things before and after he killed that young babysitter. Corrections empathy is pathetic.

T. R.: Hope he never gets out.

T. N.: Never had an issue with him

D. J. H.: Neither did I when I was working in Tecumseh[25]

||||

Studying the trial transcripts, appeals, and resentencing information, I don't read remorse anywhere in X's statements or his multiple versions of what transpired. Everything in both guys' reports to police seems premeditated, self-centered, immature, cold-blooded, and monstrous. It lacks any emotional intelligence whatsoever. It's quite obvious that the other perpetrator couldn't think for himself. X is an odious killer. I don't read sorrow. I don't read reports of regret or transformation since Christina's murder. In the transcript of his resentencing, X still doesn't admit that he acted alone, that he committed the crime.

In X's postconviction case, the district court applied preceding cases *Miller* and *Mantich* and granted postconviction relief in the form of resentencing on the murder conviction. No appeal was taken from that order.

> To facilitate resentencing, an evidentiary hearing was held before the district court. X offered three exhibits: (1) Department of Correctional Services reclassification action forms, (2) various certificates of achievement he earned while in custody, and (3) the deposition of a neuropsychologist who testified generally about adolescent brain development. X also offered testimony of a licensed psychologist who evaluated X in preparation for resentencing. The psychologist testified that while in prison, X has taken advantage of programs available to him, been both involved and a leader in a program which seeks to reduce recidivism by preparing inmates for successful release, mentored younger inmates, earned his diploma through the GED program, completed a legal research class, and performed several jobs, some of which require earning trust because sharp objects are involved.
>
> While incarcerated, X has amassed 182 misconduct reports. As he has grown older and matured, the reports have decreased in frequency and severity. The psychologist testified that young inmates often have a higher number of misconduct reports because they have to prove themselves but that the misconduct reports usually lessen as an inmate establishes himself or herself as someone who cannot be taken advantage of. The psychologist testified that X has qualified for "community custody" status every year since 2006 and opined that

X is at low risk for future acts of violence. At the conclusion of the evidentiary hearing, the district court ordered preparation of a new presentence investigation report and set the case for resentencing.

At the resentencing hearing, the State asked the court to impose a sentence "in the realm of the maximum sentence" allowed by law. The State also reminded the court that X's codefendant, who was 18 at the time of the murder, is serving a life sentence. X's counsel asked the court to impose a sentence that would make X parole eligible "if not [that day], in the very near future." The court also heard remarks from the employer's daughter, now an adult, who spoke about how she and Christina O'Day's family had been affected by the murder. X did not make a statement at the resentencing hearing, but submitted a written statement that was included in the presentence report in which he admitted "participat[ing] in the robbery, rape, and murder of Christin[a] O'Day." The report also indicated X expressed remorse for his actions.

The sentencing judge stated he had reviewed the presentence report, the trial transcript and exhibits, the police reports, the letters of support offered on behalf of X and O'Day, and the mitigating evidence offered by X at the evidentiary hearing pursuant to Neb. Rev. Stat. § 28–105.02(2) (Reissue 2016). The court acknowledged and gave credence to X's efforts to rehabilitate himself while in prison, but stated it also had "to balance the nature of the offense and what was done to that young lady." The court then sentenced X to 90 to 90 years' imprisonment on the first degree murder conviction. That sentence was ordered to be served consecutively to the previously imposed sentence of 6 2/3 to 20 years' imprisonment for use of a weapon to commit a felony. The court advised X that, assuming he lost no good time, he would be eligible for parole after serving 48 years 4 months and would be mandatorily discharged after 55 years. X was given credit for 9,440 days previously served. He timely appeals.[26]

"The evidence does not suggest X acted impulsively," the judge wrote. "He carefully planned the attack in advance and spent hours raping, beating, cutting, and strangling O'Day before she died."[27]

The public wants to know as much as possible—why do men and women commit atrocities? They can't comprehend why, if a person isn't dealt cards they like, they take someone else's life from them. You certainly don't take another human being's life because you are angry, because you are broke, because a high school girlfriend dumped you.

No, I don't ever want to talk with X. However, I hope he has learned something from his actions. What positive contributions to the public's understanding of crime and punishment could he share? What can he do to help others before they make the same mistakes? How can he contribute to the greater good? If he truly does deem himself rehabilitated—if he has any faith in himself and a higher power—then he'd better pray.

When X was resentenced in 2016, the media interviewed Christina's family members and Beth Ann, the child who listened as the brutal crime unfolded. Beth Ann told WOWT 6 News, "I mean, I wake up in the middle of the night and I can relive it all. It's on my mind way more frequent[sic] than I would like to admit." In advance of the hearing, Beth Ann added, "I kind of feel like this is a gift from Chris. This will happen, be done again, and I will move on with my life."

Sheila O'Day, Christina's mother, added that Beth Ann suffered the most. "Of all of us she suffered the most I think. She had to relive this from eight years old—just a child—how do you process that?"[28]

In another article, "She Listened as Baby Sitter Was Murdered, and She Wants Killer to Never Walk Free," by Erin Grace of the *Omaha World-Herald*, Beth Ann is quoted as saying that if X were ever to leave prison, it would be her "worst nightmare come true."

"'I've been on the bench for a number of years and heard many murder trials,' Judge Burkhard said during X's sentencing. 'This one is by far the most brutal I've ever heard.'

'I couldn't save her then,' Beth Ann said. 'But today all I can do is make sure he spends the rest of his life in jail.'"[29]

Adverse Childhood Experiences

"Didn't they have some help for you and her friends?" my wife asks. We are walking. It is dusk. We are that couple that treads very fast, exchanging ideas—the day's dilemmas and what's on our minds. It works. We walk for two miles, or about twenty minutes. We walk fast. We talk fast. Time's up. Leave it in the street. Sometimes I throw out ideas about things I'm working or dwelling on. We encourage each other, give each other feedback.

I have been studying trauma and its effects on people, paying a lot more attention to it. It is a thing some college and prison students go through. I learned about adverse childhood experiences, or ACEs, from Grammy Award–winning producer Fritzi Horstman, when she was a guest speaker at Mount Marty University. She is the founder and director of a nonprofit called the Compassion Prison Project.

A week before Fritzi's presentation I sent her a copy of my book *Bone Chalk*, which includes an essay entitled "Never Talk to Strangers—12 Years in Prisons and What Criminals Teach Me." It is the essay that inspired this book. Fritzi and I talked via ZOOM right before her presentation, as the university students filed into the auditorium. She was projected on a big screen on the stage and I appeared in a little box next to her.

She said, "I read your essay and I like it a lot."

I reiterated how much I believed in her program. I said, "It's hard. No part of me wants to talk to this guy who murdered my friend. Since I'm a writer, people automatically think I do."

"No one says you have to. If you really wanted to, you could write him a letter," she said. "Did he have any ACEs?"

"I remember hearing his dad was in prison. Or had been. That he lived with his grandmother."

"There are two ACEs right there," Fritzi said.

That night I told my wife about the presentation, about ACEs. I talked about Christina's murder. My wife asked again, "Didn't they have any help for you and her friends?"

I sometimes look over her head—not always in her eyes—when I am trying to articulate the right answer. Is that weird? This is the woman I married, and I am still trying to sound as smart as possible. The words stumbled out of my mouth.

"I don't know. I mean, I'm sure they did, but there's no way we would have talked to someone. It just wasn't cool. And we surely weren't going to act like victims. Guys didn't do that. It wasn't considered tough. I don't know if I ever mentioned this to you, but her killer was on the loose for weeks. His mom found out the police were looking for him and took him to the police station the day after the crime. They didn't charge him. Then he disappeared for sixteen days. His face was plastered on the news. His friends knew where he was hiding. There wasn't a lot of trust to talk to anyone."

I think back to that time—my long hair and *Corrosion of Conformity* T-shirt. Apathy was both a band we listened to and a word we leaned on—until we ran out of money and had to ask our folks to lend us a hand. We were trying desperately to be independent, rebelling against any system. That's what X did. He dropped out of high school, which sometimes—for all of us, I'd argue—felt like a jail. However, as cool as most of us wanted to look and act, as rebellious as we thought we were, we knew school was a necessity to get anywhere in life. We also liked the safety of our own homes, whether we admitted it or not. The high school was often out of control. Fights were celebrated. Megacrowds erupted and it took teachers or the rent-a-cops a long time to fight through a crowd if they attempted it at all. These weren't pull-your-hair screaming matches either. These fights, which seemed to happen for the most immature reasons, were knockdown, really bloody fights. At this time of my life I had been taking Taekwondo classes for a couple of years—to protect myself and also to live my fantasy of becoming Ralph Macchio's character in *The Karate Kid*.

I'm not a fighter, but I found myself in one of these after-school dilemmas. I had been pushed in the parking lot by a new kid for opening my mouth when I shouldn't have. I had made fun of his shoelaces, which had his name on them. And this is why everyone there was rooting against me—taunting both of us, laughing. A large group of my "friends and acquaintances" followed me out the front doors and heckled me the minute rumors of an after-school retaliation spread—they wanted to see a fight. All of a sudden they were on the other guy's side, which in hindsight I can understand. I had been the bully and this kid was just trying to find his way. He had a girl he liked, and some skinny punk was trying to disrupt that.

Because of Taekwondo I knew that any move we practiced over and over in class might do serious damage and would have serious consequences. I knew how to protect myself from guys who were much bigger than me. And I only weighed about a buck fifteen, so that was most of the guys in my class. Our *sa bom*, Master Kim, had drilled into us that we should not fight anyone unless it was for protection. That's why I let the guy continue to push me—until he pushed me hard into a parked car. I grabbed his shirt by the collar, closed my eyes, and didn't stop hitting him in the face until I couldn't make a fist. My best friend hollered at me that we needed to go, and he dragged me to his Trans Am. We drove off before any teacher or cop got me. I was shaking uncontrollably. My hands were numb, red, and bruised. All of it felt wrong. My friend laughed and sped away.

When I think of this after-school quarrel, I'm embarrassed. I remember my best friend calling the guy later to rub it in; he had gone to a different school with him years before. He told him to just let "us" know if he wanted to fight again. My friend liked to fight. And I was still shaking from the ordeal. I felt bad. All of this had happened because I had asked a girl he liked, and who apparently liked him, how she could fall for someone who still had his own name on his shoelaces? This was our maturity level. This was the same year X murdered Christina.

A person could draw comparisons here. As pathetic as our fight was—the kid had a problem with me because I made fun of his shoelaces—he was defending his honor because he was jealous of me. X was jealous and angry because Christina insulted his honor—she didn't like him anymore. She was done with him. The relationship didn't work. But this new kid—he didn't sneak into my house and shoot me. It makes me wonder how our reactions to life can be so very different. How does one even rationalize the idea that if they aren't getting what they want from another human being, they are entitled to kill them?

I often ask my students when we talk about crime, "Can you imagine where you'd be right now if you didn't graduate high school? What if you dropped out? What if you couldn't afford to stay in school and had to fend for yourself? Where do you think you'd be?" The classroom often grows quiet, because most of my students are still being supported either by another person or by loans, and they don't have any idea how they would fend for themselves.

If X was a victim of ACEs, it's proof that one of crime's sinister effects is to create more people who don't know they're victims and who therefore deal with life—their trauma—in random or premeditated and self-destructive ways. How many country songs have been written about guys down on their luck who continue to dig themselves into deeper holes? I know one thing for certain: dropping out of school should never be in the equation before you are eighteen years old—period.

"It's not that what they did was OK, absolutely not, it's that we have to understand the mitigating circumstances," said Fritzi Horstman. "Those men aren't bad people. They did bad things, but they are not bad people. They are highly traumatized.

"A person who executes a heinous crime doesn't see the world the way we see it. They go into fight or flight mode—trauma mode. We have to ask what was done with these people who are portrayed as monsters. Underneath every monster is a boy that was never loved."

When I talked to Horstman about Christina's murder, she said, "He took your friend away from you. To face that harm may be too much for you. But the other side of that—maybe he wants to make amends to people. He was abandoned early, which is his primary wound. Mother or father or both left him. You said he was living with his grandmother, or so you heard. There are two ACEs right there. You said his ex-girlfriend abandoned him. A major trigger. Another woman does that to him so he kills her. He sees he's not safe—it's back again—same thing he was tormented with as a child—so he reacts. Unless he was or is a sociopath, he has some serious childhood trauma. If we help him heal, then maybe he could help heal other people down the road."[30]

I don't know if I have enough kindheartedness to meet with him to discuss this. I didn't talk to him when he was dating Christina, nor do I want to now. Of all the people who work in this field, maybe I am the one who should. But I think if he wants to try to make any amends, he should start with Christina's family, and with the victim who was in the house when he committed this murder.

A part of posttraumatic stress, as I'm beginning to understand it after all these years, is a feeling of guilt and an obsessive desire to speak with the people who have inflicted crimes. Feelings invade our existence and we've done nothing to deserve them. The perpetrators of such acts of violence should be begging to talk to us. If they are truly sorry for such crimes—if they deem themselves rehabilitated—they should do everything possible to offer some form of public statement to the family, the primary victims, and all others who are suffering. The criminal makes those people and communities bear the guilt of the very acts they committed—sometimes without remorse or accountability—until they find out there's a chance they could be set free. During X's resentencing, in a presentence report, he admitted "participat[ing] in the robbery, rape, and murder of Christin[a] O'Day."

He couldn't even spell her name or the word "participating" correctly. Is that intentional? Could his lawyer not use spellcheck? The whole thing still seems so juvenile and lacks emotion. And intelligence.

I'm not the judge nor the jury. It's not my job to decide X's punishment. Was I and were thousands of other people affected by his actions? Of course we were. And it affected all of my classmates differently. We were all emotionally unintelligent at this age—we didn't have the resources or knowledge to understand what to do with feelings in general, let alone these kinds of feelings.

Was X a victim of ACEs? Maybe. Did that make him commit the crime? Research says it's quite possible. Is he a psychopath with no feelings? Possibly. We don't know. Only he and his accomplice know. We can ask all the well-crafted questions we want. Victims are haunted by such inquiries while the rest of the world isn't, nor will the rest of the world ever fathom such feelings until they become victims of trauma themselves. We can suppress our state of mind—pretend that such events never took place—or we can try to piece such feelings together, especially if we might want to help others in similar circumstances. We can do this partly to understand ourselves and such pain, and partly to try to make the world a better place. I don't believe it's the job of the wounded or the prison staff to make perpetrators answer to their victims. That should be the responsibility of those who undertook such actions. That would be part of their learning and developmental process. Could the prison staff help them find the tools they'd need to come to such a reckoning? Yes. But isn't this something we should have been doing all along? It seems so obvious. Why aren't supports like this implemented along with all of the other reforms criminals are subjected to behind bars? This is another example of the fundamental problem with our carceral systems. We are failing each other. Surely by now there are practices we've developed that support this kind of rehabilitation.

Totems

This year my mother gave me a binder full of all the creative writing and journalism pieces of mine that she had saved since I started writing. She had asked if I wanted them organized and collected in something. To be honest, I was a little embarrassed to go back and look at some of those pieces, but I did, and hey, some of them weren't as bad as I remembered. She was kind enough to organize them by year—everything I'd written in high school and college, and all the things that had been written about me or the bands I played in up to 2006, when I was finally free of the bars of higher education (except for my student loans). It's a gift I'm sure I will give to my grandkids someday.

I asked her if she could find my high school yearbooks, too, while she was at it. She gave them to me along with some of my other adolescent totems. My pinewood derby car—eighth place! Some coasters I made in industrial arts class—with my initials wood-burned into them. (I wish I still had my solar hotdog cooker.)

While I was reminiscing, I stopped and looked around for my senior yearbook. *That's odd,* I thought. *I don't see it.* And then, like a steel dumpster slamming shut, I remembered. I refused to purchase a senior yearbook. I wanted to distance myself from Millard South and the crime that had been committed there. I didn't want to remember the past.

Page 152 in my 1990 junior yearbook, which has the heading "The Same but Different," features Christina's senior picture, and on the adjoining page there is an inscription that reads: "The class of 1990 pays tribute to the memory of Christina O'Day, 1972–1990." I went back to my freshman yearbook and looked up Christina. Then I looked up X. He is there in 1988—with an awkward smile like most of us. His sophomore picture—completely different story. No smile. Chin up a bit, hair longer (like a lot of us), and a smirk that says, "Man, fuck you. Take the picture." And that would be his last appearance in the yearbook before he dropped out.

Funeral Flowers

Tonight as I sit here revising another draft of my manuscript, I have to stop. I text my friend Stephen Bell, a former LAPD undercover investigator: "When I'm writing about my friend's murder, I can only go for an hour and I have to stop. I commend you for the stuff you have dealt with. It has to be hard to compartmentalize some crimes."

He responds: "Yours is far more personal. . . . It's easier to compartmentalize when there's no relationship. That's probably why I still deal with the death of my partner years later."

I know I can only write so much, so long about you, Christina.

My wife tells me to go play soccer tonight. I have cabin fever. I've been fretting about revising this book. I have to sort these feelings. Some days I sense I should be writing something else. Why am I agonizing over this all these years later? I love writing essays where I can make people laugh; it's so addictive. But I also feel compelled—dare I say, even a little obligated—to tell society what I've learned. How else do we move forward?

I'm standing in the kitchen cutting the dead stalk off of a small bunch of Walmart flowers. You can buy a five-dollar floral arrangement that seems to last for weeks. I just keep cutting the hard stalks and placing them back in the water, and although they become shorter and shorter, they continue to bloom. My grandmother and mother have taught me these little living tricks. Flowers help. I stare out the window at a cold South Dakota evening. The wind. It's relentless. Here I am, cutting flowers.

When I was young I felt like an outsider, a stranger, especially as an only child. I was someone who was never afraid to ask why. I've never shaken that tendency. Nor do I intend to. We as humans are indecisive and unpredictable. We act out.

Christina, your murder haunts me.

As kids we were taught to never talk to a stranger. But who is he? The kid in junior high who helps you with your homework? The unfamiliar person who takes you safely to school? Who really knows?

2

Redefining Gonzo

Tattoos, Prisons, and My Friend Charles Bowden

My Tattoo

Before I spoke a word to Charles Bowden, I did a mad dash toward the table where he was signing autographs, put my foot up on it, and pulled up my pant leg. Behold my GONZO (fist and peyote button) tattoo. I shifted my eyes from the tattoo to the author. He looked me in the eyes and chuckled with the raspy, phlegmy voice of a man who has inhaled too much. He smiled as he recalled his acquaintance with Hunter S. Thompson, who popularized the gonzo symbol and brand of journalism in the 1970s. I believe he was smiling at my enthusiasm, too.

"Yeah, I knew that guy. His publisher asked me to work with him," he said, chuckling again. I must have been standing there in awe. He leaned toward me. "When I was at his fortified compound in Woody Creek, he came out of hiding a couple of times. I saw him sit at a typewriter for about a half an hour, and then he wandered back to some other part of his house. He wasn't in good shape. He couldn't work."

Before I'd left my perch at my own autograph signing at the South Dakota Festival of Books in Deadwood and walked over to the alphabetically arranged table where Bowden sat, I hadn't known what I'd say to him. I had stalked his table, watched as he talked with his fans.

"You are much smarter than he ever was," I said, a bit nervously. Chuck smiled again. He was missing a front tooth. He scribbled "Appetite is the road to life and culture" on the casino voucher I handed him, and said, "I hate gambling." That comment sounded so odd; it went against every idea I had of him. Gambling—wasn't that part of gonzo journalism, what that lived experience was all about? Everything I had read of his seemed risky, but I would later learn that while it *was* risky, it was *not* gambling. It was dangerous. Was Chuck Bowden intentionally wagering his life like Thompson seemed to do so openly and recklessly?

Journaling

Bowden detested the word *journaling* (in journalism). He said he didn't keep a diary. He was a reporter. He was responsible for fact checking, for finding the truth. He was an investigator—a detective, a witness. *You follow?* He had worked gruesome crime beats as a city reporter; he was committed to reality. Unlike Hunter S. Thompson, Bowden wasn't interested in hiding his thoughts or flaws, and he didn't create an enigma or fictionalized version of himself. He laid it all out there. His voice was brutally honest, sometimes to a fault.

Thompson, as the years went on, hid behind a facade of his own making rather than trying to find the truth, the heart of the story or subject. Thompson's style was embellishment and evasion, and his gonzo was to take the assignment and all but scrap it for his own drug-fueled farce—not what his editors had intended. The assignment inevitably would be a fictional narrative of Thompson's own adventures—tales he was so good at spinning that the reader would all but forget what the actual headline was. I rarely read Hunter S. Thompson's work for the facts; more often I read it for entertainment.

The American Dream and Disillusionment

There is an American dream that millions of immigrants reach for and that Bowden chronicled for decades. He was engulfed in the brutal conflict on the border when, just days after taking office, Mexican President Felipe Calderón declared war against the drug cartels.

The U. S. Department of Justice released the following:

EX-MEXICAN SECRETARY OF PUBLIC SECURITY GENARO GARCIA LUNA CONVICTED OF ENGAGING IN A CONTINUING CRIMINAL ENTERPRISE AND TAKING MILLIONS IN CASH BRIBES FROM THE SINALOA CARTEL

"Garcia Luna, who once stood at the pinnacle of law enforcement in Mexico, will now live the rest of his days having been revealed as a traitor to his country and to the honest members of law enforcement

> who risked their lives to dismantle drug cartels," stated United States Attorney Peace. "It is unconscionable that the defendant betrayed his duty as Secretary of Public Security by greedily accepting millions of dollars in bribe money that was stained by the blood of Cartel wars and drug-related battles in the streets of the United States and Mexico, in exchange for protecting those murderers and traffickers he was solemnly sworn to investigate. Today's verdict is a shining light for the rule of law, right over wrong, and justice over injustice for all those who have suffered as a result of the defendant's deplorable crimes."
>
> "Today's conviction of Genaro Garcia Luna clearly shows that DEA will stop at nothing to pursue corrupt political officials who engage in drug trafficking and violence," said DEA Administrator Anne Milgram.[1]

"I can't help but see again how much of what Bowden wrote looks like prophecy now. . . . A lot of what is in [his work] from ten-plus years ago foreshadows this current (and past) phenomenon of showing 'narco-cultura' as glorious and attractive—especially to the young people who take the lead on all the social media platforms," wrote Molly Molloy, a research librarian for Latin America and the border at New Mexico State University and the creator of the Frontera List, a Google news group. Molloy had been Bowden's girlfriend since I'd known him, and the two authored *El Sicario: The Autobiography of a Mexican Assassin* in 2011. "Much of Bowden's (and my own) work on Juárez aims to reveal this recurring lie about the 'glorious' lives of the cartels . . . rather than the terrifying dead end for most of those involved and their victims," she wrote in the Frontera List.[2]

Since 2007, according to data from official Mexican government sources, nearly five hundred thousand people in Mexico have been victims of homicide.[3] And according to the National Registry of Missing Persons, "as of 21 September 2023, 111,521 persons were reported as disappeared in Mexico as a result of crime."[4]

What Bowden was doing wasn't journalism mixed with hard drugs and booze to numb the impact of murder. Chuck Bowden was invested. True, he had his vices, did his own experimenting—but he didn't use drugs or alcohol as tools to propel his writing or entertain his readers. They were ancillary; the red wine he might drink after he was done writing wasn't there to thicken the plot. I don't know how much more gonzo you can get—Bowden was always there to get the story. He never stopped working. His wheels were always spinning; he was always listening, processing, working it all over in his head. He was there to uncover this drug cartel–fueled carnage until that afternoon in August 2014 when he took a nap and never woke.

Gonzo

Adventure was what I was after when I first heard the term *gonzo*. I had read the copy of *Generation of Swine: Tales of Shame and Degradation in the '80s* that my father had at home. I had read Thompson's work in *Rolling Stone*. I knew then that what little talent I had as a musician was in writing, but it needed development. The book *Hell's Angels* inspired me, too. Reading Thompson—feeling that rhythm, imagining that life—is still addictive today. When I was sixteen and I opened *Rolling Stone* and read a passage by HST, I knew I had stumbled on something unique. This kind of writing sounded like a blast. Where could I sign up? I started looking for more decadent and depraved drawings by Ralph Steadman, Thompson's collaborator, and started seeing "Dr. Thompson" bylines in magazines. I even noticed that *Doonesbury* featured a guy named Duke sitting at a typewriter—an obvious parody of Thompson.

As a novice writer, I was picking up pieces here and there, but I wasn't putting in the work. Gonzo was what I was learning and trying to incorporate as I began my college career as a newspaper editor.

You want to write about tattoos? Go get one and report firsthand how it feels instead of just observing someone drawing on someone else's skin.

Where does the gonzo—the immersion into the story—end? That is perhaps the bigger question. My journalism professor gave us a lot of free rein and encouragement, and answered innumerable phone calls from administrators when we crossed the line in our small conservative town in Nebraska. He always defended us because we were always seeking the truth. He encouraged our excitement and intense drive to dig deeper. With his support, the idea of gonzo and my shameless self-promotion heightened. I equated gonzo with me, me, me.

I also learned how crucial investigating a story could be.

| | | |

You want to uncover a rape that happened and the lack of security on campus? Grab a crowbar and break into a manhole, photograph all the open doors to administrative buildings, open doors to offices. See how the tunnels lead to most dorms on campus, too. This is how the perpetrator entered the women's building. No one comes to arrest you for breaking and entering. No security meets you at the manhole entrance when you resurface forty-five minutes later. So you go down in the tunnels again, almost aching to get caught. No one comes for you, just like no one heard a thing.

The next day you notify campus security about the lack of secure doors on campus. They do not give you a quote for your story. They tell you to call them back in five minutes. They advise against running the piece before you have the "facts." Run the story above the fold, and in twenty-four hours (as administrators threaten to kick you out of college) notice how all the manholes on campus have new secured locks on them.

Your journalism professor tells you that if the college tries to kick you out of school for writing an investigative news story about a woman being raped on campus, you can sue the college for a lot of money. You like the word "investigative." It feels powerful.

Follow the accused for months as authorities change their minds about whether or not they should press charges. He's a football player with a bright future ahead of him. And really, it's "he said versus she said," isn't it? Where's the physical proof?

Give voice to the woman who was raped and no longer feels safe at school. Give voice to the woman who leaves this small-town American college and never returns.

A year later, you will win a first-place award for investigative reporting from the Nebraska Collegiate Media Association. It will come at a time when you are flat broke, have a college degree, and are wondering if writing is a fit profession for a man. You wouldn't know because you sort mail in a warehouse. There are not many editing jobs in Nebraska. The award is enough to keep you going, to make you realize you have the hunger. You scribble anecdotes and stanzas on mail flats and return receipts. You are a witness to what is going on around you. You seem to care more than others about the greater good. With no money it's hard to see that your voice can help make positive change. But you see the light ahead.

||||

In college we had weekly deadlines, which was good. I was also working at the local paper in town, so I knew how to get in and out of an assignment. I quickly learned whose voice to capture in my stories—nobody's. From Izaak Walton fish fries to the Annual Chicken Show's egg drop, I covered the weekly realm of current events in Wayne, Nebraska. Occasionally I ventured outside town limits to meet the farmers and ranchers who really made up the county. By doing so, I developed a better understanding of where I had landed. Although I didn't know what a JD 3020 was, I decided that when I got back to the office, I'd look it up or corral someone into a confession. A tractor—*why didn't the guy say so*, I thought. I was the city paper's greenhorn. They all got a lot of laughs at my expense.

The longer I stayed in the journalism program, the more responsibility, assignments, oversight, and freedom I had. I spent some nights in the newsroom with a drink in hand (because I'd read Thompson did it—so why not?). I believed that that was what all the great writers did—cocktails to call up the spirits. Thompson was my hero at this point, and his approach would be my approach. There weren't many articles, photos, or Ralph Steadman caricatures of Thompson without a drink in his hand. Drinking seemed essential for the story.

We lived in the newsroom. Our photographer took up residence in the darkroom for extended periods of time, which worked better than paying rent; no one complained. No one praised my approach. No one stopped me, either. A few of the other editors shook their heads in disappointment and went about their business. My stories were good or atrocious, depending on my momentary focus.

Perks of an Editor

I interviewed a lot of people, most notably Adam Sandler, the Spin Doctors, and Nebraska senator Bob Kerrey when he was running for reelection. When I talked to Sandler, he was in the process of filming *Happy Gilmore*. I asked him how he liked writing for SNL, and he said he liked it, but acting was so much more fun. He spent ten minutes talking about Chris Farley. He loved Chris Farley. I put my arm around him, grabbed his elbow for some reason, and posed for a picture. When the local media stations had their cameras set up and someone insisted we start the interview, the first question that was asked was, "How do you like Wayne, America?" He said, "I have a friend here that has a little kitty. He really likes that little kitty."

The Spin Doctors' "Little Miss Can't Be Wrong" went from heavy rotation to one of the greatest hits of the '90s—it's still running its course. Chris Barron, the lead singer, was down to earth. When some arrogant rookie college reporter asked him about the band's second album and a "sophomore jinx," he said something like, "We are a bar band from New York. We are just happy to be playing music every night." The bass player ate an enormous bowl of cucumbers and ranch dressing and wasn't happy because something was missing from his food request. I remember thinking, *This is Wayne, America, man. Cucumbers and ranch we have; most other stuff—don't count on it.* Barron was thoughtful when we asked him what it was like to be on the cover of *High Times*.

NORML (National Organization for the Reform of Marijuana Laws) was making waves at the college; they had more members than the Young Republicans. The subject was conveniently broached in interviews with public figures. When we asked Senator Kerrey, he said, "I have no problem with legalizing marijuana for medical purposes. There has only been one other individual who has brought this topic to my attention. That was Willie Nelson, and it seems to work for him."[5] That quote from Kerrey brought us a lot of media attention during his reelection campaign. I even got a visit in Wayne from someone on his campaign staff.

All of these stories made me aware that writers have special access to people of influence. I was hooked, but I was idealizing a fictional persona developed by Hunter S. Thompson. I had done one serious investigative piece. I ached to rub elbows with famous people. I wanted my picture taken with every person I interviewed. What I hadn't understood yet was that to realize the power of the written word, I needed to take myself completely out of the story and get to the truth.

Was I Really a Writer?

Being young and naïve, and diluting my senses on a regular basis, made being a writer seem attainable. However, after graduation I rarely put in the work. I had this idea of lived experiences—of immersing myself in the plot as it thickened—but none of that applied if you were at a desk working and revising. I was oblivious to the fact that hard work, practice, and committing my ass to the chair were key. Writing, failing, revising, writing more—that's what I should have been doing.

If you study Chuck Bowden, you know he woke early and wrote. Most famous writers do—they have a routine. Discipline was something I lacked as an aspiring writer. When I reminisce about my undergraduate college career, I remember how some of my mentors were more interested in partying and talking at us than providing the tools we needed to be successful. That's one side of the story. The other is that I distanced myself from the teachers who *were* providing those tools, and it's more than likely that I failed to pay attention. I always believed that my engagement in entertainment was where craft and creativity collided. I didn't see myself returning to school for graduate work. Soon after graduation I discovered that if I wanted to work in a newsroom, I had to either start with writing obituaries and want ads or go to graduate school.

When someone from the Associated Press visited our college, I was engrossed. I wanted to go to work for him immediately. After his presentation, I asked him about employment. He didn't miss a beat—said they wouldn't even consider me unless I had a master's degree. But I refused to go back to school for three more years of study. Plus, I didn't have the grades to get into most graduate programs. The first time I applied to the University of Nebraska–Lincoln, where I would eventually get my doctorate, I applied to the MFA program. At the time I didn't even know the difference between an MA and an MFA. That's how rushed I was. I never stopped to read the directions. They didn't even have an MFA program in writing. That first rejection letter encouraged me, rather bluntly, to learn about the programs I was applying for.

I began to put my time in, writing for money. It was better than the countless other jobs I was applying for and not getting. I reminded myself that it was better than sorting mail flats in a warehouse. I was writing puff pieces for clients, showcasing some, depending on how much they advertised within the glossy pages of the magazines I was editing: *Strictly Business, Strictly Health,* and *Strictly Working Women.* Herman Cain sent us a lot of Godfather's Pizza after we wrote a feature about him. This was the school of hard knocks, the real life of a writer. I discovered that the American dream for some was wealth, glad-handing, and greasy pizza delivered in a box. There was an American dream and disillusionment that Thompson uncovered and then almost seemed to embrace throughout all of his work. Both Thompson and Bowden liked to travel—both were flight risks. Both had a command of their craft.

How Hunter S. Thompson Became a Legend

Nearly fifty years after the publication of Hunter S. Thompson's *Fear and Loathing in Las Vegas,* Patrick Doyle recalled the following in *Rolling Stone*:

> *Fear and Loathing in Las Vegas* became Thompson's defining piece, and a defining literary experience for generations of readers. It had begun as an assignment from *Sports Illustrated* when Thompson was asked to go to Las Vegas to write a 250-word photo caption on a motorcycle race, the Mint 400. Introducing himself as a "doctor of journalism," he chronicled the fuel he brought along: "two bags of grass, 75 pellets of mescaline, five sheets of high-powered blotter acid, a salt shaker half full of cocaine, and a whole galaxy of multicolored uppers, downers, screamers, laughers . . . and also a quart of tequila, a quart of rum, a case of Budweiser, a pint of raw ether and two dozen amyls . . . Not that we needed all that for the trip, but once you get locked into a serious drug collection, the tendency is to push it as far as you can."
>
> The trip became less about covering the race and more of, in Thompson's words, "a savage journey into the heart of the American

dream." When he submitted 2,500 words to *Sports Illustrated*, the piece was rejected, along with his expenses.[6]

Thompson was a character who became an enigma. His first book, *Hell's Angels: A Strange and Terrible Saga*, took readers inside the life of a gang, which was all but forbidden to outsiders and which almost cost Thompson his life. This may have been as close as he came to true gonzo. The book garnered a national following. In 1971 *Rolling Stone* ran the first part of *Fear and Loathing in Las Vegas: A Savage Journey to the Heart of the American Dream*. Readers were itching for an inimitable voice. Hunter S. Thompson was it. Nikki Finke of the *Los Angeles Times* announced in 1987 that Thompson had said goodbye to gonzo journalism, that "drugs were always integral to his creative process," and that "the drugs have been cut way back."[7]

One could argue that after Thompson's heyday, "America's most alarming writer" Charles Bowden came to town. He published his first book, *Killing the Hidden Waters*, in 1977—eleven years after Thompson's *Hell's Angels* was released. Bowden was not a fictionalized version of Thompson—the "doctor of journalism"—or of any other persona. Bowden's work was real gonzo, the core of what I had wanted to embrace and believe in, what I thought Thompson was doing but upon closer inspection realized he wasn't.

Thompson loved to rant on the page. I never met him, but the rhythm of his work—the momentum—was addictive. He made sentences read like he had just dashed them off while searching for the next high. Like so many aspiring young men, I bought into the myth—believed singeing myself was part of the process. I tried writing while drinking. Drinking and then writing. Writing about drinking. It was ugly. All the while, and especially when the buzz wore off, I wondered why Thompson didn't try for social change with the same passion he had for self-indulgence. He ran for sheriff and almost won. He never left the midway carnival action; he was always shooting himself out of cannons. He inspired readers to do the same. I know; I read his work like an instruction manual, bought tickets and took my own ride. I wore T-shirts that read *Still Crazy After All These Beers*. I was thirty years old. I belonged behind a booth at a carnival more than I deserved to be behind a keyboard—I'd have done a better job. And the problem was that I didn't have much of a body of work. Thompson did. He had a bestseller. He was being given assignments. The only assignment I had was to sit down and try to write, anything. But first I needed inspiration. Let's go to the bar. Surely it was there among the flies and liquid courage that these altered universes and stories were found.

Somehow, during all of this, I kept publishing poems. I gained a lot of lived experience. And I earned a PhD in creative writing and published my first book of narrative poetry. I began teaching college. When I was asked to start a creative writing program at the federal prison in the city where I was teaching, I jumped at the chance. I had little knowledge of what our prison systems were made of, and I equated most prisoners with X. After a few years of intense study and immersion, I learned what our war on drugs—our war on race and poverty—really was. And I realized that my passion for writing and my interest in crime were coming full circle. I was writing poetry about men who were incarcerated and understanding more and more about what led some of them to jails and prisons.

Stats

If it bleeds, it leads. You've heard this saying before. I wonder about intention versus attention— the media's devotion to crime. The general public has an "it doesn't affect me" attitude when it comes to prisoners, but in reality most all of us are guilty of crime, petty or not. Some of us just never get caught. Check out the organization We Are All Criminals.

Why should I care? There are eighteen hundred state and federal correctional facilities and thirty-two hundred local and county jails in the United States, according to Christopher Ingraham of the *Washington Post*. To put these figures in context, we have slightly more jails and prisons—more than five thousand—than we do degree-granting colleges and universities. In many parts of the country, particularly in the South, more people live in prisons than on college campuses.[8] I work at two prisons within a fifty-mile radius of my house. Both prisons were colleges less than forty years ago. Each year, we spend billions on criminal justice but increasingly less on education.

I was eating lunch with my friend Bob, a Philly transplant who has been a local in my city longer than I have been alive. He's the former baseball coach at the university where I teach, the former interim dean of the university, a guy they named the new baseball field after. He's a smart man and a good coach. He understands that life, just like baseball, is a game of failure more often than not. Most times you go to bat you aren't a success. I said, "I wish I had a quick comeback for people who ask me why I do this work at the prisons." He didn't blink an eye and said, "If we all aren't trying to chip away at the iceberg, what's our alternative?"[9]

First Time Reading Bowden

During my second book tour, the award-winning writer Kent Meyers asked me if I had ever heard of a guy named Charles Bowden. He recommended a cover article in a recent issue of *Harper's Magazine*. In the 2009 article, "The Sicario: A Juárez Hit Man Speaks," Bowden writes the following:

> I am ready for the story of all the dead men who last saw his face.
>
> As I drank coffee and tried to frame questions in my mind, a crime reporter in Juárez was cut down beside his eight-year-old daughter as they sat in his car letting it warm up. This morning as I drove down here, a Toyota passed me with a bumper sticker that read, with a heart symbol, i love love. This morning I tried to remember how I got to this rendezvous.
>
> I was in a distant city and a man told me of the killer and how he had hidden him. He said at first he feared him, but he was so useful. He would clean everything and cook all the time and get on his hands and knees and polish his shoes. I took him on as a favor, he explained.
>
> I said, "I want him. I want to put him on paper."
>
> And so I came.
>
> The man I wait for insists, "You don't know me. No one can forgive me for what I did."

He has pride in his hard work. The good killers make a very tight pattern through the driver's door. They do not spray rounds everywhere in the vehicle, no, they make a tight pattern right through the door and into the driver's chest. The reporter who died received just such a pattern, ten rounds from a 9mm and not a single bullet came near his eight-year-old daughter.

I wait.

I admire craftsmanship. . . .

We meet in a parking lot, our cars conjoined like cops with driver next to driver. I hand over some photographs. He quickly glances at them and then tells me to go to a pizza parlor. There he says we must find a quiet place because he talks very loudly. I rent a motel room with him. None of this can be arranged ahead of time because that would allow me to set him up.

He glances at the photographs, images never printed in newspapers. He stabs his finger at a guy standing over a half-exposed body in a grave and says, "This picture can get you killed."[10]

Traveling

Traveling was important, even if it meant leaving reality for a brief time to enter a state of disillusion. In his book *Red Line*, Bowden writes, "I usually begin by running away from something. Soon I forget what I am fleeing. Actually, I am not too sure about this matter of fleeing, but flight, to speak of flight, is a convention of our time, and so it is easier to shout about escape than to admit or face real motives."[11]

This was true gonzo—true immersion. This wasn't a circus; this was reality. Bowden had all the qualities that I admired and wanted to emulate—the rhythm, the drive, the daring adventures—but they weren't make-believe; the circumstances he wrote about were real atrocities. This was investigative reporting at its finest.

Motive

What was my real cause? Like Thompson and Bowden, I wanted adventure. Fun. Thrill. Excitement. The quickest way to reach any of these is by ingesting the liquid or chemical that will take you there. It's a yearning. It's a hunger. Maybe some are born with a natural talent that can take them to another level, which in turn gives them this high, this adventure. But some of us are average or, perhaps more importantly, lack the discipline to achieve a natural high. And when the going gets weird, we have ambition but not the self-control to turn pro.

I wish I'd had then the discipline I have now. An old proverb. That was something I learned after failing and watching the thin line run long too many nights. Some musicians argue that "the road goes on forever and the party never ends." I've spent fourteen years in classrooms with prisoners who have tested this theory. These are men and women who have graced my classrooms not for a grade but to tell their story (or at first, maybe, just to get access to a computer). Inmates who have PhDs and GEDs. People who have stolen millions—embezzled—sold—extorted—used—and have believed in outlaw tales. The road for them did in fact stop.

One night after class I googled half of my students who I knew were in prison for serious federal crimes—one of them had even been featured on the show *American Greed*. I added up more than $140 million of defrauding between six of them and stopped. I couldn't believe it. And this was after hardly any digging. Some of them even wrote about their wild rides. I wanted to believe that most of them felt remorse for what they did. I wondered if they thought it was worth it. It seemed to me that the fantasy they were chasing was the American dream and disillusionment. Gatsby and his shirts—Thompson and his Great Red Shark. Now Bowden—his American dream had weight. He was searching—yearning—hungry for a better place and interested in how we treat one another. His appetite was gonzo, yet disciplined. He knew to sit down and write. He knew to stay to get the whole story. He knew to keep his mouth shut. He knew to listen.

In the tribute book about Bowden, *America's Most Alarming Writer*, his friends say the same. Here's a man who woke before most (3:00 a.m.), drank the strongest black coffee he could brew (Jim Harrison said you could stand a fork in it), and hammered it out. He went and lived the story, but he also knew to write every day, and there's a body of work to prove it—over two dozen books. He was generous with his work. He coauthored many titles. He shared his stage with photographers and artists. All of this speaks volumes about a man who gave up domesticity for the written word. He writes in *Red Line*, "I will walk away from family instantly and call this desertion work."

Objective

Bowden was objective. He was seeking facts. True reporting—to be true gonzo—is to be objective, to witness and see how subjects ("the other") and ourselves ("our other") coexist and how passion and drive fit into this quest. The hunt is an assignment. The pursuit, an answer. It's finding a better place. Gonzo, immersing yourself in the story, is exhausting. It's addictive. Vices can make it bearable at times, the baggage a little easier to schlep on some days. But the passion is inherent. You have to be both angry and eager. You have to want to keep chipping away at the iceberg. You've got to have rhythm. You have to feel the pulse, feel a heartbeat in your eyelids that you can't turn off. The ivy, the itch and scratch.

Suicide

When I was in my twenties, the illusion was in full swing—I was failing to find myself. I blew through my thirties without any regret. I was working, succeeding. In my forties, with children and a mortgage, I started to realize that life is short—it's time to kick it into high gear. If I'd spent a fraction of the time writing that I did partying, where might I be now? I'm fifty. People close to me have died too young. Thompson writes about age and longevity in his suicide note, later published in *Rolling Stone*:

> No More Games. No More Bombs. No More Walking. No More Fun. No More Swimming. 67. That is 17 years past 50. 17 more than I needed or wanted. Boring. I am always bitchy. No Fun—for anybody. 67. You are getting Greedy. Act your old age. Relax—This won't hurt.[12]

In all my interactions with Bowden I never found him talking about time or how much he had left. He worked and talked about work. He would talk about breaks, needing rest, needing the desert and long walks to sort it all out. Thoreau wrote, "Pursue some path, however narrow and crooked, in which you can walk with love and reverence."[13]

If Thompson had spent more time on his subjects than on himself, he might still be writing today. He would be eighty-nine. Imagine his wisdom if he had reined it in—the amazement in articles on Trump, sports doping, what our America has become. Thompson's wit would have uncovered Trump's deceit before he became president. That's what I have found myself pondering. I miss the pure entertainment of his voice—even, at times, his enigma. Some new "Hey, Rube" articles proved he still had it in him to entertain and edify. I'm angry that Thompson committed suicide, maybe because I've seen the ugly side of things and have encountered so many men who've turned their lives around. Addiction is a painful thing. No amount of money or fun can cure it.

Lessons in Reporting

I've been hungry for years, investigating our culture of fear. If you want to be an effective writer, you have to be hungry. You have to be willing to immerse yourself in the story. Bowden, in his earlier years, was rebellious. He had his indiscretions. I knew him during the last six years of his life. He was passionate about everything that we talked about, whether it was sandhill cranes, poor Mexicans being kidnapped and slaughtered on the border, NAFTA, or the poetry of Carl Sandburg. When we first hung out that night in Deadwood, he talked about the importance of interviewing people and meeting them face-to-face. He said, "Always let them run the tape recorder. Show them how it operates and where the on-and-off switch is. Ninety-nine percent of the time they will keep the recorder running. And always try to talk over food. People like to eat."

Chuck was genuine. When I met him in 2009, it was as if we'd known each other for some time. The writers Daryl Farmer and Neil Harrison were also attending the book festival, and we had presented at the nearby Western American Literature Conference that day, where Bowden, the keynote speaker, had presented "Living on the Edge of the Matter." Daryl said later that night, "I knew when I came into that casino you'd be sitting with Bowden. You're a stalker. I knew you'd hunt him down."

Having passion for your subjects can be poisonous, leading you to walk around in prisons of your own making. Gonzo reporting has its consequences. Critics called Bowden one of our country's most dangerous writers. He often would write and talk about holing up, sometimes for a month at a time, finishing stories and projects to feed his hunger. When you truly care about your subjects and realize that time isn't on your side as a writer, passion quickly turns to addiction. When you are reporting on the cartels' slaughter of hundreds of thousands of innocent men and women on the border and the ugly monster our criminal justice system has become, it consumes you.

Both Bowden and I knew our jobs had a hold on us—it was a bond we shared. He was interested in my mission; I was curious about his. Maybe Bowden saw me as a fellow traveler—a guy undertaking more than just selling books or making a name for himself. When I first started teaching in prisons, I used to brag to my writing colleagues that I was going to San Quentin or New Folsom. I thought it was cool. As the years went on, it became my calling. I wasn't just a teacher. I wasn't just a journalist. This was gonzo. I had become a listener, an advocate, a counselor, and a reporter seeking to uncover what really goes on inside prisons and who the men and women are. There are constraints in taking on all these roles. I can't be just a reporter—I am their teacher, too. Once a month someone calls my university office and asks me to speak to their community group about my activism. A few times a year someone from my community will question or criticize my role working in prisons. "Why do you care about helping these people? Lock 'em up and throw out the key," some say. Prisons quickly became part of my identity. And I was standing on this new ground with men and women who were accustomed to saying, "If it flies, it dies."

Prison Tattoos

I want to believe so badly that the man with *REDNECK* and a confederate flag tattooed on his forearms will get the tattoos removed. He's sitting in the front row of my Writing for Reentry class in this medium-high security prison. With inviting southern hospitality and a cordial voice, he shares stories about his family and his children. It's evident that he misses them, that he cares about them. But I can't get past the symbol and word he has tattooed on his body. Why this guy? Why do I keep coming back to him? Because he's human just like the rest of us. He cares passionately about his kin—the roots, he tells me, run deep. If that's the case, I wonder if the tattoos are just a projection. In here, ink is a shield. Inmates portray particular personas for protection. Like a lot of men in prison, he's outta shape—and if he doesn't scare me, then I doubt he scares many at all.

Each week his writing gets better and we talk more, and I am compelled to ask if he considers getting his tattoos removed. Very calmly he says, "That's not happening—ever." It's clear to me that this is part of his identity, one that seems particularly odd in this day and age. What is it he is specifically promoting with this word and symbol on his body—that he is a racist? That he is a good ol' boy?

It could be worse. It could say *INMATE*. He could have *SHIT* tattooed across his forehead—or *F-U-C-K* or *P-A-I-N* tattooed on his knuckles. I've seen those before. I suppose there are worse things than a Jeff Foxworthy punchline. A southern what? Tradition? In seven years, with no violations, he can be completely off paper. There are over three hundred free and low-cost tattoo-removal programs for those formerly incarcerated—a chance to remove another barrier and get a new start at life.[14]

Contact with Former Federal Inmates Is PROHIBITED in Any Form

After they are released, I cannot have any contact with the federal inmates I work with. These are the rules. As a teacher, I always wonder how they are doing and hope they are well. As a scholar, I feel like this is a missed opportunity to research and write a qualitative study about my former students. But federal rules are rules, and I don't want to jeopardize my job, which I know helps these men. However, I can and do speak with a few former students from the state prisons where

I taught, and if there happens to be a former inmate at the university where I work, I often ask them how they got back on the right track.

A few formerly incarcerated students in my classes at Mount Marty University have written or spoken with me about constructing façades—that you have to do it if you want to survive in prison. They speak of finding a good community of peers inside, which is key. And of course programming—taking classes of any kind helps.

One student, a person of mixed race, said he had made the mistake of trying to belong to a certain group when he arrived in prison. It didn't work. Racism is endemic in prisons. Men have told me they immediately felt the need to conform to one group for survival, even if they didn't believe in the systemic ideologies. Eventually, this student found that cutting hair allowed him to make friends and stay off anyone's radar as long as they were happy with their haircut.

Another student, who had been incarcerated at many facilities, said that at the first place where he was locked up, men got their last names tattooed on their backs. He said he wasn't sure why, but he decided he would follow suit—he wanted to fit in. Now he thinks this might not have been the best idea. He later got his first name tattooed on his belly. When his dad came to visit him, he showed him the tattoos and his father gave him a puzzled look and asked, "Why?"

San Quentin, 2008

I have seen extreme discrimination and segregation at San Quentin. In 2008, the first time I went out into the yard, men stood in the corners of their little territories, keeping guard. There were a lot of turfs. All these little cubes—men in corners, standing watch in their box of concrete. I observed in amazement. There were more gangs than I could count. I couldn't believe this form of segregation still existed in America. Over a thousand men in the yard stood guard—protecting each other from one another. The correctional officers seemed like the last thing these guys were worried about. I've been to New Folsom and San Quentin during lockdowns. Prison gangs communicate with each other. When there is a riot at one facility, another will lock down as a precaution.

Brasso Man

It's a beautiful May afternoon in South Dakota; the sun is out and everything at the prison camp is green. At the beginning of the quarter-mile walking track, inmates are directed which way to walk—Mondays, take a left; Tuesdays, right; and so on in alternation. There's good reason for this: men complain of muscle loss and mental health issues, so it's good to break up the monotony of a simple walking track for their well-being. What is not good for their health are the signs posted around the perimeter of the prison camp: "Unauthorized Contact with the Public is PROHIBITED."

The guy walking with me is leaving in a week to be transferred closer to his son, closer to his home. He'll spend another year in a higher-security prison. "This will be my third location in ten years, but I'll be closer to my son," he says. "In a year I will be able to be his father—maybe from afar, but I will be there for him in case he needs me. Who knows? Maybe his mom will even give me another chance."

I was instructed early on to never get close to any inmate. I understand why. This guy has been in my class for four years. I've learned a lot from him. He was a wealthy man and greed got the best of him. He ended up here for manufacturing and distributing methamphetamine. Like most men and women when they are finally convicted, he realized that chasing paper isn't what it's all about.

He says, "They told me before I even went up for my first year that I could get off, maybe not get any time at all if I cooperated and told the authorities who was supplying me with the large quantity of drugs. I wasn't about to give up my 'friends' and 'business associates.' Why ruin someone else's life when I already ruined a big chunk of my own? Hell, this place has been a blessing. I've learned a lot about myself and life."

We continue to walk the track together. He hands another passing inmate some *Wall Street Journal* crosswords. "That's all I've got for you, friend. Next week I'm going on the merry-go-round to Kansas. One more year, I'm done." The merry-go-round is a program of check-ins at various locations at the prison camp before one leaves—protocol prior to release.

A large man pushes by us, huffing and sweating; I move out of the way so he can pass during his workout.

"It's been a pleasure having you in class," I tell my student, and he smiles.

"I got one for you, Doc. See that man right there that just passed us?"

"How could I miss him?"

"He used to be the Brasso man. He would polish our belt buckles for a stamp. We don't have much here, but we like our buckles to shine for family visits. He's not the Brasso man anymore, but he made good shining things for us, passing the time."

Mike Durfee State Prison and South Dakota Women's Prison, 2018

I want to believe in the smiles on the men's and women's faces when I talk about writing mechanics and revision and how reentry and happiness are real—that the smiles continue to be contagious and that the men and women are not just putting on an act so they can get ninety days off their sentence. I know that's why most of them are here, but I believe I am helping them come to terms with their life through writing. I have to believe. Teacher, reporter, counselor, journalist—objectivity, neutrality, detachment. The plot thickens as my years of involvement increase.

It's obvious that the guy with the *REDNECK* tattoo and so many other men and women here are hiding behind this badass veneer—that ink is their brand. It's tribal. I'm positive some don't know what their true identity is. The values some possess are very shallow. Very selfish. I often show a Martin Luther King Jr. quote in my classes, and I pray that they think about it: "Nothing in all the world is more dangerous than sincere ignorance and conscientious stupidity." This is something I share in all my classes at the prisons and university.

Small-Town Stereotypes

So many of the people in rural America are born on little islands—tiny towns of two thousand or fewer. They throw the anchor in and never leave home. There are guys I've known for a large majority of their lives who might venture to the big city for a weekend, or even four years for college, but they come back and continue on with a narrow view of the world—purposefully oblivious and maybe even frightened about what they learned by leaving their small communities. It's a high school clique they never shake. Willful blindness. Cultural immersion is difficult for some people, so they go back to what they deem comfortable. They want a world where outsiders are not welcome, whether they admit it or not. I have lived in these towns. And the moment I didn't conform I was judged as an outsider again. If you didn't drink beer in the machine shed every night, if you didn't go to a specific church, if you didn't believe in the norm, if you rode a bike instead of driving a vehicle, if you didn't laugh at the jokes and nod in approval, you were marked.

I fear this is not just small-town USA but a part of the provincialism everywhere, including small communities in urban areas that are essentially closed to new ideas. If all you know is one way, it can be hard to enter into a new place or ethos because you might actually feel like a foreigner. But that's what lived experience should be. You should step outside your comfort zone, move from your lane, your county, your state. This in essence is at the heart of gonzo—it's a way of approaching life, being open to new adventures and experiences.

This kind of openness and acceptance is ingrained in me, possibly to a fault. When I was very young, my father told me to never, under any circumstance, use the N-word. Why would I? As I grew older, I had friends whose parents used the word without batting an eye. I heard men purposefully use a buffet of racist words to get a rise out of people. As an adult, I lived in a small town where the word was used and I never quite understood why. The place was 99 percent white. The men using these offensive words had never spent time with any person of color, yet they were quick to label and degrade—an obvious sign of insecurity. All because of a color.

If you are a Christian, if you are a human being with a heart, it makes no sense, but there is hypocrisy everywhere. The two-faced good ol' boy brand is a learned and unfortunate stamp of ignorance. Why are people (good, hardworking Christians) so quick to cast judgment and throw stones at "the other"? The problem isn't just with small communities; it's a way of thinking and doing that is rooted in institutions and enterprises everywhere.

Investigative journalist Bill Conroy writes that "too many of our democratic institutions have been infected by entrenched good ol' boy networks that have their own internal caste systems and systemic treachery. They operate with impunity to ensure self-preservation—screw up; you move up. And these largely white-male good ol' boy networks also maintain power and build fortunes through a seemingly unfettered access to the revolving door that connects government and private-sector power centers. Ultimately, they feed off the taxpayers in the bargain."[15]

Charles Bowden tried to understand all cultures—including the poor Mexicans and their killer, the *sicario*. He treated them equally, evil and good, without judgment. As an objective reporter, Bowden interviewed the sicarios and their associates. For one of his last works, Bowden spent a good deal of time talking with a hit man who admits that he murdered hundreds of people. The publisher's summary of *El Sicario: The Autobiography of a Mexican Assassin*, edited by Molly Molloy and Charles Bowden, is poignant and chilling:

> In this unprecedented and chilling monologue, a repentant Mexican hit man tells the unvarnished truth about the war on drugs on the American. El Sicario is the hidden face of America's war on drugs. He is a contract killer who functioned as a comandante in the Chihuahuan State police, who was trained in the US by the FBI, and who for twenty years kidnapped, tortured and murdered people for the drug industry at the behest of Mexican drug cartels. He is a hit man who came off the killing fields alive. He left the business and turned to Christ. And then he decided to tell the story of his life and work. Charles Bowden first encountered El Sicario while reporting for the book "Murder City." As trust between the two men developed, Bowden bore witness to the Sicario's unfolding confession, and decided to tell his story. The well-spoken man that emerges from the pages of *El Sicario* is one who has been groomed by poverty and driven by a refusal to be one more statistic in the failure of Mexico. He is not boastful, he claims no major standing in organized crime. But he can explain in detail not only torture and murder, but how power is distributed and used in the arrangement between the public

> Mexican state and law enforcement on the ground—where terror and slaughter are simply tools in implementing policy for both the police and the cartels. And he is not an outlaw or a rebel. He is the state. When he headed the state police anti-kidnapping squad in Juarez, he was also running a kidnapping ring in Juarez. When he was killing people for money in Juarez, he was sharpening his marksmanship at the Federal Police range. Now he lives in the United States as a fugitive. One cartel has a quarter million dollar contract on his head. Another cartel is trying to recruit him. He speaks as a free man and of his own free will—there are no charges against him. He is a lonely voice—no one with his background has ever come forward and talked. He is the future—there are thousands of men like him in Mexico and there will be more in other places. He is the truth no one wants to hear.[16]

The truth is that Mexican reporters are still in grave danger ten years later. Celeste González de Bustamante and Jeannine E. Relly's book *Surviving Mexico: Resistance and Resilience among Journalists in the Twenty-First Century*, published in 2021, is the latest investigation:

> Since 2000, more than 150 journalists have been killed in Mexico. Today the country is one of the most dangerous in the world in which to be a reporter. . . . [González de Bustamante and Relly] examine the networks of political power, business interests, and organized crime that threaten and attack Mexican journalists, who forge ahead despite the risks.[17]

It's as if the whole world knows about and is feeding this corruption and no one cares to put an end to it. Why is that? Well, there's too much money being passed around. The drug war and mass incarceration are billion-dollar enterprises. And for hit men, it's a living.

Top Ten Cushiest Prisons in the Nation

In the "cushy" federal prison where I teach, fifteen out of twenty-two guys in the class are inked. Blue-black brands, their inimitable statements. The forearms of one of my students are a mess of calligraphy.

When I read his arm horizontally, it says *LIFE*; when he turns his arm upside down, it says *DEATH*. "Interesting," I say out loud. Someone put a lot of thought into that. I ask the other students in class to write down what their tattoos say on a piece of paper, or show me if they prefer. One asks, "Do you have a tattoo, Dr. Reese?" I put my leg up on the desk, pull up my pant leg, and push down my black sock. *GONZO*. "What does that say? Gonzo? What's that supposed to mean?"

"It means immersing yourself in the story. Instead of writing about someone getting a tattoo, you go get one yourself and tell everyone how it feels to be permanently marked."

What I don't say is that I still believe in the message—that one must live or try to be part of the story, objectively, before they begin to tell it. My students have joked but also been serious when they've suggested that I should just stay at the prison to get the whole picture. Every couple of years *Dateline* or some other show sends the host inside a prison for a day and night to report on the living conditions. A night, even a week—I don't think that's going to show viewers the psychological costs and repercussions of imprisonment.

I am a student at heart, and I have a lot to learn. I pray that never ends. The most important thing I've discovered about writing is this lesson (and I learned it from Chuck, not Hunter): Gonzo reporting and immersing yourself in the story are necessary. It's painful. You carry your subjects with you most days. You wake with them. They get inside your skin. They crawl through your brain. People will warn you to never get too close to your subjects. Chuck made me realize that being defiant off the page, living dangerously and pushing my limits, wasn't the answer. The enigmatic man he presented on the page in his early books was not the man I observed when I was with him. The writer I observed was working and never out of control. The pen pal I had for years kept digging for the story, looking for what motivated him and me. He was a subtle and excellent teacher. Bowden exposed himself to danger but also knew how to keep his distance. When questioned about the time he spent reporting in Juárez, he brushed it off. Mexican reporters, he said on numerous occasions, were the people in danger and the ones losing their lives.

At our first encounter in Deadwood, after a couple of glasses of red wine, Chuck gave a reading in a packed ballroom. I sat in the back at a table with Molly Molloy, Daryl Farmer, Neil Harrison, and some other acquaintances. The banquet was a celebration of Dan O'Brien, his South Dakota memoir *Buffalo for the Broken Heart: Restoring Life to a Black Hills Ranch*, and the bison he raises to restore the Great Plains. We were all excited to eat the buffalo. Rick Bass was there reading for the celebration, as were other environmental writers. Bowden read an important passage from his book, and if you were paying attention, you realized the enormity of his presence among these other writers. They all cared passionately about the land, its inhabitants, and the places they brought to life in their books.

I was still in shock that I had spent the previous two hours with Chuck. After he finished reading, I wandered the streets of Deadwood and then crashed at the hotel. My intention was to wake the next morning and catch Bowden at another of his presentations. It didn't happen. I slept in. I was hungover. But the next week I reached out to Bowden and our correspondence began. I wish I had realized that night that partying wasn't the key to the story. I wish I could go back to that evening and shake myself awake. The misinterpretation of gonzo—the idea that you *need* drugs and alcohol to *fuel* creativity—is some real bullshit. There's just no truth to it. You put your time in like you do with any job. You do it honestly and the best you can. You engage yourself. You become the story. You capture people's authentic voices. You listen to your gut to get what you need. You revise and continue to ask questions. You never quit asking why. That's gonzo to me. And maybe it's time to redefine the drug-fueled and author-centric writing style. The power of gonzo, as exemplified by my tattoo, resides in the fist, not the peyote bud. Gonzo asks why. And you try never to settle for "just because" as an answer.

Back Inside

Outside this prison, body art is a statement, a mark of authority: *M.O.B.* [Money Over Bitches]. *LOOSE LIPS SINK SHIPS. WHAT IS, WILL BE. LOYALTY. BORN 2 FAIL, DESTINED 2 SUCCEED.*

Inside the prisons, I watch men peel off layers of themselves, stripped of freedom, some trying to find redemption. I am not afraid to question them. I begin asking them to write down their tattoos and explain what they mean. Many are hesitant to respond, but the following are three of their submissions:

> My 6-point tattoo, because it represents 6 different points in my life that I live by: knowledge, wisdom, understanding, love, life and loyalty.
>
> My initials are tattoos in puke green on my forearm. It's a reminder of a bad decision at 16 given to me by the only friend who ever posted my bail.
>
> The tattoo on my back that says "pure Chicano," which means pure Chicano. It lets everyone know that I am of Hispanic descent and that I belong to a group of people, my second "family."

"Who the hell has the tattoo *FUCK THE ATF DEA US MARSHALS*?" I ask. I see a student put his head down; his face turns red. He slowly raises his hand, kinda grins.

"I seen it," a classmate of his says. "It's on his back."

Immediately, I flash back to high school, when I was in a cramped apartment drinking a forty with some Nazi punk with *SKINS* tattooed across his forehead backward. I tell the class the story. How we all hated the kid but didn't know what to do. They laugh. Cuss under their breath. Shake their heads. The student is deadpan, looking out the iron window.

At San Quentin I read the eyelids of one man. When he shuts his eyes to show me, the two tattoos on his eyelids read *GAME OVER*. At the state prison in South Dakota, the eyelids of another man read *LIGHTS OUT*.

"It used to be that tattoos were big in the military and in prisons, places where you don't have the freedom to do what you want, where other people are in charge," writes author and veteran Neil Harrison. "Now everybody's getting tattoos, like they need something to give them an identity outside the power structure they have no real say in."[18]

||||

At the women's prison, the inmates' tattoos seemed more spur-of-the-moment. Here too, I asked the women to write down or describe their tattoos and why they got them. "One of mine is of a band. I used to like them a lot. Now I don't. What can you do?" Men's names loitered on their necks and arms like most unforgiving exes do. Children's names under ears, above hearts, across their chests, they said. A few of these women pushed up their sleeves to show me and describe their ink:

.38 SPECIAL
47K ("My prison number.")
Pot leaf and crown ("I'm the queen of bud!")
M.O.B. (Money Over Bitches)
Virgo sign ("A prison tattoo gone all wrong.")
JINX ("It's my nickname.")
Left hand—*BEAUTY*
Right thumb—semicolon (;) ("Stands for suicide awareness.")
Inside left wrist—*THINK AND THINK* (with a heart)

There were numerous ring tattoos. Green and black. Numerous girlfriends and husbands. "Everyone has a girlfriend," one woman said. "There's more girlfriend drama than any other kind in here," another said. "Everyone will tell you they love you. That love becomes an almost empty term thrown around to try and make meaningful emotional connections inside these walls."

In the crook of one woman's elbow was a tattoo of a red *X*. "That's where the fun begins," she said laughingly. "You have good veins," she told me. "I noticed that right away. You and I could have a lot of fun." This was the same woman who told me later in class that when she and her friends ran out of dope one night, they decided to shoot ice water into their veins.

Bowden's Visit to South Dakota in 2014

Shortly before his unexpected death, Chuck Bowden and his girlfriend and writing companion Molly Molloy co-wrote a letter to my students at Mount Marty University. This was after another visit to South Dakota, where we screened the documentary *El Sicario, Room 164*, which was based on Bowden's 2009 *Harper's* article and Bowden and Molloy's 2011 book, *El Sicario*. The film and the book are a cumulative project representing more than ten years of investigative reporting. In their letter to my students, Chuck and Molly wrote:

> A lot of your comments refer to some idea of the risks we take in our work. We'd like to get rid of that impression. We are not at risk. Mexican citizens are. . . . Journalists in Mexico are frequently threatened and murdered. . . . And these deaths are not investigated and no one is arrested, tried or imprisoned for the crimes. Organized crime in Mexico is big business. . . . Increasingly because of migration, friendship and love, we are one family and our relationships and emotions cannot be repealed or deported. All the problems of violence, drugs, smuggling and poverty must be faced, and by that we mean that we must look to the root causes and fix them, not simply denounce people, ideas and policies we don't like.[19]

What is so intriguing to me about this letter is the frank nature with which they address reporting. Molloy and Bowden spent more than a decade covering the "murder capital of the world," Juárez, and the killings in Mexico—the slaughter of nearly five hundred thousand Mexicans since 2007 and the disappearance of innocent people—where innumerable murders never get fully investigated or solved.[20]

Molloy writes about Juárez in the article "Give Us This Day Our Daily Massacre . . .":

> Some people will insist that focusing on the numbers denies the humanity of the victims and of those working for social change in Juárez. I disagree. The actual victims of the slaughter happening in Juárez disappear in the pages of commentary and policy analysis from government, academic and law enforcement experts in both the United States and Mexico. Poets and critics say that perhaps "Juárez has become a metaphor, an emblem of the future of the U.S.-Mexico border . . ." ["Juárez Is Dying, Prominent Journalist Warns," *El Paso Times*, April 10, 2010.]

> But Juárez is not a metaphor. It is a real place of great neglect and great suffering. It is a place where gangs of killers—organized and otherwise—commit murder with no fear of punishment. It is a place where the citizens can expect no protection from their government leaders or from their institutions.[21]

Chuck and I were fighting the same war, but I hadn't connected all the dots when we first met—"All the problems of violence, drugs, smuggling and poverty must be faced, and by that we mean that we must look to the root causes and fix them, not simply denounce people." Well, that's exactly how to fix our problem of mass incarceration, now, isn't it? Face it and fix it, although the "how" is always the hardest part.

I've spent fourteen years teaching men and women in prisons how to write, how to come to terms with the actions that brought them to jail. I am one of five artists-in-residence throughout the country who are part of the National Endowment for the Arts interagency initiative with the Federal Bureau of Prisons. I established Yankton Federal Prison Camp's first creative writing workshop and publishing course, editing the annual journal *4 P.M. Count*, which features creative writing and visual artwork by inmates. This is a vigorous course. I teach men, very quickly, how to go into their dark caves, how to knock the crows off their shoulders, how to deal with the things they carry wherever they land—how to live with their past. And in doing so, they become richer, wiser, and better equipped for reentry. I've spent these years working in federal and, more recently, state prisons. I've worked and presented to inmates in San Quentin, the Allegheny County Jail, and the women's prison in Pierre, South Dakota.

Chuck taught me to get the facts, present statistics, and repeat them often.

Facts

"Almost one in three Americans of working age has some sort of criminal record. The United States accounts for 5 percent of the world's population and 25 percent of its inmates."[22] According to RAND, every dollar spent on prison education equates to five dollars of taxpayer savings.[23] The vast majority of men and women incarcerated in America are nonviolent offenders; this is why you should care.

Both Charles Bowden and I knew the war on drugs didn't work. And we set out in two different parts of the United States to try to bring to light this epidemic that is affecting the poor, the powerless, the incarcerated, and persons in need of rehabilitation. In response to his experience with my students at the prison, Chuck wrote:

> i was struck by how most of them tried to make sense out of their lives and how they refused to let the court and prison system define them . . . and i couldn't help but notice the fear some had of harder drugs being legalized lest they become addicts again—a thought i have heard expressed by friends who have been all but ruined by cocaine. such desires speak of a hunger for a better world, one where temptation has been removed. such a world is not near at hand and i think those who are tempted by illegal substances must face the same struggle as those tempted by alcohol and tobacco. . . . i see no escape from the present system except to legalize drugs. i see no magic cure for the poverty and violence . . . and I see no reform of the prison system so long as it is largely devoted to warehousing the poor and the powerless . . . you have helped educate me and I am grateful. this War on Drugs will eventually end. not because of truth but because the policy costs too much money. this abandonment will never be admitted.[24]

When I shared Chuck's response with the men in my prison class, they reiterated how aware they were of the oppression they had witnessed in our society, as free Americans and as incarcerated men. They weren't arguing that they were innocent of any crime. They were expressing their concerns about a fair and just system. Some had serious addiction issues and were now enrolled in classes to help them with their disease. Some described how dead set on destruction they were, that prison was their lifesaver. Some were victims of their environment who honestly hadn't thought they'd live past their eighteenth birthday. They were happy Chuck responded to their letters, and his response started a dialogue within the class. No one was denying that they had done something wrong, and they all understood that our collective voices could help foster positive change. By sharing our stories—communicating and listening to each other—and with education, we could see, right in front of our eyes, attitudes changing for the better.

When I give talks about my work in prisons, I am often asked if I believe drugs should be legal. My short answer is yes. If we legalized drugs, we could then discover and look at the root problem. Where is the need for drugs really coming from? Previous trauma? Anxiety? Depression? Boredom? All of the above? Prison has saved some of my students' lives. However, I think there are far better options than locking addicts up. Every year more organizations form to help those in need. The federal prison system has a valuable residential drug and alcohol program. A large number of state prisons don't have much programming or training. But innumerable opportunities exist to create life-saving institutions to help ourselves and our communities. The problem is that there's too much money in mass incarceration. This war on our people is systemic and won't change until we all fight for positive transformation and real rehabilitation.

Prisons, Floods, and Cancer

South Dakota Magazine publisher and author Bernie Hunhoff visits my prison classes once a year to talk about craft. In an email he wrote to me in 2012, he made the following observation:

> One day this summer, I visited the Federal Prison at Yankton to speak to inmates about writing and publishing. That same afternoon, I learned that one of our best friends was diagnosed with a serious cancer.
>
> Later, at the office, I asked a co-worker who has survived cancer, "What's it going to be like for her?"
>
> "She'll feel all alone at times, no matter what people do to help, because it's something you have to ultimately face alone," said my co-worker. "She'll walk down the street and feel sort of disconnected from everyone else as they go about their daily routine, smiling and laughing."

That same week, I also traveled up and down the Missouri River, meeting with victims of the historic 2011 flood. By coincidence, one landowner used the same street analogy as he explained his predicament. "You walk down the street and you think, 'These people have no idea I might be losing my house and farm. They have no idea what we're going through.'"

I've spoken to classes at the Yankton prison for a number of years, and on every trip I leave with somewhat the same message that the flooded farmer and the cancer survivor expressed. Prisoners are crammed on a campus or cell-block with hundreds of other inmates as well as guards and staff, and yet there is a palpable atmosphere of aloneness, despite the hail-fellow camaraderie. . . . Prison. Cancer. Floods. Droughts. Fires. Poverty. Alcoholism. Mental illness. There are a hundred types of prison cells. We are on solo paths, but perhaps we're seldom as alone as we feel.[25]

Sharing Ideas

What I so admired about Chuck was his eagerness to share his ideas and his time. He did this with his friends and the people he came in contact with. He was a giving person. Unorthodox—which of course was refreshing to read and hear. He was my favorite pen pal. He relentlessly championed and was passionate about the things we talked about. Out of the blue, he'd do something unusual, like type up a poem or a few paragraphs from a book he was reading and email it to me. "Read this," he'd say.

Once, he typed up a page from a James Jones book. "I have been reading the new restored edition of James Jones *From Here to Eternity* and stumbled on this passage about blowing taps on a bugle." And in typical Chuck fashion, he shared it with me:

> This is the song of the men who have no place, played by a man who has never had a place, and can therefore play it. Listen to it. You know this song, remember? This is the song you close your ears to every night, so you can sleep. This is the song you drink five martinis every evening not to hear. This is the song of the Great Loneliness, that

> creeps in like the desert wind and dehydrates the soul. This is the song you'll listen to on the day you die. When you lay there in the bed and sweat it out, and know that all the doctors and nurses and weeping friends dont mean a thing and cant help you any, cant save you one small bitter taste of it, because you are the one thats dying and not them; when you wait for it to come and know that sleep will not evade it and martinis will not put it off and conversation will not circumvent it and hobbies will not help you to escape it; then you will hear this song and, remembering, recognize it. This song is Reality. Remember? Surely you remember?[26]

This passage rang true to both of us. As writers, Chuck and I were both trapped in our own prisons—we knew and understood this. We recognized that we wouldn't be leaving soon. Is this gonzo, or is this in-depth reporting? This passage speaks to our communities—the oppressed, the teachers, the addicts, the police. It's a tug-of-war that connects us all.

When I first started teaching in prisons, some of my family members didn't want me to talk about it. But it was as if I'd entered a new world. I was visiting San Quentin on a yearly basis. I was meeting with advocates throughout the country. I knew the power of education. What I was learning wasn't at all what we are fed on television, on social media, and in the news. These were real people—people who made mistakes and needed serious help. I couldn't and wouldn't stop talking. I kept listening and learning.

I'd been teaching in the prison for maybe seven years. I had passed the point of bragging about this work, and I was carrying a lot of baggage home with me. A lot of atrocious stories about abuse were told to me in confidence, but the men spoke about some of it in class with their peers. I had become a counselor as well as their writing instructor. The personal space to share some of our deepest secrets and confront our fears grew in those first years and served as the foundation of my program. I developed a deep understanding of how close I was to being one of these men behind bars and paranoia about how many times I never got caught. We are all guilty. Working with men and women who are behind bars really heightens this awareness and fear.

But I was working and successful. My second book had been published, and I was riding some unusual waves. My daughters were healthy and getting older, and I was digging, quite rapidly, into my own addiction. I dealt with these stories, my responsibilities, and my growing anxiety not through discipline, exercise, and writing but by drinking. On most days, as soon as my work was done, I'd head to the liquor store. I suppose I'm no different from a lot of men and women. I see liquor and beer bottles littered on every road I run on now.

One day, before that 3:30 bell rang to dismiss my class, I was in the prison having one-on-one conferences with students. My hands were beginning to shake. My body wanted what it wanted. I would sit on my hands sometimes to hide the fact that I was beginning to go through withdrawal. I was inside a prison trying to help men, while meanwhile my life was falling apart. I knew it. And I kept fucking lying to myself.

As I popped open a soda in front of my student, my hand was shaking uncontrollably. I was ashamed. There was no hiding this. The student watched me. He was in his mid-forties, maybe a little older. I grabbed the can with both hands because I had to. I took a drink. He said, "It looks like you needed that drink." I looked him in the eyes and said, "I did." I couldn't tell you the name of that student. But he knew just as well as I did that my game was up. I wasn't fooling anyone, certainly not those close to me who had brought this problem to my attention on innumerable occasions.

I have never written much about this. I can tell you that I drank like most people, because it was fun. I equated fun with alcohol. And alcohol is legal and alcohol is everywhere. I liked to chase that high. I drank because it calmed my nerves, and it worked well until it didn't. The liquor, I thought, was a way to dull the worries and concerns I had about all of it. The horrors I heard about in classrooms and my constant anxiety to do more and be more. I drank to make my excuses plausible. I spent a lot of time in my head. I dabbled in regret on a daily basis and got used to it. I wish I could get that time back. It would be another year or two before I completely hit bottom and turned my life around. I suppose it was pure luck that I never got pulled over and put in jail. I was fortunate to have people who cared about me and encouraged me to get help. They could have walked away, but they didn't. A lot of the men and women in my classes have never had a support system or been given the tools to deal with common life problems in a constructive manner.

That passage in *From Here to Eternity* can make a guy think late at night, after a few too many drinks, that he is no different from the next guy—his problems are real problems: "This is the song you drink five martinis every evening not to hear. This is the song of the Great Loneliness, that creeps in like the desert wind and dehydrates the soul."

It's funny how literature does that, how words we create become other people's freedoms and fantasies. Their songs. Words free us from others and ourselves. Was it year seven in the prison that I showed my true self? Or had they seen it all along? Was it year seven that I truly realized I was no different from any man in that prison? "Remember this," the supervisor of education told me my first year. "Any of us could have wound up here after a few bad decisions."

What's absurd and interesting is that working inside prisons gave me this delusional feeling that I was walking the edge. I was almost ready to step off that cliff, but then I was pulled back into reality—into a prison to help men. Surely I was okay. My problems weren't as bad as these guys' problems. When you treat drinking like a part-time job, your brain starts playing tricks on you. You don't think clearly.

After I was sober a few years, I decided to tell the whole class about my addiction. I can't remember how the discussion led to my opening up. What I remember is that I looked down after telling the class about my own trials. I felt a bit ashamed and told them as much. I said something like, "I'm a professor. Maybe now you don't think I am as smart as you thought I was. Maybe now you don't respect me as much. But I thought the truth mattered. There are no socioeconomic divisions when it comes to addiction." One student, and I do remember his name, said, "I respect you a lot more now than I ever did. Thanks for sharing your story."

Going Deep

Chuck and I had shown up. We weren't just blowing through some city with an agenda. We were sticking around and getting to know the people, asking all our questions until the whole story was told. That's what turned me on to Bowden's work: his true and often painful investigation. I truly believe in immersing yourself in the story before claiming to be an expert. You have to live and breathe and work with your subjects, if you can. The work becomes important if you can invest that kind of time. Every day, writers and reporters show up at events with an itinerary, questions, and, perhaps, preconceived notions. Agendas. I know I showed up with all of this when I first started teaching in prisons.

When I was in my first year, there was the inmate who said, "Man, you weren't born a criminal—you don't understand." And another who said, "What's the difference between poetry and prose?" I knew I had to find a beginning, a level playing field. Maybe that's when I let my guard down, allowed myself to be trapped, consumed by my subjects, my fears and failures. Both a prison arts activist and the contract I signed to enter San Quentin prison reiterated that my job should always be about the art—that I should have a very narrow definition of my role inside. Both warned me to refrain from having any personal connections with the students. As a teacher, as a writer, as a human being who cares, I just could not come to terms with that. There's a reason the words "art" and "humanity" are often grouped together. I vowed to treat my students like I'd treat any other person—with respect.

I have been asked by audience members how I connect with people of color in my class. My response: no differently than with white students. Maybe a better answer would be what University of Washington teaching professor Teddi Beam-Conroy once said to me: "I try to meet students where they're at."

I once had a presentation canceled in Omaha, my hometown, because someone on Facebook protested, saying I surely didn't know what I was talking about because I was white, implying that my fourteen years working behind bars didn't matter. I had never met this person in my life. I was still paid for the keynote. What's wrong with this picture? It would have been a perfect opportunity to share what I know as a teacher in corrections.

I have been made fun of and talked about because I help criminals. "Fuck 'em. Keep 'em locked up. Why should we be wasting tax dollars to help prisoners—people who broke the law?" I have carried my job home with me since I started it. I have made family members, people who care about me, uncomfortable in various ways. Anger. Entertainment. Curiosity. Research. Compassion. Money. Empathy. Because it became an obsession.

I wished for years that I knew the cold hard facts. I didn't really learn about the millions of incarcerated people and what over fifty years of the war on drugs have done to the bedrock of our society until I started listening. I had to throw out my plan, my syllabus, my prepared questions. I didn't know that I could silence critics and ill-informed people with facts and statistics—with our stories. So I learned. I studied. I visited notorious prisons. I asked questions. I taught for three years at medium-high men's and women's prisons. I put in the time and I continue to do it. "When the going gets weird, the weird turn pro." Hunter S. Thompson wrote that. How much of the idea of hard work, which is at the foundation of that statement, has been lost to his philosophy of crazy exploits?

I got the gonzo tattoo when I was in my early twenties. I debated it for a year. I loved the idea of the open highway and all the stories out there—who doesn't? I wound up working at the end of that road with men whose drug-fueled adventures put them in prison. That idea of "go big or go home" has landed millions of men and women behind bars. Isn't that what essentially happened to Thompson in the long run? He found himself in his own prison, and he believed his only way out was suicide. I've seen hundreds of men in similar situations who have still turned their lives around. I truly wish Thompson had been able to do the same. Hunter S. Thompson, at his core, was a very gifted writer—one of the best.

How My Gonzo May Be Different than Yours

"True gonzo ultimately seems to be living one's writing life as one's own, not someone else's," said Kent Meyers.[27] It means having the courage and daring that Hunter S. Thompson modeled, and perhaps even a bit of the risk, yes. And it means the discipline, hard work, time, and commitment that I saw Chuck Bowden put in. I remember Bowden saying something like, "If your writing doesn't put you in some sort of danger, it's not worth doing." I believe that. I have questioned a lot of my own writing, and as I've grown I have asked myself, *Why are you doing this?* The answer is simple, and it's a philosophy I will forever live by. The assignment should always be about discovery, not display.

Gonzo means that the writer makes the quest their own, that the writer "doesn't imitate or idolize or slavishly copy a method or life," says Meyers. "Put briefly, you learned from Bowden and Thompson—but you are now doing things differently than either of them," he continues. "Bowden says he would abandon his family and consider it work. You have chosen not to abandon your family but instead pull them into what you consider your work. The border you cross is not out of the nation but into the prison. . . . So, you're gonzo to yourself, but you're not just imitating either Bowden or Thompson."[28]

LOVE Your WORK

A friend asked me one time if I knew how to spell *love*. I looked at her like you might imagine.

"Go on," she said, "spell it." So I did.

"L-O-V-E," I said.

"No, that's wrong," she said. "W-O-R-K."

I shared the advice Chuck emailed me about investigative reporting:

> Investigative reporting is based on anger and appetite. You can't do it unless you really have a hunger to know something and you can't do it unless lies really make you angry. . . . I've learned a few things over the years.
>
> 1. Never go to a press conference. . . .
> 2. Most people want to tell the truth, they are simply shopping for someone who they can trust with their lives and experiences. . . .
> 3. Never be the expert. . . .
> 4. Never break your word. . . .
> 5. Never trust a story that does not explode under your hand. . . .
> 6. Always meet a person face-to-face if possible. People are animals and want to look into your eyes. . . .
> 7. Admit mistakes. . . .
> 8. Never give up. . . .

9. Never stop making notes. . . .
10. Love your work. I have never known a good investigative reporter who didn't love their job and work very long hours. You can't do this without love of the work. Reporting is both a craft and an art and if you love your work, you will always be getting better at it and always be learning. And one day you'll look around and notice most other people don't love their work. Think about that for a moment, and then get back to your work.[29]

I had the pleasure of publishing some of Chuck's last essays in our university journal *Paddlefish*. We have a small budget and he sent me these essays for next to nothing. They were incredible. "See, I'm easy," he said, on more than one occasion. I loved soliciting Chuck for new work. Here in South Dakota, the border war and real immigrant stories aren't reported—except, of course, Trump's plan to end DACA and build a bigger wall. Even with all my education, I didn't know anything about what was going on at the border until two writers, David Cremean and Kent Meyers, brought Bowden's article "The Sicario: A Juárez Hit Man Speaks" to my attention. I read it over and over. I couldn't believe I'd never heard any of this. In my critical writing classes, I'd spent weeks trying to speak with authority on a subject that was foreign to me. But my students and I were learning together.

Chuck Bowden lit a fire in me. This was when I started asking myself, *What are you doing working in prisons? What's your purpose as a writer? What kind of legacy will you leave?* It was when I realized that working in prisons was, dare I say, my calling. Gonzo. It was the ink I had branded myself with years ago, but now I started truly living it. Expression. Obsession. Insight into my core that developed over the years and went much further than skin deep. Gonzo is my intimacy, my empathy, my connection to the greater good. My tattoo was never a front—it was never meant as a brand to ward off strangers or enemies, or to welcome confrontation. But I have grown into my tattoo as a way to live that represents me and my writing.

Every once in a while, I'll be walking down the street and someone will yell, "Hunter!" Or someone will lift a sleeve of their shirt and show me their gonzo tattoo. "Brothers in ink," one guy proclaimed. I'm sure there are thousands of us spread across the world. I hope the tattoo means more than the peyote button to them, too. What permanent message will I leave?

The last time I saw Chuck, when he visited my university and spoke to hundreds of people, I studied him carefully. I stopped at his hotel before any of his presentations began. I gave him a copy of Michael Forsberg's *Great Plains: America's Lingering Wild*. After his lecture and film screening, he and Molly were heading to the Rowe Sanctuary in Kearney, Nebraska, hoping to see the sandhill crane migration. Chuck wasn't smoking. He drank very little when we went out to eat one night. On his last afternoon, after lunch, I hugged him. "Alright," he said. I hoped we'd see each other soon.

How well did I know Chuck Bowden? Does it really matter? As readers, our heroes become our associates, don't they? Sometimes we even meet them and a friendship grows. We think about them. Want to steal from them. Want to be them. I love my work. I continue to get better. I am hungry. If you are driven, you will continue to win. The good ones—we fight, we witness, we get better, we push through the crowd. *You follow?*

I think Chuck would want me to reiterate the words he wrote on that casino voucher he autographed for me on the day we met, which is now framed and hanging in my office, right underneath the poem "The Hangman at Home," by Carl Sandburg (which Chuck sent to me in the body of an email): "Appetite is the road to life and culture."

3

Crime as Entertainment

It's show time! I'm with CJ Box, Craig Johnson, and some other commercial crime writers, each of us serving as a keynote speaker representing a different crime genre. I'm reading poetry about prisoners—about coming to terms with why people are incarcerated. The grand event is being held in the historic ballroom, which is packed with hundreds of people paying banquet prices for a good cause. When I finish reading my poem, the master of ceremonies stands up to retrieve the microphone. She wants to stop my presentation short. It isn't commercial enough. I don't hand the mic to her. Instead, I read another poem about the war on drugs—on race, on humanity. When I finish my ten-minute presentation, I hand the microphone to the MC, who looks the part here in the West—shiny and stiff cowboy hat, everything amazingly gunslinger chic.

"Well, that was depressing," she mutters while covering the microphone. She smiles and turns back to the crowd to attempt another joke and reassert the idea that crime is just show business, entertainment, mostly fiction, just made up. And for so many gathered here, she is right—most of this is entertainment, mostly fiction, mostly made up. I like it just as much as the next person. I can't wait to finish revising this manuscript so I can go binge-watch a few episodes of *Yellowstone*. However, when people are traumatized by crime and punishment, they don't disregard the truth and horror of it so eagerly. The authors on stage know and understand this. In fact, that was the reason I was invited—to read about the hard realities of punishment.

All over the country, people pay admission to see parodies of the Wild West and mafioso-gangster reenactments. This is part of what crime fiction is about—it's a commodity. And good mystery and suspense authors use their real-life experience to craft their stories. I remember best-selling author Marc Cameron, a thirty-year law enforcement veteran and former man tracker for the U.S. Marshals Service, telling me, "Real crime writers are men and women who are using their experience to write facts with fiction." The reason my students like the writer Allen Eskens so much is that he was a criminal defense attorney for more than twenty years, and he understands people who are down on their luck. His 2014 debut novel, *The Life We Bury*, which has been translated into more than twenty languages, is by far their favorite. It was rejected by 148 agents before being published, and now it is being made into a movie.

A few years after the conference, I am in another city presenting at a book festival and I make a point to go listen to a recent Edgar Award winner. His details and description are very good. I am captivated by his honesty when he admits that he doesn't know a lot about crime. After his presentation, I see him walking into a banquet room, riding a high after the day's events. I introduce myself, tell him I enjoyed his reading and appreciate his craft. "Oh, you are that prison writer. I totally have to pick your brain to find out what criminals are really like," he says. It's the third time a famous crime writer has said this to me.

Crime is glamorized—we know this. There's always a journey—a before and after. There's always suspense. Thrill. A wild ride. A climax. Who doesn't want to be part of that? But in real life, there's not always a resolution. There's not always a happy ending. We have industries devoted to these genres. Millions of fans turn on, tune in, and watch, listen to, and read these stories. We don't always hear about the victims, but we are starting to. That is the intrigue with documentaries, with true-crime podcasts, with unsolved cases. We are starting to see the realities, and sometimes we are able to watch them as they unfold through real-time texts, live surveillance, recorded videos, and police body cams. The problem is, some people in the industry are insulated from the reality of their subject.

When I first started teaching in prisons, I knew I'd write about it. I thought I had scored the golden ticket. I was so excited to go to San Quentin on my first assignment that the organizer from the William

James Association was concerned about my eagerness. And my interest was all about me—how my poems and stories could get me into the stadium of this industry. And then, when I read this paragraph in the department of corrections (DOC) manual, reality hit:

> DO NOT WEAR DENIM OR BLUE TO THE FACILITY. Never allow yourself to be without staff or security. The DOC does not tolerate sexual harassment—notify authorities immediately. Do not engage in personal transactions with any inmate. Do not discuss personal affairs—confine yourself to teaching art. Our program depends on a narrow and conservative view of our role in the facility. It is a felony for anyone to assist in an inmate's escape. Bringing guns, weapons of any kind is prohibited—this includes tear gas, explosives, and also cocaine, liquor or any other narcotics. The CDCR will not negotiate for you in a hostage situation.[1]

||||

Stage fright doesn't exist. Say yes when the Arts ask you to leave your daughters at home and read for and work with the hardest of men. "The correction officers will not negotiate for you in a hostage situation." Hear and understand this. This isn't a game. Read the contract—black and white. Think urinal gassings, homemade shanks, and newspaper daggers. Pack your funeral shoes and black boots. YouTube San Quentin and bypass Johnny Cash. "You are a skinny little white man," a colleague says. "They won't leave you unattended." This trip is nonrefundable. You understand?

"Don't forget your lube!" the small-town cop in Nebraska says.[2]

Welcome to San Quentin

"They will try you, immediately. They will see how far they can push, how much you will let on, how much you will provide. Believe me. I see it every day," a correctional officer says. Hop off Sir Frances Drake Boulevard and just like that, you're in their world.

"Prime real estate in San Fran," the driver says. Pass through the first armed and guarded entrance after they check the trunk, into the 432 acres that house California's only gas chamber and death row for condemned inmates. Park the car in the neighborhood where staff and their families

live (some in trailers they pull behind their pickups because it's too expensive to live anywhere else in Marin County, California).

When a prisoner picks you up in a state vehicle, drives you to the sally port, act like it's all natural. Watch him patiently change the dial of the radio. There you will show ID *and be hand-stamped with an invisible marker as you are received through three separated and locked iron-gate corridors.*

Hear a man tell you about the problems prisoners face with parole boards, the governor's inevitable final say. Hear him laugh, kind of, and tell you how this place, demographically, is compared to the country of China. "China." Hear the echo. "China—a country—get that, man! We get the newspaper here. Get a lot of things you probably don't want to know about. State made chicken coops bigger, on account they weren't humane for a chicken. Made them cages bigger. We petitioned. Did the math. Proved our holes aren't large enough for a Labrador Retriever. Shit, I suppose I shouldn't complain—360 guys sleeping in my room—the gymnasium. Believe that. I can show you, you want."

"Whose house is this? Our house!" Fear the Mexican Mafia over the three-story barbed and fenced courtyard doing their hour-long session of strenuous organized calisthenics. See their shadows—push-ups, deep-knee bends. "Hoo! Hoo! Hoo! Hoo!"

You are outside with the pigeons, but locked in. There is a memorial garden for slain officers to your left and a chapel to your right. Walk through the courtyard and keep your eyes on. The convicted men are in blues and T-shirts.

"Fresh Fish. Fresh Fish!" A line of new prisoners in their fluorescent orange jumpsuits single file—heads slumped—eyes zig-zagging. "Fresh Fish!"

Arrive at the entrance of the prison arts program. "My name is Bird Man. Bird Man," an old gray man says. "Birds like me. Land right on my shoulder."

"It's the truth," another prisoner says.

"Of course it is. Of course it is. Why he lie about birds. You see it, right here."

Walk with your group inside. An inmate immediately approaches you.

"You ever have that dream, the one where you have to choose your ears or your eyes? Which one would you pick? Here," he says, "we try to forget both."[3]

||||

The first time I went to San Quentin in 2008 to visit the Arts in Corrections program, we arrived when the warden was hosting his own retirement party, which featured a kazoo band. As part of the festivities, the live band would soon be playing in the yard. San Quentin is half the size of the small city I live in. The yard is huge. A four-hundred-meter track, where men run marathons, surrounds it. There's a field for baseball and even an old medieval cavern where you can find shackles still hanging on the wall, if you know where to look.

The yard is controlled by segregated plots, each claimed by a different gang. In the 2014 article "How Gangs Took Over Prisons" in *The Atlantic*, the reporter states, "Gangs effect this justice on the inside in part by circulating a 'bad-news list,' or BNL. If your name is on a BNL, gang members are to attack you on sight—perhaps because you stole from an affiliate on the outside, or because you failed to repay a drug debt, or because you're suspected of ratting someone out. . . . One sign that the BNL is a rationally deployed tool, rather than just a haphazard vengeance mechanism, is that gangs are fastidious about removing names from the list when debts are paid."[4]

Here in San Quentin's yard, men work out, bullshit, kill time, and, on occasion, try to kill each other. At the corners of everyone's turf are guys standing guard. Not far from these plots is an open field, and this was where the band played—a parody cover band who claimed to be from a fictitious California prison.

The members of the band, at least fifteen of them, wore an array of prison blues and played kazoos along with their chosen instruments. They sounded good. They were a theatrical collective. They reminded me of the ska band The Mighty Mighty Bosstones, horns and all. The men moved in unison and had rehearsed their show—a lot. They jumped and moved; the stage shook. I had the privilege of opening for the Bosstones when I was in college, and I've spent a lot of years watching and playing in bands. This was the most absurd cover band I'd ever seen. And the gonads on these guys were a bit terrifying. I really thought a mosh pit might erupt, and it wouldn't be a good one. I knew Johnny Cash had played at San Quentin and that it had helped to solidify his badass persona, but this kazoo band was absurd. However, it *was* entertaining.

I have to fact-check my memory—who were these guys? Here is what I found in the *San Quentin News*:

> SAN QUENTIN RECEIVES 'THE OPHIR PRISON MARCHING KAZOOBAND & TEMPERANCE SOCIETY'
>
> December 1, 2008 by *San Quentin News* Staff
>
> Bizarre events were happening in San Quentin. Warden Robert Ayers, Jr., stepped up to the microphone on the lower yard and announced that the California "State Prison" at "Ophir" was closed, and the members of the marching band were transferred to San Quentin. In a gesture of good will, these newly arrived (volunteer) "inmates" decided to put on a concert on the lower yard. . . .
>
> . . . The music was tight, playing familiar tunes. A SQTV video showed them on temporary community release marching in local parades. In the end, the inmates were applauded loudly by San Quentin prisoners. A reversal in the transfer must have come about, being that they marched back up the hill under heavy escort, never to be seen again.[5]

I had boarded a golf cart with an extended bed for more passenger seating, and I rode down the track until we parked close to the stage. I got off and looked around. I wondered if guards were going to escort me onto the playing field near the stage. The group of five of us looked dazed and confused. The band started to get fired up after their first song, the Kingsmen's "Louie, Louie."

"Up yours, San Quentin!" one of the kazoo players hollered before the band broke into their next number.

About this time, men started walking down from the yard to get a closer look. I felt real nervous and completely out of place—no doubt I stuck out. I saw a familiar face coming toward me—a young Hispanic man I'd met earlier in the day in the Arts in Corrections room. I knew it was him because I was dumbfounded by how young he looked, in his baggy prison blues, when he spoke with me about his crime. Because I was young and naïve, only thirty-six, I asked all the questions I wasn't supposed to. He said, "Wrong place, wrong time. A drive-by. I was standing on a porch with some of my cousins who shot back." He looked so innocent to me. As he approached our group, I moved close to him. "What is this?" I asked.

"The Jefe's last hurrah. He's decided to throw himself a party and I guess he gets the last laugh. Not many of these guys are impressed." And after another cheesy song I asked him, "Where is everyone? I mean, here's a band in prison. Doesn't everyone show up, even if it is a kazoo band? What else do they have to do?"

"No, ese. Just like at home. People like to chill in their cell. Watch TV."

His answer bothered me. As politically incorrect as this band was, I expected a crowd. I mean, this gave people *something* to do. I would think about this moment often after my return home. The more I visited San Quentin in the following years, the more I realized that it *was* home for many of the men. Men who had standards. Men who wouldn't help celebrate the warden's retirement by dancing and clapping along to a kazoo band.

Later that day, when the band quit and we were going to get lunch outside the old-school iron-gate entrance where the staff eat, I saw the members of this parody band posing for a photo with the warden and some correctional personnel. One of the men in the band had a plastic keg attached to the top of his head. *This*, I thought, *is what hell looks like*. And I couldn't help but laugh.

||||

When I returned to San Quentin for the second time, I still didn't understand that I was going into the inmates' home and asking them some very personal questions right out of the gate. Who did I think I was? I was naïve, anxious, and eager; this was totally gonzo, I thought. I felt so empowered to tell anyone who would listen that I was training and presenting my own creative work at San Quentin. I thought I was Cash, a bad ass. In fact, though, when I first read some of my work at the Arts in Corrections facility, one inmate in class fell asleep. I was in for some astonishing discoveries. Here I was, the National Endowment for the Arts Writer-in-Residence for the Federal Bureau of Prisons, and my very captivated audience was yawning and even closing their eyes.

After I had told about four or five anecdotes and followed each with a poem, I was disturbed that the young Native American inmate fell asleep. I was talking about the Great Plains, for Christ's sake, and the people who populate that area. He had family from Pine Ridge. But my work didn't do anything for him until I read some funny pieces, and then he finally opened his eyes. I later joked with him about it; my ego wouldn't let it go.

"Everyone comes in here and tries to be serious and read this heavy work—poetry. Man, I'm in prison. Make me laugh, I pay attention."

||||

"Do you have a chance of ever getting out of here?" I asked a student in class.

"Son, how old are you?"

"Thirty-six," I replied, looking right back into his eyes. He shifted, stepped closer, and answered, "I've been in here since you were five years old. I'm never getting out."

"Okay," I replied, awkward, cold, and uncertain.

I was still living in this fantasy-land façade of what prison actually was—the fiction I'd googled and read about as opposed to the reality of what was going on right in front of me. I knew crimes could put a person behind bars for the rest of their life—X was behind bars for murdering Christina. His accomplice was never getting out. But I hadn't quite comprehended that I was in a room with a lot of lifers. I went in feeling cocky and very much believing I was a better person because my credentials said so. Not many people get an escort around San Quentin—or rides in golf carts to kazoo bands—unless they are a big deal.

I wasn't prepared to understand the reality that a crime can put a person in prison for life no matter how he acts once he's there. Maybe what I should have said was, "I'm sorry. I realize now this is home for you—you who have been fundamental in resurrecting the *San Quentin News* after sixteen years, been instrumental in changing attitudes inside and outside the prison walls, been the writer who has found the pen a mighty fortress." I was naïve enough to think that things like the prison newspaper or arts programs could matter. As I continued working in various prisons, I questioned how many of the facilities really cared about rehabilitation and how many were doing just enough to get the occasional sound bite or press release. I knew what was cut from the prison journals I edited—and it very much depended on who you reported to. The "truth" of what happens behind bars is not always reported. We know this.

A few years later, I went back and found the man I had talked with who said he was never getting out. I read him my poem about our encounter, which had since appeared in a book of mine. I told him I was sorry for acting the way I had.

If you pay attention to San Quentin, you may know that it is one of the prisons in our country that is making great strides in rehabilitative programs. I can't think of another state prison that allows so many visitors in and out or that is doing such unique programming. I am very interested in returning to "the Q" once the San Quentin Rehabilitation Center is up and running. Today the real pulse of the Q is fueled by the *San Quentin News* and many other unique programs. The newspaper's website includes this description: "*SQ News* prints 35,000 newspapers each month and distributes them to all 30+ CDCR prisons, university and public libraries, to thousands of subscribers across the country. Through a partnership with Edovo *San Quentin News* is made digitally accessible across the country in more than 740 facilities, free of charge. The state of California does not fund the paper. It is funded by grants from foundations, generous private donations and fundraising events hosted by Pollen Initiative. You can follow us on Twitter: @SanQuentinNews and Instagram."[6]

|||

I stand in the sally port—this old-fashioned gateway in and out of the prison. The word *port* means a place where people set off and return from their voyage. A *sally port* is a small secured entryway to prisons or other fortified compounds. What an interesting name. Here is a detailed account from another educator, Bill "Woody" Woodward, who works with the incarcerated and who was in the Q in 2023:

> You park in the prison's "lower lot," a huge parking lot at the bottom of a long uphill walk to meet up with the small crowd of graduate students (less than half male), and an occasional old person. Your pockets must be empty except for a driver's license or passport (a cell phone could get you arrested) and you cannot wear any of the prison colors (orange, blue, gray). After a short wait we cross the first threshold gate holding our credentials in the air for the guard to see. Another walk to the main entrance follows, to have credentials checked against a cleared persons list, to get stamped with invisible ink, and to sign in. Then into the "Sally Port," a 12 × 12 × 15 ft. cage with heavy bar doors on each end, one of which is always locked. Gathered in there, with both sides locked, we again show credentials to the guard behind the (likely bullet-proof) glass and then the inside bars open and we exit through a 500 lb. solid, antique steel door into a beautiful courtyard with roses, palms, succulents, and many flowers for the walk to the education center. San Quentin, California's oldest prison started as a sailing ship to house the bad people from San Francisco. Those inmates began building on land in 1852 and there still remains a "dungeon" dating to 1854 (a tour stop in the dungeon for the lucky few will surely bring nightmares). San Quentin has this country's (the world's?) largest death row (around 700, but shrinking on account of old age and dismantling by Governor Newsom); it's been many years since the death chamber (another ghoulish tour stop) was in use. Death row inmates have been housed in a separate old building with the words "Condemned Row" in 24 inch high, old-English style letters over the barred door. These mostly ancient prison buildings are unexpectedly quite beautiful, with a front that dates from the 19th Century and many "antique" doors, cells, and other spaces. The newest part is a modern hospital, built in response to class action lawsuits.[7]

I have wondered if the sally port and other things have changed. By his detailed description, it doesn't sound like they have.

Pruno

I notice one of many signs hanging on the old stone walls. "Don't forget to buy your San Quentin T-shirt—*TODAY ONLY*." I remember my colleague insisting, "Bring me back a souvenir this time and don't be cheap about it."

I'm standing in the parking lot overlooking the San Francisco Bay, inhaling its salty shell breeze. San Quentin's 432 acres are the most desired waterfront property in San Francisco; experts believe that developers would pay two billion dollars for it.

I approach the CO (correctional officer)—the T-shirt vendor—and like everything here, it's surreal. There is a line. There are hoodies, various apparel—all for sale, with proceeds to help sustain the San Quentin Honor Guard program. I buy two identical T-shirts that replicate a Jack Daniels bottle and that read:

San Quentin Prison
Penn No. 1
1852
Cell-brewed
Pruno

"So," I say to the CO, "you're selling T-shirts that promote a crime within the prison to raise money for the Honor Guard?"

"Yeah."

"Fair enough," I respond, as I turn and enter a vehicle driven by an inmate who will escort us off the grounds—a few blocks away—to one of the lucky employees who happens to live on the grounds.

When I am buckled up in the passenger seat, I flash the inmate the T-shirt and ask him if he wants one. "No way, man!" he says in disgust, a bit surprised. "I'm living this hell."

||||

Despite all the weirdness I encountered at San Quentin around that time, I continue to report on it today, to donate to various programs, and to subscribe to the SQ *News*. I am excited to say that *Ear Hustle* is the first podcast ever to be created and produced from inside a prison. It features "stories of the daily realities of life inside California's San Quentin State Prison, shared by those living it. Co-founded by Bay Area artist Nigel Poor alongside Earlonne Woods and Antwan

Williams—who were incarcerated at the time—the podcast now tells stories from inside prison and from the outside, post-incarceration."[8] Created in 2017, *Ear Hustle* was still producing new episodes as of 2024, and Episode 90 was a finalist for a Pulitzer Prize in 2020. The shows aren't the typical fare of crime fiction books. The "ten essential" recommended episodes include "Cellies," which highlights how tough it can be to find a roommate, especially in a five-by-ten-foot space; and "Kissing the Concrete," about how the weeks and months after release from prison can make or break you. Other episodes examine living a meaningful life, even if it will be mostly behind bars, and the solace in finding a critter—a bird or bug—to take care of in prison.

Another inimitable San Quentin program is the former Prison University Project, which is now an associate of arts degree and college preparatory program that is free of charge to people at San Quentin. Since 1996 nearly four thousand students have taken at least one course with the program.[9]

And the last encouraging development was the creation of the San Quentin Rehabilitation Center. According to the *San Quentin News*:

> The San Quentin Rehabilitation Center aims to provide the prison's 3,900 general population residents with lifestyle-changing programs and skills to help them return to their communities safely and avoid recidivism, San Quentin's Public Information Officer Lt. Guim'mara Berry said. The planned changes "would make San Quentin the premiere rehabilitation center of the world," Newsom said, speaking in an area of the prison that was once a furniture factory, soon to become a hub for the innovative new center. The current system has "failed for too long" to keep the public safe, he said, referencing the nearly 50% recidivism rate for released prisoners. The reform is about "real public safety, keeping communities safe," and getting "serious about addressing crime and violence in our state," Newsom said. . . . "This is about reducing recidivism in this state, keeping people safe, and making sure that victims feel respected through that process," said Newsom.[10]

There's more, of course—and as amusing, frightening, and eerie as I thought San Quentin was, from my first visit I understood that they were doing the unusual things our country needs for progress in prisons. It's really that simple. Sadly, prison is a rite of passage for many young men in this country. If it takes getting locked up to turn your life around, we'd better make it a rehabilitative, educational, and, dare I say, interesting experience. Maybe then the men and women can find a sense of self-worth.

Craig Johnson

I admire *New York Times* best-selling author Craig Johnson because he not only is a fantastic writer and showman, he also works the land—gets his hands dirty and understands the places and people he writes about and represents. I've stayed in touch with him since our first presentation. He's authentic. Maybe that's why his Western crime fiction show *Longmire*, which originally aired on A&E and is now streaming on Paramount+, is still such a hit. He's got some unique characters who continue to enthrall. The television series contains a lot of the grit that characterizes the books. But the entertainment business is unusual, and one can only wonder why the network would not renew the "highest-rated original drama series" on A&E after the third season. Netflix picked it up and ran with it for another few seasons. Was Walt Longmire not commercial enough? Even as a character in the highest-rated show? Did Walt not pique the prime-time target audience? TVwriter.com reported that Craig Johnson believed A&E canceled the show because it wanted to own and produce all the shows it airs, but when they tried to buy it, the producer wouldn't sell it. In an interview, Johnson said, "A broadcaster can make a lot more money off a show if they own it, rather than leasing it from a studio, but Warner Brothers knew they had a hit on their hands with 'Longmire' and wouldn't sell. . . . A&E, in a fit of pique, decided that if they couldn't buy the highest-rated, scripted show they'd ever had—[they] would cancel it. Which they did."[11]

Johnson continues to crank out Walt Longmire books, and his fans are ecstatic about them. According to Tyler Stephenson of *Oil City News*, "One of the biggest things that he hopes readers take away from his new book is an awareness of the situation with missing indigenous people. According to the FBI, more than 5,600 Native America women went missing last year. . . . There's a lot of responsibilities that go along with being a writer. You have a job to entertain, and to provide a good read. But you also have responsibilities like anybody else in culture."[12]

And that inevitably is the backbone of Craig Johnson's success. He's not writing a series just to make a buck. He understands the complexities of his characters and their traditions—something as simple as a cowboy removing his hat when he enters a room. He lives in the place he writes about and understands its history and diversity. That's one reason his characters resonate and have made the transition so well from page to screen. It's his own sense of gonzo and immersion. Johnson can't write well about the people and places his characters inhabit without living among them.

At a recent festival in Deadwood, South Dakota, I listened to Johnson address an arena of fans at the Deadwood Mountain Grand. As festival organizers rolled in a few more pallets of chairs for the standing-room-only crowd, Johnson talked about his research on drug cartels and areas of Mexico that are riddled with crime and murder. He knows. He's putting his time in. Like Bowden, he's putting himself at risk to get the story right. That's immersion—osmosis—gonzo. It is one of Johnson's trademarks and explains why his fans like him, too.

In early May of 2023, Johnson posted on Facebook a picture of his television screen, on which were listed the shows that were trending on Netflix. Right above the top ten shows that were highlighted as "trending now," there was *Longmire*. He wrote, "So last night, like an old friend you check-in on periodically, I switch over and find *Longmire* on Netflix either trending or popular just about every night. You would think that Warner Brothers with all their cancellations and one-season wonders would figure it out, wouldn't you." One very blunt comment out of the 451 I observed when I was scrolling said, "You give them too much credit."

The Family Next Door

Our fascination with crime is infectious. Kieran Nicholson of the *Denver Post* writes, "A documentary on the 2018 murders of a Frederick woman and her two children, killed by her husband—Christopher Watts—who was the father of the two girls, is now being shown on Netflix. *American Murder: The Family Next Door*, a story of a familicide . . .

Using raw, firsthand footage, this documentary examines the disappearance of Shanann Watts and her children, and the terrible events that followed."[13]

When I show this documentary in my Crime, Literature, and Film class, the most chilling scene for me occurs during the afternoon of the crime, when Watts is notified of his wife's murder and he returns to the family home, apparently coming from work. The police body cam shows Watts in a fairly collected state. He doesn't look like someone who just murdered his pregnant wife and two daughters with his bare hands and then dumped his daughters' bodies in an oil tank. It's chilling. His denial. His composure. This is what a psychopath looks like. We see how a person can disregard life so easily—his own children, spouse, and unborn child. Watch the documentary and tell me if you think this family annihilator should get a second chance at life.

This is what Gavin Newsom (a policymaker), victims, and society must wrestle with when making decisions about crime and punishment. Rehabilitation and reparation are what we need to make our world a better place. Fiction series and movies often leave this element out. Readers and viewers are interested in seeing the crime solved and then moving on.

This documentary struck a chord with me, reiterating the importance of reporting what we know—about trauma and how it affects us and our communities—so we can learn from one another. Chris Watts's father was allowed in the interrogation room with him—a risky move, but Watts wasn't under arrest at the time—and it was here, with his father present, that Chris Watts somewhat confessed to the crimes. His father had flown across the country to be by his son's side—to help him cope with his missing family. We watch as the father keeps asking his son questions. "Do you know what happened?" And then his father is dumbstruck when his son lies about how his daughters were killed by their mother, yet admits choking his wife to death to get revenge. "Oh, my God," his father says.

I can't imagine what that confession did to Watts's father. As a parent, as a human being, to hear anyone confess to the worst of what's possible is unfathomable. And to realize that your own son did the inflicting—

there are no words to describe that feeling. These interrogation room videos are as real as it gets. A cold-blooded psychopath was lying to his own father and trying to cover up his evil deeds. Chris Watts would later confess to all the murders in a very detailed five-hour interview from prison.

I am shocked and mortified. How could a person commit such crimes against his own family? Against anyone? Chris Watts's lack of empathy and compassion shows just how shallow and self-centered some people are. He looks like a decent person, but this could be one of the most horrifying examples to date of how evil presents itself. Watts's father said at his son's sentencing that he didn't understand why his son committed the crimes. "I hope one day, Christopher, you can help us," Ronnie Watts said that day.[14]

It makes me think of X—how he lied and went on the run for weeks after he raped and murdered Christina, and then later kept changing his story. He was not going to admit the truth. How chicken-shit is that? These men who have no empathy for others—and who can take a human life—don't have the strength to come clean. That is a denial that I'm glad I'll never be able to wrap my head around. This kind of remorselessness reminds me of O. J. Simpson in the courtroom, when he did not testify in his own defense but was able to speak to the court and televisions throughout the world without the jury present.

> "I have four kids. Two kids I haven't seen in a year. They ask me every week, Dad, how much longer . . . before this trial is over?" Simpson said.
>
> In the front row, Simpson's grown daughter, Arnelle, sobbed.
>
> Across the room, victim Ronald Goldman's father clenched his hands into fists and muttered, "Murderer. Murderer."
>
> "Mr. Simpson," the judge said, interrupting the monologue, "you do understand your right to testify as a witness and you choose to rest your case at this time?"
>
> Simpson nodded.
>
> "All right. Thank you very much, sir," Ito said.[15]

||||

I continue to question my intentions, as any good reporter should. *What is the discovery for the reader in this book? What is your point, Jim?* What I believed to be a book of prison anecdotes about what I learned from teaching behind bars has turned into something I had not envisioned. Rick Rubin writes in *The Creative Act: A Way of Being*, "We don't need to make a point of making a point. It will appear when it appears. The true point is already made in the innocent act of perception and creation. . . . Great art is created through freedom of self-expression and received with freedom of individual interpretation. Great art opens a conversation rather than closing it.

And often this conversation is started by accident."[16]

||||

You want to call what you are doing "great art"—or art all the same. You remember the radio broadcast and you knew a retrial was inevitable. You want to give voice to your friend who was taken from this world. All of this discussion of crime—all these years in prisons perhaps started by accident—terrible accidents—then coincidence—to find yourself where you are now behind this screen, writing your fears? Is it happenstance? Or are you, like Rubin says, the vessel and the filter? When you are scared—when you question yourself—remember what Rubin writes: "If a piece of work, a fragment of consciousness, or an element of nature is somehow allowing us to access something bigger, that is its spiritual component made manifest. It awards us a glimpse of the unseen."[17]

||||

As of 2023, more than nine books—some by the same author—had been written about Watts's crime since it took place in 2018. I wonder how many books speak to the trauma he inflicted as opposed to his crime and the gory details. When I first saw the documentary, I wondered if there would be a sequel about how Shanann's family is coping, how Chris Watts's family is coping, how any family could understand the atrocity a son and son-in-law could inflict.

When I discuss this crime and the documentary with Javier Murguia, special agent at the South Dakota Division of Criminal Investigation, he says the guy looks guilty. "You can see it immediately. It was the manner in which he reacted. The lack of emotion when hearing what should be the most devastating news imaginable. The reaction looked rehearsed."

A year later, the documentary is still a favorite on Netflix. I give my students the option to choose their own show to watch or podcast to listen to for their final exam. Even with the thousands of true-crime documentaries, podcasts, and series, fourteen out of twenty-six students chose to watch *American Murder: The Family Next Door*.

I can't help but wonder how many classes about victimization are offered at colleges and universities in this country. Perhaps if more were available, our interest in the perpetrator and evil—that is, interest in the dark side—would subside. I'm as fascinated by these grisly cases as the next guy—probably more so. As soon as I added the word "crime" to my Crime, Literature, and Film class, it became one of the most popular class electives on campus. It really shows the power one word can have.

It's always a challenge to decide which movies, film noir, or documentaries to show. Themes such as gender, masculinity, sexuality, and class structure in films like *Silence of the Lambs* and Alfred Hitchcock's *Rear Window* are still important and relevant today. Voyeurism in film was an important theme when the films were released and is much more so now, especially considering social media and its impact on society. There are in-depth and grotesque accounts in documentaries on Ted Bundy and other psychopaths and serial killers—it's all relevant. I may need to add an Advanced Crime, Literature, and Film class or cut all the black-and-white films, as some students have suggested. Some of the older classics are boring to them—too long—and aren't as entertaining as the films of the twenty-first century. The old ones don't have the students on the edge of their seats and are not realistic enough.

When I ask students to reflect on why crime is so fascinating, they say things like, "the storytelling is so engrossing," "the tragedy or victory outside of our own lives," "the psychology behind it all," and "I wonder why someone turns to a life of crime. Were they born a criminal?" One student says, "I'm very interested in taking a class that plays into a hobby of mine." Another states, "I don't like to read much, but I like to read books that involve crime." The fascination with evil is a predominant theme. Throughout the semester, three students say, "My dad is a cop." A handful of students each semester tell the class, "I want to be a cop. I want to be a detective." The fascination with crime is something we can easily discuss as an academic exercise. "No matter what, we can't look away from the accident. We are interested in the macabre," another student says.

King of Horror

I read an interview with Stephen King in which he states that almost every one of his ideas is from his own life or from headlines he reads, including the inspiration for *Mr. Mercedes*, a true story about a woman driving her car into a fast food restaurant. Adrienne Tyler wrote in *Screen Rant*, "Stephen King takes inspiration from a variety of sources—whether literary classics (like *Dracula* or *Salem's Lot*), popular horror creatures, real-life tragedies and serial killers, and more. However, there are some stories that were inspired by his own life, whether by traumatic experiences, unusual but harmless ones, his own personal struggles, and people he has met."[18]

All of the ideas that crime writers pull from come from real life. But crime in literature and movies is very different from crime in real life. In fiction, in the movies, we don't see and hear from primary and secondary victims or from first responders and communities affected by a crime unless their perspectives might thicken the plot. In real life, we don't usually hear from victims because there is no happy ending. Victimization is a state of being, a thing that just is. It's been over thirty years since Christina's murder, and although the criminal justice system has tried and retried X and imprisoned his accomplice for life without parole for the crime, there is no clear resolution. Crime fiction has to have a climax and a resolution—that's how the structure of the novel ultimately works. But true crime and its repercussions are felt and lived—they're ongoing, a state of being that reaffirms our need and craving for closure.

Ride-Alongs

When I was doing ride-alongs with police, there was one call that I'll never forget. It was related to a woman whose boyfriend had an extensive rap sheet. The boyfriend called 911 claiming the woman had jumped from his moving vehicle and was lying on the side of the road. Within twenty-four hours, the scared and finally willing victim would confide in a very talented female officer that this boyfriend had repeatedly hit her while he was driving and then had thrown her from the moving car, pulled over, gotten out, and smashed her head into the curb. Her face looked like the Elephant Man in the old black-and-white movie. However, this wasn't Hollywood or make-believe. It was in color. It was a reminder of the cold hard truth of victims in emergency rooms who are afraid to speak because they fear for their lives. After finally opening up, her fear must have taken over again, and she said, "Maybe my head accidentally got smashed against the curb. He owns me."

It was one of many occasions where I witnessed victims who were afraid to talk because they knew charges would be dismissed, pleaded down, or not brought at all, and the perpetrator would be free to hurt them again. Many cases I encountered during my ride-alongs would get dismissed—especially domestic violence cases. If perpetrators know they can get away with abuse and aren't going to be held accountable, they won't stop and victims will continue to feel helpless. Many people in law enforcement see this problem day after day—it's no wonder so many police suffer with depression, anxiety, alcoholism, and even suicide. Despite the few bad cops doing bad things, most police officers (more than eight hundred thousand in the United States) are there to serve and protect. Public safety is their number one concern.

I remember a CO at San Quentin who was a textbook prison cliché. His chain holding keys to various facilities was longer than required, his hair was buzzed, and he carried himself with an unusual chip on his shoulder. Or so I perceived. This guy fit the description of every prison guard I'd seen portrayed on television. I asked him how he coped with working at the Q. He said very matter-of-factly, "I get off work, take four or five Tylenol, take a bath and I have my Budweiser, of course." Alcohol shouldn't be the mediator. Why can't we do something about this? I later felt a little ashamed of my stereotyping, my prejudging. My preconceived notions were wrong. He was just a guy like me—genuine and really, really stressed out. So he drank every night after work. So did I back then. Who was I to judge?

We don't hear from many victims because of the way our justice system works—and this isn't the police's fault, although they are the only people victims see when something horrible happens. It's not the police's fault that cases get dismissed. After a year of ride-alongs and following up with questions after specific calls, and then hearing that the cases had been dismissed, I found that a tremendous amount of gloom followed me home most mornings after these overnight observations. I felt depressed and sad, and I didn't even have to write a report about what I'd seen. I would most likely never see the victims again. I would never have to testify in court that I followed procedure and protocol. I could feel the heavy baggage the sergeants and officers carried. Crime in real life looked pretty chaotic whenever I saw it unfolding. It was hardly ever a story with a satisfying ending or resolution.

On many occasions I said to a few of the sergeants and officers I got close to, "I don't know how you all do it. I couldn't. Not for the amount of money you get paid. Even if you paid me triple your salary, I'm not sure I'm brave enough to do it." But man, I was hungry for the action and liked being there to help when I could. It was addictive. I became wrapped up in my ride-alongs and found it so enthralling and fascinating that I also enrolled in and passed the citizen's academy. I was then asked to join the newly developed reserve officer program. I was interviewed for and passed the Minnesota Multiphasic Personality Inventory, an exhausting conglomeration of 567 true-false questions—the most researched psychological test in existence. I consulted with professionals in the field about whether I, a writer and professor at Mount Marty University, should become a part-time officer once a month and on call. After a hundred hours of training, I would find myself carrying a Glock 17 nine-millimeter handgun—the standard issue firearm for police agencies across the country. I'd be equipped with a Taser and a bulletproof vest—twenty-five pounds of gear and a license to serve and protect.

COVID hit. George Floyd was murdered by police. The country was and still is in turmoil. I was still backing the blue, but I found myself at an intersection—I was deeper than I ever expected to get. I just wanted to see the front end of crime, to see men and women caught in the act, so I could learn and understand more. I phoned my father and told him that as part of the background check, he might get a call from a lieutenant or commander about my interest in becoming a reserve officer. There was a pause on the line and then he said, "Well, don't get shot. If you do, your mother will kill you."

I got a little lucky that COVID happened. Everything was paused and it gave me a lot more time to think about what I was getting myself into. I knew I had a book—I already had a year of notes, and this would be another golden ticket I could write about. It could become more than just a chapter in this book. But if shit went south, there would be no guard to call to come rescue me—I was the guard. And in the end, I had to be honest with everyone involved. I didn't feel comfortable carrying a gun; I wasn't sure how I'd react under extreme pressure. Too many times during ride-alongs I turned around and walked away or back to the police cruiser because I was going to either say something I shouldn't or lose my temper. The sergeant I was observing and the officers who worked under him didn't lose their cool. It was astonishing to witness the care and control they had. I didn't think I could do it. I knew I couldn't. For my safety and yours, I declined the offer. I wasted people's time getting that far into the program, but it was in the public's best interest that I wasn't carrying a gun.

I miss the energy, the unknown around the corner, the fear and excitement of it all.

| | |

You are in the passenger seat of a police SUV when an emergency call—a signal 1—comes over the channels. You grab the holy-shit handle with your right hand and instantly move your left arm across your stomach, grip the passenger door handle tight—all the while screaming at the tail lights in front of you growing closer. You try not to scream at the sergeant to slow down. All the while, his body camera and the cameras and mic inside the car are on. He passes the truck and slows enough to make a right turn. You are not sure where the accident is, but you look hard, hoping to spot it first.

The inside of the car is lit up—the console of controls and a computer—shotgun mounted in the center. You look out the passenger window into the dark night. Try to decipher what's real and what is a reflection bouncing off the inside windows. You can see two silhouettes of people in the windshield—it is not make-believe, it is a reflection of the sergeant and you. You turn back to the front of the vehicle and see tire tracks where it looks like the driver lost control. Tire tracks snake up from the glare off the windshield. You follow them down into the ditch to the culvert where they disappear. "It's gotta be right here. This is the area," the sergeant says. The nearby pole and the moon create a white translucent floor of snow. You spot the car ahead of the lost tracks, upside down.

"There. Right, there!" You holler at the sergeant who is peering out his side of the cruiser.

An eyewitness will claim to have seen the car pass her with no headlights, swerve toward the ditch, hit a roadside culvert, launch, and go airborne, Dukes of Hazzard style—then crash and topple end-over-end before landing where it is now, at least eighty feet away from initial impact.

The car is upside down—thirty feet off the street. The roof smashed. Duffel bags, backpacks, pillow, blanket, little plastic baggies, shoes, and parts of metal from the vehicle litter a flat terrain. The car engine is smoking. The sergeant hits the brakes and is out of the SUV *running a beeline to the car to make sure no one is trapped inside. You get out and start to run, too. Try to keep a flashlight shining on him, but also keep your distance. You are just a ride-along. The snow's surface is a thin sheet of ice. With each step you feel your feet crunch—the top layer brittle and breaking like a used Styrofoam cup.*

As you approach the vehicle, you stop and stare hard at the car engine to make sure you don't see fire—that you don't see the smallest spark or flicker. Against the white glare of the snow, the shadows of three lone street poles in a nearby parking lot stretch gray into the distance. Your eyes play tricks. You look closer at the black object on the ground. It's a man's body, splayed out and with no shoes—approximately seven feet from the car.

You get close enough to hear him moan, see his jeans pushed up one leg to his quad. One shin twisted, torn up, and bleeding. His head is cocked sideways—you listen for another breath. You hear the sirens of emergency responders coming from different directions. You know not to touch or move him. You look back at his bleeding leg. Broken, but nothing severed.

"There's no one left in the car," the sergeant says as he moves toward you. It's unnervingly quiet outside. There's an apartment complex just across the street. Where are all the people? Could there be others? There have to be. Who has this much shit in a car unless they are living in it?

You see a hiking boot. A cellphone. You look away from the snow, which seems almost hallucinogenic. You glare harder at where the car cleared an eight-foot industrial fence. You move toward it. There are two more bodies. "Two more over here!" you scream, and you are upon them, kneeling, looking at them lying face down in the snow. You can hear them snoring. Really?

Another first responder is running toward you and the sergeant. What you will learn later is that if a human suffers severe brain trauma, the body shuts down and often snoring ensues. Snorers. It's the body's way to cope with disaster.

Snorers. I will never forget that word.[19]

Anthony Hopkins

I want to bring gonzo, alcoholism, *Silence of the Lambs*, and Anthony Hopkins to your attention again, because they represent popular triggers that consume us—crime, addictions, creativity, and our inner selves. Interestingly, Anthony Hopkins quit drinking over forty-five years ago.

In the documentary *Inside the Labyrinth: The Making of the Silence of the Lambs*, the narrator states, "Dr. Hannibal Lecter is the greatest villain in popular fiction; he's like Sherlock Holmes' arch rival Moriarty. He's completely out of his mind. He's utterly insane and evil. There's a danger almost that he's a cartoon character. So he has to be played by a really great actor."[20] In the documentary, Anthony Hopkins says,

> Jonathan Demme came over to see me in London and I asked him why he wanted me to play the part and he said, "Don't you want to play it?" Yeah I do, but just curious, why cast me? And he'd seen me in a film called *The Elephant Man*, and I was playing the part of Dr. Treves. That's what convinced him. Treves is a very good man. I think Jonathan's reply was, as far as I can remember, as well, "That's what I want for Lecter. He's [a] compassionate man. He's a humanitarian. He's a good man, locked inside this insane mind." And for some, God

> knows what reason, I understood the man, how to play him. I knew he was the shadowy figure that lurks inside all of us. And I don't know why I have an instinct about those things, but I do. I'm fascinated by the shadow side of our psyches, because they are also the most creative sides of us. If we didn't know the shadow side and the dark side of our nature, [we'd] live a pretty bland life or a destructive life because they come out in some form or another.[21]

It seems to me that Hopkins is backing up what Charles Bowden said—that we all have an ugly side, a dark side. Most of us don't act on it. We see it a lot, though—people in our lives and, more specifically, people at our jobs who try, in very calculated ways, to make people unhappy. They are actively disengaged and willingly make others miserable. Maybe it's their misery or their sense of not having enough control. I've always wondered if such unfortunate and aggressive people act the way they do because they don't have any creative outlets and if they drown themselves or self-medicate after work as soon as possible. It's a ruthless cycle. I know— I dabbled in it. Without any creative or "good" outlet, destructive thinking and doing catches everyone. It is latent in all of us. One could argue that this aggressiveness is a predictable unhappiness that becomes twisted and evil.

Think about it: Police are protecting us, trying to make our country a safer place. They deal with and arrest criminals, but when the crimes are dismissed, what happens to police officers' creative thinking and doing? They become depressed, and the addictive cycle of self-medication kicks in. We have systems in place that are not working. If correctional officers and police don't have the opportunity to turn the darkness they experience into something better, our country continues to be confused. And this extends beyond police and corrections.

The Gallup organization's most recent yearly study on U.S. employee engagement states that "in 2023, 33% of employees were engaged. Not engaged or actively disengaged employees account for $1.9 trillion in lost productivity. . . . On a positive note, the percentage of actively disengaged workers has declined from 18% in 2022 to 16% in 2023. Active disengagement—what we could call 'loud quitting'—reached an all-time low of 13% in 2018 and 2019. In 2023, 50% of employees were not engaged (quiet quitting)."[22]

A lot of people won't acknowledge the dark, ugly, perhaps malicious side of themselves, but I believe it is the magnet that pulls us to crime fiction and film, that we are drawn there to understand the shadows that lurk in all of us. We all have them. We are all criminals in the sense that we have all broken a law. But most of us have an inner voice that prevents us from doing bad things, stops us from saying what we might want to say and subconsciously what we might want to do. Not long ago, a good friend of mine said sarcastically, "There [were] a lot of bad things running through my head today. Everyone should be happy to know I didn't act on them." This was her way of coping with stress—through humor.

When I was younger, I equated my dark side with my originality. I especially bought into the gonzo myth that singeing my brain with alcohol and drugs would open doors to creativity. Well, that's bullshit. Although the dark rebel and evil villain are entertaining, often going for wild and engaging rides, they too are fiction. Creativity might come from one side of us—perhaps the shadowy side, the dark and sinister side—but that does not mean that feeding it or nourishing it makes us creative. We have all kinds of personas and voices, and I agree with Hopkins that we should be open to all of them and their rights and wrongs.

I'm exploring the very darkest sides of my psyche as I write this book. It's not easy. In fact, this exploration often disturbs me. I can't sit down at just any time of the day to write. It's usually late at night. I put it off. There are twenty other things that I don't like to do, but I do them instead of writing because writing is not easy. I caught myself vacuuming behind our dryer the other day—thinking, *I have to get back to editing the book. I'm a writer. I know and have experienced things firsthand that need to be shared.* Can you imagine a world where no one ever learned or spoke of their past?

I joke with my friends, "Why can't I build birdhouses or something?" My cousin David says, "Because you are too smart to build birdhouses." I have to transport myself to another time and place. I've done a good job of suppressing but obviously not forgetting—there's a side of myself I didn't know I had the luxury of exploring. The memories of my friend's murder—of a serial killer—still scare me. And I wish I could drink the thoughts away. I wish I could keep quiet. I can imagine people throwing up walls and saying, "Let it go, man." A concert of crows squawks loudly some days. Critics and black ravens—all made up, of course.

What about this? What about that? What if you make someone unhappy or scare them with your words?

When you work in prisons for fourteen years, you think about crime every day. You think about criminals. It becomes a second skin. It's the Midwesterner in me who chooses to be quiet. I've been raised to keep it to myself. It's a prerequisite for living in these parts. But we are all open books, whether we admit it or not. Tough personas never last. I know because I've hung around and worked with thousands of tough motherfuckers and badass women in prisons.

The shadows we carry are often hard to deal with and they come out in unproductive or criminal ways, and that's why you see judges, teachers, psychologists, and psychiatrists trying to encourage perpetrators to explore the shadowy parts of themselves—to write it down. This is why arts in corrections works. This is why art therapy works. When you can teach people to unleash the inner self in productive and creative ways rather than in crime or victimization, everyone wins.

During my first weekend at San Quentin, I wrote a passage in my moleskin pocket notebook—the only thing I was allowed to take inside the prison. I can't remember if it was something I heard someone say or if I read it in the San Quentin newspaper, but it stuck with me. It was a mantra I have lived by in prisons ever since. It went something like this: *You can lock people up and let them out after their time is served. Maybe during their incarceration you teach them a trade—that's great. What you also have to do is help them tap into the emotional instabilities that brought them to prison in the first place. If people never come to terms with themselves, you are just going to send angry people right back out into society.*

They Want to Be Like Thompson and Bourdain

Anthony Bourdain took us to parts unknown. He gave us an hour of escapism—that American dream and disillusionment through the boob tube. He was the Kerouac traveler, a Dharma bum, the gourmet savant and connoisseur of adventure. We empathized with him, too. Many of us have sweated behind an apron—cleaning tables, bars, and dishes, bleach peeling back layers of our skin for years. We have spent time in minimum wage jobs—peeling potatoes, mopping grease, perhaps moving up from busboy to sous chef—and maybe even commanded a kitchen ourselves. Most of us have had working-class jobs. Behind the façade, Anthony Bourdain embodied that work ethic. Maybe some of the students in my prison classes are like Bourdain, and they just made some stupid mistakes on their journey.

The traveler who can't wait to leave and can't wait to get home—the great curse, the great quest. Bourdain was an underdog as a chef standing next to a hot grill, and then he was catapulted to the Sahara Desert with a film crew and he was a star. He understood hard work, had battled serious drug addiction, and had come out the other side—an alcoholic, but "rehabilitated" all the same.

In the documentary *Roadrunner: A Film about Anthony Bourdain*, Bourdain says, "I'm not going to tell you here how to live your life, but I got very lucky." He's dead now, of course. Suicide. But fifteen minutes and twenty-seven seconds into the documentary I was still grinning. We follow him as filmmaker Morgan Neville examines his quick, virtually overnight success, telling the truth about how he was living paycheck to paycheck, cooking and sweating under the grill. Twenty-five minutes into the film they ask him what he wants. "I don't know, maybe I can buy something that'll fill a void, but hell, my rent is paid. That's all I ever wanted was to be an average person." His creative director talks about his persona on camera and how he seemed to be able to engage with anyone he met.

A few of my students, usually in the federal prison, knew who Charles Bowden was. They'd heard of his writing about corruption on and below the border. Some of them were found guilty for running drugs for the cartel. But if I mentioned Hunter S. Thompson or Anthony Bourdain—well, that was like preaching to the choir. Not only did my students want to live those lifestyles, many had embraced them and tried. Both celebrities lived on the wild side, did too many drugs, and committed suicide, in the end revealing the true dark side of gonzo and the irresponsibility of it. Both Hunter S. Thompson and Anthony Bourdain were enigmatic characters who had produced entertaining myths about themselves, but they failed to put the brakes on, which eventually hindered their creativity. Don't get me wrong—I am one of their biggest fans. They both did fantastic work, but as time went on, it seemed to lack substance. In the end, what they were creating didn't have the energy and nerve they wanted, and they weren't happy with the self that had emerged—to the point that they ended their own lives. It is one thing to embrace the dark side, but to refuse to do something positive with it is frightening. Bowden, on the other hand, not only completely engulfed himself and those he wrote about—hitmen, the cartel—in mayhem at times, but he fueled his fire through hard work and discipline, cranking out over two dozen books of prose, sometimes with other artists, to help save innocent Mexican citizens, the environment, and people everywhere. Bowden is the most dangerous writer the world never knew. His work is prophecy.

Forty-one minutes into the documentary, Anthony Bourdain is remarried. His thirty-year relationship with his high school sweetheart is gone, and now he is a father with his second wife. Second chances and lucky breaks are themes men and women gravitate toward. Coming and going, trying the buffet of life. "Be a traveler, not a tourist." Another famous tagline. Bourdain was always rushing to get into the scene and out of the scene—rushing to go, even if he had no place to go, one of the director's mentions.

In a haunting scene that begins at around fifty-seven minutes, Bourdain and Josh Homme are cruising down a desolate desert highway in a convertible (*Fear and Loathing*-style picturesque). Later, at a bar, they clink glasses and pop a shot. Homme says, "I was thinking. Yo ho ho, a pirate's life for me."

Tony asks, "You've been touring since you were . . . ?"

"Since I was eighteen."

Tony says, "You know, it's weird. I'm home and I'm ridiculously happy for a week and then I start getting crazy like I should be doing something."

Homme says, "I call it the bittersweet curse. Nothing feels better than going home and nothing feels better than leaving home." (Laughter.)

"Yeah, you got a point," Bourdain finishes.

When I think of Hunter S. Thompson, Anthony Bourdain, and Ernest Hemingway—their machoism, especially Bourdain's swagger—they inspire. But all three committed suicide. All three suffered from apparent mental health issues. Booze will do that. Drugs will do that. Fame, unhappiness in a perceived world of glamour, riches, and glee, a contending itch to be more and do more, will do that.

When I was still drinking, I was lucky that I never felt so bad that I wanted to take my own life. But I slept like I was dead. And I loved that coma. I could eat up a whole day in bed. By day two I'd be so riddled with anxiety and paranoia (because I wasn't doing anything and hadn't had a drink to calm my nerves) that I'd almost always make up problems for myself. It was a delirious cycle. A great friend of mine once said something like, "Booze is funny. We chase it. It consumes us. We feel like shit for a day or two and then we run right back to it." I laughed. I knew he was spot on. But I was rarely giving my body a day or two to recover. I was full on traveling—watching the thin line run long and crooked.

At an AA meeting I attended when I was finally getting help, one person asked a particularly disturbing question: "Isn't alcoholism its own form of suicide?" It was a solid fucking question.

||||

You might not have wished it upon yourself, but you knew you were slowly killing yourself. You knew running to the bathroom that your body was physically telling you something. You knew you were risking your life—pushing yourself well past what was healthy or normal. No normal person drinks Pepto Bismol on a daily basis. And that doesn't work either after a spell. But you keep the charade going and you continue to lie to yourself just like a criminal because the immediate reward is what you want—eventually what your body can't live without it. Maybe you were dabbling with regret. Maybe you were just cleaning a gun in the morning. Running. Swimming. Traveling. A sucker for life, dead set on destruction with no self-control.

| | | |

Bourdain, Hemmingway, Thompson, and others make it all look glamorous until we read about them in the past tense. In a review of David Wills's book *High White Notes: The Rise and Fall of Gonzo Journalism*, Kevin Mims makes the following observation about these singular personalities:

> There always seems to be something inherently phony in people whose shtick is authenticity—as if the effort to play themselves becomes too much to bear. Hunter S. Thompson, Spalding Gray, Anthony Bourdain, even to some extent Robin Williams—these guys all specialized in solo performances of their own public personae. Wills repeatedly refers to Gonzo journalism as "a one-man genre." A book about monologist Spalding Gray is called *Cast of One*. Williams was a manic one-man stand-up comic. Bourdain was best known for being the only regular cast member in a string of reality food programs in which, as he put it, "I travel around the world, eat a lot of shit, and basically do whatever the fuck I want." That kind of freedom, the freedom to just be yourself, probably feels at first like the perfect gig until it doesn't. There's only one sure way to escape a role like the ones they were playing, and in the end they all chose it.
>
> But finding yourself stuck in a seat next to Spalding Gray or Anthony Bourdain during a long plane flight might have been interesting. Those guys could at least do humility and interest in other people (sometimes the interest even seemed genuine). But being stuck in a seat next to Hunter S. Thompson during a long airplane flight sounds like a good reason to request an urgent reassignment.[23]

The men and women in my prison classes also "specialized in solo performances of their own public personae." That is essentially the plot my students enacted. They thought they were specialists and they were their own one-man shows—illegal charades that landed them behind bars. They embezzled, stole, sold, cheated, lied, and in some cases even killed to get what they wanted. And they wanted it all—their fountain of frosting and to swim in it, too.

So many of the people in my classes have stated that they were getting away with it and didn't know how to stop. When that happens, you start to believe your own lies, the ones you tell yourself to feed an impulse, hunger, and lifestyle you could never have imagined. Anthony Bourdain got extremely lucky and went on a never-ending tour of the world at someone else's expense. He embodied the escapism we most likely will never experience. He was madly in love with a woman who cheated on him. He made a shit load of money and then killed himself.

Crime Scene: Do Not Cross

Crime equals tension—heightened momentum, blood coursing, heart pounding, stomach turning. Add suspense to some good ol' storytelling and you have a narrative that not only captures our attention but also offers the worst-case scenarios, and we can't stop reading, listening, watching, staring. It's inherently infectious—the same way we can't look away from an emergency vehicle, from a crime scene. We are tempted to crawl under the yellow CRIME SCENE DO NOT CROSS tape to see for ourselves. Fiction and fact. The characters a writer develops—the people that enact these atrocities—are unbelievable, and the horrors push far beyond conventional ideologies and empathy for others. We know there's a tremendous disparity between real crime and crime as entertainment, but it has its hook in us and is more popular now than ever.

4

What They Do Not Tell You about Prison, Part 1

River Birch

I really like the student I'm talking to on the track. He's a lot more honest than most people I know outside of the prison. He means what he says. He's the kind of guy you want on your side. He's a good listener. He's in here for drugs, and honestly, I don't care. My job is to help him never come back here. He's an amazing writer, spinning yarns about his deep woods Missouri kin. It's surprising to me when he asks me the name of the tree in front of us with the bark peeling off its trunk.

"River birch," I tell him.

"That's it. How did I forget that? You know, before I got here I was at a different prison. Most of us trickle down the system to get to a place like this, if we are lucky. And most prisons aren't like this. I never saw anything green. Just concrete, dirt, and razor wire. I remember arriving here in a minivan. The instant I got out I saw this tree. I walked right toward it and touched it. I grabbed ahold of it and squeezed. The guard said, 'Get back here; I need to process you!' I told him, 'Just hold on a second. I haven't seen a tree in three years.' And I wrapped my hands around its trunk. Squeezed so tight. I'm a country boy. To be denied the outdoors was like a death sentence for me."

Pine Ridge

I talk with the men and women about trust and believing in themselves when nobody else will. I talk about our collective voices and how we are building our own community in the classroom. Some of the writing prompts I pass around class are questions we answer and turn into lists that we print in the prison's creative writing journal. Today's prompt: What they do not tell you about prison.

Someone says, "It's a revolving door." Three out of the nine guys raise their hands and say they believe they will be coming back to prison after being released. This baffles me, and I blurt out, "What? You don't have any faith in yourself? You are already giving up?"

South Dakota has an incarceration rate of 824 per 100,000 people (in prisons, jails, immigration detention, and juvenile justice facilities), meaning that it locks up a higher percentage of its people than any democratic country on earth, according to a 2021 Prison Policy Initiative report.[1] In 2024, according to the South Dakota Department of Corrections, the state's three-year recidivism rate was 44 percent.[2]

I'm challenging myself to try to change my students' thinking, which seems like an insurmountable task. Some of my students are from the Pine Ridge Reservation, where alcoholism may be the worst in the world. You can't buy beer on the reservation because it is outlawed, so residents go to nearby Whiteclay, Nebraska, described in the *Nebraska Quarterly* as:

> a ramshackle collection of forgotten souls, abandoned buildings, urine-soaked sidewalks, squalid streets and four thriving beer stores. In the last decade, those four stores in an unincorporated village of 12 residents have sold the equivalent of nearly 42 million 12-oz. cans of beer. Placed end to end, they would stretch from New York to Los Angeles. Nearly all of those cans were consumed by residents of the nearby Pine Ridge Reservation—a hauntingly beautiful landscape of rolling prairie, rugged bluffs, badlands and canyons. But in that stunning vista also lie some terrible truths. On this South Dakota reservation, where the sale and consumption of alcohol has been illegal since 1889 (aside from a few months in the 1970s), the Oglala Lakota live in the poorest of America's 3,144 counties, according to a 2014 U.S. Census Bureau report. In 2015, 55 percent of its roughly 30,000 residents were unemployed, according to the U.S. Census Bureau. A decade before, the Department of the Interior put the number at 89 percent. Here, men die on average at age 47, according to Rainey Enjady, former

> interim CEO of the Pine Ridge Hospital. That's a shorter lifespan than any other country in the world, according to the World Health Organization. Its women fare better. On average, they live to 55—on par with Angola, Nigeria and Somalia.[3]

How can I encourage these men to think positively? One expression I hear today is, "If you want to get out of your hole, you have to quit digging."

|||

It's week three with our first cohort of students; the pilot program is over and we are in action. Seven out of the nine men share their writing in class and everyone has turned something in, which is a great sign. If we can build the students' confidence and get them motivated, it will be a blessing. As they share their writing, we can see the lightbulbs turning on. I have to continue to build their trust. I tell them they might not believe in anyone else here, but they can trust me. I reiterate the purpose of the class. After two hours, men are handing in more work for us to read. I shake their hands as they leave class.

We got into a pretty heavy discussion about men who have been incarcerated for over twenty years and have been in and out of prison—men who, if they get one more felony count, will be in for good. One student talked about being out, back at Pine Ridge. He had some groceries in a sack, and within eight seconds of his leaving a store, some men pulled their car over and began beating him up. He said they stole his food. He said he was depantsed. He mentioned, nonchalantly, that he happened to put his wallet in his grocery sack after checking out.

I wasn't sure what the depantsing meant. Was he raped on the reservation? Was he only concerned about his wallet? If I'm learning anything, though, it's to keep my mouth shut when my students begin to tell stories.

He said it's tough out there and he said living in prison is a lifestyle. It might not be what you want, but it is a life. He said people have friends and it might be easier than trying to find a job on the outside—especially at his age. He talked about not having any Social Security because he's always been incarcerated and has worked very little.

During the same class, one of the unit managers who watched over the men in my class told a story about being a white guy, growing up on the reservation, helping guys in prison. He said to the student who didn't have hope, "You DO need to believe in yourself." This unit manager seemed to really care. He enjoyed helping men in prison. "If you can help one person, that makes all the difference," he said.

VIEWS OF WHITECLAY MIXED, A YEAR AFTER THE BEER STORES CLOSED

> Outside the Family Dollar store in Whiteclay, Anna Dawn, says she likes that the town is quieter, with less loitering. But she says reservation residents are still getting alcohol. "I think they're just going to Rushville, and Rushville's probably making more money now," Dawn said. Rushville, Nebraska is 21 miles south of Whiteclay. Rushville Mayor Chris Heiser says the closing of the beer stores has changed things. "Since the beer stores have closed, more people have died on the roads. That's a fact," Heiser said.[4]

Library Card

When I shared a statistic with another prison educator about the lack of books in inner city kids' homes, she told me about a former student who had been working hard on his GED. The student was eager to learn but had never had the opportunity before he was incarcerated. He was reading all he could get his hands on. If he didn't understand something in one of the books he found in the prison library, he corralled one of the teachers or other inmate students to get the answer.

This was a guy directly affected by adverse childhood experiences. His dad never liked him because he didn't want to have a son. When he was young, he was ordered to sleep in the shed out behind the house. He didn't like sleeping in the shed. Eventually, he left and found a new family—gang life.

Although he hadn't completed his GED before being released from prison, he still wanted to finish it. The last time he and the educator had spoken, he had said, "When I get my own place, my own money, I'm going to buy a book case and start putting my own books on it."

The educator knew money would be a problem for him, like it is for most men and women who are released from jails and prisons. He told the guy, "All you need to do is get a library card. The card is free and all the books you want are free."

"A what?" the man asked.

"A library card. Any town or city you move to has libraries, and you can go in them and check out any book you want for free."

"You mean, they have the same kind of books out there that you got in here. Like the room down the hall, there? I thought that was just a prison thing."

Those of us who are educators and writers understand the power of words—how a passage from a single book can give us great hope and strength. There are millions of worlds written on pages, amazing characters who show us how to dream. And the Library of Congress adds thousands of new items to its collection every day.[5]

General Equivalency Diploma

"Hey, I passed—I really did it!" Two inmate students high-five each other. "Way to go, man! I told you you'd do it." The one pats the other on the back, happy to be graduating. Their smiles frozen on Polaroid—ear to ear to sky, soaring alone now—FREE.

"GED test result day is always fun here," the education director tells me.

This Isn't Dress Rehearsal

I am visiting my daughter's fifth grade class to talk about poetry. I'm trying to maintain my cool factor, and the stakes are high today. I'm trying not to embarrass my kid. Since I won the Allen Ginsberg Poetry Award, her teacher believes it would be good if I would talk about my work. I don't want my hands to shake and I don't want to look out of my element. I teach in prisons, for Christ's sake, and these kids I've never met before have me sleep-deprived. Upon entering the classroom, I wave to my daughter in the front. "Hi Paige. It's Dad from home." She smiles, her face beet red.

I show them how levelheaded words can be. How their voices, even now, really matter. How in writing, their favorite objects (besides their phones) can take on a life of their own. "What's that called, class?" the teacher asks after one example. Hands fly up in the air. I point to a boy in the back. "Personification," he says.

"Wow, mom, look, cow," they say in unison.

"What was that?" I ask.

"A cheer!" The teacher responds, smiling. I think, *These kids already know what words can do.*

In the back of the room there's an unusual arrangement of bookshelves they call the Golden Porch. Room for only two. An actual porch—full of books—where students are eager to sit during reading time.

I do my best to find my own fifth-grade-appropriate poetry. One poem is about girls and softball and my daughter's team opening up their first can of whoop-ass against their competition. I break a rule and say "whoop-ass." My face flushes, unlike those on the wall of famous figures in the room: Albert Einstein, Cesar Chavez, Jane Goodall, Pablo Picasso, Amelia Earhart, Miles Davis, Jim Henson, Dr. James Watson, Mahatma Gandhi.

I read them a poem I wrote about their playground, about dads standing in line, waiting to pick up their kids. The poem may be too much for some fifth-graders, too heavy. Maybe it hits it square on the head for others.

This Isn't Dress Rehearsal

It's fifty-three degrees this afternoon. Tomorrow time
will spring ahead. In five minutes the still obnoxiously loud
grade-school bell will alarm the neighborhood.

In line at the chain-link fence with some other fathers who
have shown up, I'm waiting for you, my daughters.
Today, recess should never end.

In two months one of you will leave this place for middle school,
the other will ascend to second grade. Some things never change.
I claw my fingers into the chain-link

that seems so much shorter now. I see the tire-swing, basketball
hoop without a net, blacktop and worn tetherball.
I'm not old enough to wish I were back in your shoes,

not with the math homework you're assigned. But, there's the aching
for some of that freedom. Maybe that's why none of the fathers
standing here say a word.

When I shared the rough draft of this poem in class, a prisoner said,
That's one fence I never minded being behind.
Girls, do you know how much I'm going to miss

these days? This magical moment on all our faces when we see
each other between these boundaries,
waiting to go home?[6]

Before class I had been thinking about this poem and about prisons—about the corruption some children see at an early age. I was thinking about inevitable osmosis, the school-to-prison pipeline.

I asked two of my daughter's teachers, "What do you do when you know a kid has it bad at home?" One said, "There's not a lot we can do except report things to the authorities." And the other said, "I tell them, you're in fifth grade now. You know right from wrong; you're not kids anymore. If what mom and dad are doing at home is bad, don't do what they do."

When I return to the school at the end of the school day, I stand outside the same fence as the bell rings. A few kids from the class wave to me, smile, and talk with each other. I see a woman with neon purple hair, smoking and talking loudly on her cell phone in her car. There's a whole line of cars, mostly young parents, some middle-aged. I'm a grown adult, still a bit worried, hoping I haven't let my daughter down. She sees me and smiles, runs to where I'm standing. In the car she says, "You did a great job. My friends came up to me at recess and said, 'Your dad said 'whoop-ass' in class!' You got a 'Whoop! Whoop! Hip hip hooray!' on the playground."

The Real "Orange Is the New Black"

The real "Orange Is the New Black" is not what you see on Netflix. I spend four and a half hours at the women's prison. It's my first time inside a women-only prison. Women wear red or orange uniforms, depending on their security clearance and what level of offender they are. It's like a sporting event—all the noise and commotion, all the same colors. But not many are rooting for this team.

Author Sarah Shotland, who co-founded Words Without Walls at Chatham University, told me to give them this writing prompt first: Finish the statement "No one ever asked me . . ." I read them the prompt, and they begin writing almost immediately. I reiterate to them that their stories carry more weight than they might think. I truly believe, and my gut tells me, that a lot of these women are in prison for addiction issues or simply hanging out with the wrong person.

I continue to give them writing prompts. I present my lecture about the rape of a woman on my former college campus and how, as an undergraduate reporter, I reported on the crime and the lack of security on campus. I tell them how my investigative reporting helped make the campus a more secure place. I speak with pride about how using my voice for the first time as a writer made all the difference for me.

One of the five women asks, "Do you really think giving somebody some advice is going to help them? That it's gonna change anything?"

"Yes," I said. She mocked me, said something I couldn't hear and looked away. What I know about this particular snickering student is what she shares about her family—that most of them are drug users. During our class, the educational supervisor on duty separates her from another woman—they are sitting too close and touching each other. I can tell this student isn't afraid to ask or say whatever is on her mind, which I appreciate.

Another student talks about being raised by her grandmother and raped by her uncle and grandfather. After that, she was sent away to a foster family. At the end of her one-page piece, she apologizes to her grandmother. The essay is disturbing and sad. It wasn't her fault that her uncle and grandfather molested her. She doesn't owe anyone an apology. Here she is in prison, apologizing for being raped—unspeakable trauma that fueled an addiction as she tried to forget her past. Hearing and reading stories like this continues to make me question my faith in people. How on earth do these things continue to happen?

Another talks about getting right with the world. Says fentanyl is her drug of choice. Went from oxycontin to fentanyl to carfentanil—an elephant tranquilizer. She says she never did heroin.

"What's the point?" I ask. "You can't get out of bed. You need a fix so bad and then when you get it, you black out—it knocks you out."

"Yeah. Scary," she says. She also says she has about thirty tattoos. I can see she has a pot leaf on her knuckle. It's green, of course. It looks like she got it a long time ago, but all the women in this class are thirty and under.

The space I'm in is a tiny white-cinder-block room. To get here, I enter the control center and wait to be buzzed in. Then a giant black door opens. I wait in an interior corridor and another door opens automatically. I wonder what would happen if the electricity went out. When I am finally inside, I pass a cafeteria and the commissary room on my left. I don't go too far down the hallway. The education rooms are to my right. During class the rumble of women waiting in line to get their commissary supplies fills the room. It's always loud.

During a break, I ask to see the library and the women's living quarters. The person on staff takes me farther down the hall to a room full of books—their small library. This is encouraging. Through another locked corridor I see a wall of glass and can look into a large area where some of the women are housed. One story above me is another control center with tinted windows for monitoring this common area. As I stand at the glass wall, I can see that the women's rooms, their cells, don't have doors—instead, they have what look like shower curtains. They are all open. I see women sitting at round tables that are bolted to the floor. Two women turn to look at me and smile. One is missing some of her front teeth. It's an odd and uncomfortable feeling standing at these heavy glass windows staring into a world I know little about. It feels intrusive and also a bit powerful because I know I am not and do not have to be contained in there.

The South Dakota Women's Prison is located in Pierre—it houses more than 350 maximum, medium, and minimum security offenders. The complex is composed of multiple law enforcement buildings, part of the Solem Public Safety Center.

Driving to our state capital from Yankton feels like being out in the middle of nowhere. It's all wide open, what's left of the American frontier. No stop lights—no stop signs—no street lights; or at least it feels that way most of the trip. About two million people visit Mount Rushmore each year. Most of those visitors head west through South Dakota on I-90 to see the presidents' faces blasted and carved into a mountain. Not many of the drivers take the Pierre turnoff. This is where the movie *Dancing with Wolves* was filmed, near the Triple U Standing Butte Ranch outside Pierre, on Route 14 at the Missouri River. It's about a forty-minute drive off I-90. You don't want to run out of gas during a blizzard on this road. The atrocities of our country's past—the decimation of Native Americans—what's left of our prairie—it's all here on your way to the women's prison.

The man who helps me and stays with me the whole day today is a former grade school principal. We talk briefly about the mission of education behind bars and the greater good. A few days before this, the state recorded its coldest temperature—twenty-nine degrees below zero in Aberdeen.

Lunch with a DOC Official

I had lunch with a South Dakota Department of Corrections official today, one who makes the decisions for all of us who work for the system. My program is in limbo. After ten years, I've run into this problem at the prisons where I teach; the program is up and running, but once the initial funding is gone, the facility usually doesn't renew it. "No money in the budget," I've been told. Or you bid for the program through a series of tedious forms and procedures—all after you acquire your DUNS number (a unique nine-digit identifier for a business) and fill out innumerable SAM (a system used for registering to do business with the government) forms.

Working for the state or federal government involves way too much paperwork. We could save billions by reducing the amount of paperwork the government requires and not treating people like they are suspicious or guilty because they want to work for governmental organizations. Something to think about. This is your tax money.

One time, during an intensive background check, the administrator conducting my two-hour interview kept tapping her pen on the table and then finally asked me, "What are you hiding?" It was straight out of a detective show. I thought about it for a minute. There were plenty of things I'd never been caught doing, but I wasn't quite sure where to start. I just smiled and said what most would likely say—"Nothing." I wish I knew what covert operation they were trying to stick me with. The paranoia about Big Brother watching you is real. It's probably good that George Orwell's *1984* was one of the first books I read.

After fourteen years, I find the government's tedious and redundant paperwork ridiculously annoying. Ask anyone that works for government agencies. I once had to do three drug tests in one year for my creative writing contracting job because the contract was renewed, not awarded, then awarded, then on hold. But maybe, like a lot of the government systems, the program is set up to run just as everyone intended. After all, this bureaucracy is job security and these piss tests can be quantified.

My particular program at the state prison is funded through the South Dakota Department of Labor and GED classes. During my lunch with this official my hands are shaking a little as I try to spoon some fettuccini into my mouth. I'm obviously worried about the future of the program, and there's a lot riding on this conversation. When I express my concern for the second time, the official says, "In most instances, if I believe in a program continuing, people who work for me try to make it happen."

The official is pro-education and seems to care about the future and helping people. He worked in law enforcement for over twenty years, was tough on crime, and now sees the benefit of education behind bars. He visited my class early in the morning before lunch. The women were sharing some of their writing and it was evident that the program not only works but works well. It helps the inmates deal with trauma and misdirected decisions. Pierre is home base for most officials in the system, but visiting a class is not something they do often. When this one visited my class, you could tell immediately that the women in class were happy to be heard.

One particular student sticks out—the same one who was using carfentanil. They were all sharing important stories—or, as the late poet Don Welch, described it, we were "writing from our hidden heads." She talked about her children. She wrote for nearly five minutes without thinking, just getting it all down on the page. Welch's assignment is simple—you don't edit, you just write from your "hidden head." You write the secrets you keep, the ones you are afraid to face. You let them materialize without overanalyzing.

She completed another prompt called "An Exercise in Empathy," developed by the writer Daryl Farmer. Here the writer tells a story from another person's perspective. Trying to write in someone else's voice, often the voice of your opponent, helps you see another person's side of the story. This time the student wrote from her son's perspective, how he was afraid to live with her because he was afraid she would just fail again. He feared the needle in her arm *again*—the blood in the syringe. Can you imagine finding your mother nodding off with a kit sprawled across the floor? The son's voice was a cry for help like I haven't heard. Or have I? One could argue that this is the same story that addicts and the family members of travelers have been telling each other forever.

This woman's story was repackaged in the voice of a child. Even in the telling of this story, there were hints of a craving, of the hold the drug had on the mother. At one point she chuckled when she shared what she wrote. This still amazes me. How far down does one have to go to realize that life can be really, really fun without any drug? I said, "Again, you can't get out of bed. You need someone to go score your dope for you. They arrive. You shoot up. Which by the way, is an elephant tranquilizer you are writing about *again*. Then you black out. I don't get it. Doesn't sound like fun to me at all. Sounds like suicide." This time she didn't say anything.

I remember eating at a restaurant in Spearfish one evening. There was an attractive waitress most of the guys couldn't stop staring at. She had some black bandanas tied around her wrists. She also had some bruises up and down her arms. They looked like large track marks. Someone asked her what happened. She chuckled and said, "Oh. I was just throwing pumpkins." As high as I might have wanted to get sometimes, I'd never stick a needle in my arm. Maybe once you see a few young people you grew up with or hung out with in your twenties die, you start singing a different tune. And maybe we need to hear from the victims more. Maybe the child's voice will catapult a new cure.

I asked the class how many of them were under the influence when they committed their crime. All but two raised a hand. I hope and pray that the program continues.

I could see that the DOC official was listening with the ear of his heart. He was somebody who had seen the front end of crime, who then was tough on crime when he worked on the parole board. He was appointed by the governor and realized the true value of programming and good rehabilitative services. We need to put a lot of things in play here in South Dakota, a largely conservative state, because being "tough on crime" doesn't work. "METH. We're on it." Have the results of that slogan and the $449,000 campaign been quantified? If you want true public safety, you have to do things the smart way. Every kid and every adult needs someone to believe in them when no one else does. So many of our offenders need rehabilitative services—not to be locked in holes.

New Folsom Prison Blues

I've seen men in prisons who were bandaged at the throat and belly—cutting for attention, cutting for a ride in an ambulance, to see some form of life besides the despair behind bars. Traffic, congestion, horns. Anything. When this was brought to my attention at New Folsom in California, a facility that houses difficult maximum security prisoners who have long sentences, a staff member told me the logistics for responding when these complications occur.

"You have EMTs, a correctional officer, police, all inside the ambulance, plus a motorcade with highway patrol in front and back," the staff member said. "Also, take into account the medical personnel and doctor when they get to the hospital." New Folsom houses heinous criminals. The cost for each incident averages about twenty grand. "The state is desperate to give even these guys an outlet to create. Art, music, poetry, yoga, sports, anything besides trying to harm themselves or others."

There are few words for razor on flesh—blue, cut, black, wet. Few words for scream.

Prisoners can endure the pain they inflict on themselves to get the care they will receive from those attending to them. This emotional and physical cost is a means to an end—a way to get out of their narrow, confined world, if only for a few hours. Everyone is needy—we want attention and we desperately want things to hold our attention. Understanding positive outlets and implementing forms of creative expression is key. When we are absorbed in it, by it, attentive to it, art transcends and transports us beyond our present realities. Whether on a field, a court, a canvas, or a stage, craft forces one to get out of one's head and be captivated by the piece they are making. Enlightenment.

||||

It's our third visit to New Folsom Prison. Riot. Lockdown. Well, at least we made it into the parking lot. While we got out of the van to stretch, cuss, and complain, a man who hadn't been taken inside yet threw a basketball over a tall fenced concrete rec court to get our attention.

A volunteer guitarist at New Folsom told me at a recent Arts in Corrections conference, "You need to come in the winter. During the summer we are always on lockdown. There are riots. They are always in trouble."

When New Folsom went into lockdown today, San Quentin did, too. Gangs in prison communicate between facilities in different cities. So much of what goes on is known inside and unknown outside its walls. Gangs often run the show. I never saw segregation in action until I went to San Quentin. In the Arts in Corrections room at San Quentin, everyone comes together as a class and helps each other—no matter their race or beliefs. But once the men walk out the door of the classroom, it's back to their gangs. There is no disputing this. It's a matter of life and death.

Since New Folsom is in lockdown, we get back into our rental van and head back to Marin County—to San Quentin. Although San Quentin is also in lockdown, they let some guys out of their cells to come to the Arts in Corrections room to work with us.

California Dreamin' and the Sky is Gray

"Hell, man, up in here we got over two thousand mainline inmates. Find our home while we do our time. It's all segregated. Can't smoke after each other. Blacks on one side, whites on the other out there," says John, a student in the arts program, as he points to the door. "They left us this arts center. That's something. More than most people have. Helps, you know. Racism—you get that? It's a decade into a new century and it is still enforced by staff. It's easier to control us that way. When you arrive here, they literally study your skin color—red, brown, black. Southside. You are marked by your hood. Your people."

I grab a Speedball linoleum cutter, battleship grade. Get the two-inch roller. Press down hard. I roll it back and forth over the project. I ask John, "What's your opinion on them trying to close the art programs here?"

"Man, it's a political punt. Budget cuts. Legislation has to cut millions. Who you think they going after? No staff cuts. No construction going on up in here. Schools cut on the outside. Home health and social services cut off in the communities. When they hear that prisoners are getting an education, when they hear we are making prints up here and using watercolors, they get pissed off. If you already have a negative view of prisons, well then, they'll shut us off first.

"They want to get rid of Steve, cut his salary after we've made this model program work for all these years. People up in here making art, trying to better themselves, going to school, getting their GED. Hell, man, this place gives us hope that we won't never have to come back here, that we can do it on our own. Cutting his salary, cutting these programs—that's pennies in the bucket.

"Repercussions. Well, they'll be huge. A man has got to come to terms with his own demons. You know? It's all connected. Art. Redemption. You ask someone how it feels. What will it feel like if this program goes? Well, we've all been stripped pretty much of everything here. Most things gone. Lost families. Referred to as a number. You lose your sense of direction. Someone's got to slap you silly, or maybe you wake up one day and don't want to sit around no more. Tired of feeling sorry for yourself. Decide you gotta rebuild. Some people will never see the light. Half of us want to work on our lives. About 50 percent don't. This place is all they know. So, if they want to solve something, they solve it with these." John raises his fists.

"Bare knuckle blues. First couple of months I didn't know what to do. Had to find something—a challenge. Conflict means resolution. I know what it's like when people give up on you. Hadn't talked to my son in over six months. I had to turn inward. I asked for a lot of forgiveness from the higher God. Been pushing on that pull ever since."

||||

Punishment in prison is being secluded from society. It's not the old lock 'em up, work farm mentality that is portrayed in so many movies and tired television series. One of the better wardens I worked for at the federal prison camp (they rotate every two years) said, "I don't like the movie *Shawshank Redemption*. This isn't *Shawshank Redemption*. That place, for the most part, doesn't exist."

On the federal prison grounds, there's an old gymnasium where most of the recreation programs are held. Yoga classes. Art classes. Music therapy. Leather craft. There are free weights, cardio bicycles, and elliptical machines. Lots of things to keep the men occupied. Proverbs says, "Idle hands are the devil's workshop." It makes sense to keep busy. A student from the women's prison told me that boredom was the reason she continued to use and abuse drugs. Isn't boredom why so many free Americans drink in excess?

The federal prison camp has established various reentry programs to help the men prepare and succeed upon release. One of these programs is the mock job interview fair held in the big gym. Nine tables are set up so men can alternate and interview with three different groups of business leaders from the community. I often take college students from my university writing classes with me to this afternoon event so they can learn "do's and don'ts" to help them prepare for their future interviews. Each man has about twenty minutes at each table to interview; then we offer constructive criticism to help them improve their skills.

After an interview with one inmate, I tell the man that his honest voice works. He's forty-five years old. He tells us this. He says he's a grandpa. He looks entirely too young to be a grandpa. I tell him, "You sold some drugs. You got caught. You are doing your time. Life goes on.

"Try to look me in the eye—don't move your face and do that scrunchy thing when someone asks you what crime you committed. Some people will ask. Don't tell them you manufactured and distributed methamphetamine. It sounds like you're celebrating your crime. Say you made some misdirected decisions and mistakes and you are ready to move on with your life and be a productive member of society. Own it. Say it straight."

He curls his frown of uncertainty into a smile.

||||

Rita F. Pierson, in her amazing Ted Talk "Every Kid Needs a Champion," said, "Teaching and learning should bring joy. How powerful would our world be if we had kids who were not afraid to take risks, who were not afraid to think, and who had a champion? Every child deserves a champion, an adult who will never give up on them, who understands the power of connection, and insists that they become the best that they can possibly be."[7]

There are hundreds of thousands of adults who need champions, too. We all need to be reminded that we are capable of wonderful things.

"Today's Special"

I ask students in all my classes to read a short essay called "Today's Special." It helps them understand poverty and crime a bit better. The author, a former student in one of my prison classes, wrote about skipping school because he got picked on. He got picked on because he didn't have a chance to wash his clothes—he smelled. He couldn't wash his clothes because his mother didn't make enough money as a waitress for a decent place to stay—often they'd have to sleep in the cab of the cook's truck.

It's a heartbreaking story that took a lot of courage to write. This student looked to be in his sixties when he was in my class. He didn't say much at first. He shut himself off from most people. But a floodgate opened on the day he responded to the prompt that inspired his story. He couldn't quit writing. I reassured him that his story was important, that all of our stories are important. They are, after all, what make us human. They define our lives.

The writing helped him heal. It helped his family. It inspired many other students to tell their own stories. And the last time I heard from him, he was giving public speeches about what he learned in prison and how writing and education helped him change his life. If he were here, I bet he'd say that it's never too late. His name was Timothy Neal.

||||

IOWA MAN SENTENCED TO PRISON FOR KILLING GIRLFRIEND'S FATHER

PLEASANT HILL, Iowa (AP)—A Pleasant Hill man has been sentenced to 10 years in prison for killing his girlfriend's father. Twenty-seven-year-old Ricky St. John was sentenced Friday. In a deal with prosecutors, he pleaded guilty to voluntary manslaughter in the November death of 46-year-old Timothy Neal of Glidden. St. John had been charged with first-degree murder in the case. Multiple witnesses told police they saw St. John strangle Neal on the ground until Neal stopped struggling. The witnesses say they then saw St. John kick Neal in the head. Neal was later pronounced dead at Iowa Lutheran Hospital.[8]

Students in University Classes vs. Prisons

Very rarely have I felt intimidated by students at the prison. Usually it's the opposite. I've felt energized. I always tell guest writers who speak to my class that these "criminals" will be the best audience they've ever had. A captive audience (a tired joke).

Last year, for a brief moment, I felt more intimidated by a freshman at the private Catholic university where I teach than I ever have by even the most hardened criminals at San Quentin or the Allegheny County Jail or any other prison I've visited. This student couldn't control his temper, so I asked to speak to him in the hall. I couldn't call a correctional officer. He kept arguing with me because I asked him to revise his paper. In the hall I told him he wasn't welcome back in class. When he continued to be confrontational, I turned around and walked back into the classroom. The following week, almost like nothing had happened, he apologized for taking his anger out on me.

Fast forward to 2022: I was in the university hall asking a student who had spent weeks being disruptive in class why he didn't revise his paper. I'd given him an extension to complete the revisions and I'd given him suggestions on areas I thought were strongest. "I'm not fucking perfect like you!" he said. "I'm not a fucking perfect writer!" And I walked him to his advisor's office, which happened to be right next door to the classroom. I explained the situation and then asked if he had anything to say to me. "No comment," he replied. He was not permitted in my class again.

||||

For a long time I used my hardest writing prompts at the prison—those I thought were too personal for a beginning composition class at the university. But I was wrong. If students feel comfortable and safe, they want to tell their story. These stereotypical assumptions are completely wrong. People are people, no matter the building they are in.

"If I spend too much time with my daddy, he just wants to slay me like he did my mom," a student says in my office during one of her semester conferences. I don't know how to respond. I wait a few seconds and say, "I'm sorry."

"It's not your fault. I'm used to it."

I move uncomfortably in my office chair. I am at a loss for words.

"Can I do anything?" I ask.

"No," she says matter-of-factly and then adds, "Are we done?"

"Yes."

And this is before we have any protocol in place to report unusual comments or writing that is alarming. I want to believe I said something to those in charge, but to be honest, I can't remember. I can't remember her name or see her face. But her words still haunt me.

Singing "Little Red Corvette" in the Alleghany County Jail

We parked in a parking lot adjacent to the Allegheny County Jail in Pittsburgh and ducked under a ripped chain-link fence to get in the side entrance. Through the door we entered, in this secured area, there was a small room painted government grey, with a metal detector and conveyor belt for scanning bags. From the interstate, the Allegheny County Jail looks like a cluster of four high-rise project buildings. From a distance, the windows look like they have been converted to cement peep holes—small enough so no one can jump out. The windows are black. If there was a yard for recreation, I didn't see it.

I was a guest speaker for Words without Walls, a program through which Chatham University MFA students taught creative writing at area correctional institutions and a residential drug and alcohol treatment program. After I was escorted down multiple cement corridors and hallways, I entered a large room with maybe 150 chairs. The correctional officers instructed inmates to fill the three sections of seats in front of me. Adolescents to the right. Men in the middle. Women to the left. The correctional officers (at least two per group) then stood behind each section. They left their walkie-talkies on. You can always bet your money on two sounds in jail—walkie-talkies and keychains worn by the correctional officers.

Allegheny County Jail has its own school system. According to the jail's website, "Juveniles at the Allegheny County Jail attend the Academic Institute School on a daily basis. The school is managed by the Allegheny Intermediate Unit and partners with Pittsburgh Public Schools to enable students the opportunity to achieve credits toward a high school diploma. Courses offered are in line with the curriculum at the Pittsburgh Public Schools and they're taught [by] a staff of 11 Pennsylvania-certified teachers employed by the AIU. A licensed professional counselor and a special education teacher are also on staff."[9]

It was hard to contain the room. It was hard to get them to listen. "Don't mistake kindness for weakness, ladies and gentlemen," yelled one of the men in charge. "I will take you back to your unit if you can't quiet down!"

I started my presentation by reading a few poems, talking off the cuff about why I was there. I could hear the chairs squeak and the adolescents start to laugh and talk. The correctional officers called some of them out by last name and tried to keep them quiet. I probably said something about expressive writing being therapeutic and how it can help people heal. Then I read my go-to essay, "Little Red Love Machine." It would either kill or bomb, but I had to take a chance. I wanted to make them all laugh. I wanted to read something that had some weight—humor and tragedy—that might inspire or at least capture their attention enough to take them to another place.

"Little Red Love Machine" is an essay about how I learned about sex—an awkward experience that most people in the room had gone through or thought about. "Learned" is the key word here. The essay highlights my roller skating days and teenage exploits. How I learned from some uneducated examples. At one point in the short essay, I sing a few lines from Prince's "Little Red Corvette." After I butchered a few verses of the song, a kid to my right said, "He nailed that." Now more of them were leaning closer to hear what I had to say. The essay killed. It's a fun piece to read and it makes you think about how we all fail and learn by bad examples. My vulnerability and willingness to share personal stories is at the heart of that essay. I'm not afraid to talk about embarrassing moments.

After I read the essay, I answered questions from all sides of the room. I read another couple of poems, and then everyone was excused and led back to their cells. I had learned an important lesson. No matter your audience, if you want to get their attention, be vulnerable, be yourself, be a human being. And if you have something funny, read it. I learned that in San Quentin. Beginning writers think they always have to be serious. There is this notion that you have to sound like the smartest person in the room. That's not true. No one gives a rip how smart you are.

Confrontations in Class

Every Tuesday evening when my prison creative writing class is over, I pack up my things quickly and drive across the city to pick up my youngest daughter from dance. Tonight I'm frustrated. I am carrying the classroom home with me. I'm angry with two students who disrupted the class—and one of them in particular (who is about to be released), who decided to go on a rant when he was supposed to workshop some new material. His rant was all about how I didn't know what the students needed, how I was not teaching them the correct material, and how that was why three students had recently dropped (or stopped showing up). *Dropped* is a word used if you are taking my class for credit or you paid for it. They weren't. But I didn't mention that.

Everyone, according to this disgruntled inmate, wanted to learn how to write commercial fiction and screenplays. He even went so far as to provide me with a syllabus he had constructed. Week three, writing the romance novel. Week four, writing the mystery novel. He provided fourteen weeks. I wanted to ask him where his plans were for the rest of the year—but the syllabus was "filed" for me by a supervisor who heard the whole fiasco over WebEx, which is how we are conducting class during a worldwide pandemic and how I presume this student got his confidence.

My daughter can see I'm angry when I pick her up from dance class. She asks, "What's wrong?" I have been teaching in this prison since she was born. She is older now and understands, I believe, why I do what I do. She asks, "Are the men in your class killers?"

"Not that I know of," I tell her. "Most of the guys at this prison camp are in for white collar crimes—embezzlement, fraud, or selling a lot of drugs."

"Good," she says, a little less worried.

I've worked with prisoners in San Quentin and the South Dakota state prisons who have murdered people and done some very heinous things. Maybe some of the men in this class have murdered someone, but if they have, if perhaps they were involved in gang activity and someone was murdered, they haven't been caught. My daughter looks out the window. I can see her face reflected in the glass. It's pitch black outside and the light from her cell phone projects her image against the passenger window and the darkness of the night.

I've had students write about gang activity. I've had students in the prison camp allude to murder in discussions. They have talked about shootings. But as far as I know, no one, even if they trickled down the system to get to a place like FPC Yankton, is serving time for murder. If you go fifty miles away to the state prison, it's a totally different situation. I never asked why my students were in the medium-high security prison. But inevitably the correctional officer assigned to my classroom would tell me who the sex offenders were and who had murdered someone. This happened in every single class, as if they couldn't help themselves. As if, and I often wondered if this were true, when they saw the men and women begin to change for the better, they were angry.

I'm a teacher. I have one job. To help these men and women write. To perhaps (at the state prison) teach them to come to terms with their crimes in a short three-month period. And I can tell you, the heinous criminals weren't as disruptive as the two guys who decided to try to take over the classroom via a computer screen.

I've never been this angry when I've thought about teaching in prisons. I've let a few very disgruntled students get under my skin. So I am doing what I ask them to do, which is to write through it. These two students seldom write nonfiction. In fact, one has never written the truth, as far as I can remember. Both students have been in class for the past three years, which is part of the problem. They are upset because they are seeing some of this material for a third time.

There was a tradition of respect in my classrooms, but in the past couple of years, there's been increasing angst—the jealousy that comes from amateur and beginning writers wanting what the teacher has, which is experience and publishing credentials. They want books. They want to be in the front of the room. And hey, I want them to have books, too.

And I understand their anxious energy and skepticism because I was once them, criticizing the expert in the room. Back then I wasn't writing. I was talking about writing. To make matters worse, these two guys are in prison. They lack emotional intelligence and would rather argue with me (three years in) than just write. They would rather argue than trust that I am listening to them, trying to provide new material for them to consider, trying to teach the class as I have for the past thirteen years. I am them. I crave what other writers have. All I want to do is get paid to create. But the difference between me and them is that I've grown up.

Maybe I'm wrong—that's what one student told me two weeks ago. He said that I didn't understand the wants and needs of the students—that they are fiction writers, they care little about telling their truths, and they want to write for the big screen. This veteran student went through a litany of all the things I was doing wrong and should be doing differently—no more writing prompts, for example, unless there are hard deadlines, and no more constant revision. More character development, more on plot structure and dialogue—everything he presumably wants. This is a guy who for the past year, during COVID, was provided with screenwriting exercises and innumerable articles on craft. Just for him. But I don't remind him of this.

There are a few problems with all of this. First, because of COVID, I am not allowed in the prison. Second, this student is leaving in two weeks and has decided to write to me and then lecture me via WebEx. We are in a pandemic, so my class is delivered via a computer screen and monitor in two different classrooms, which are in two different units in the prison. The entire prison is still divided because of pandemic restrictions on the compound. We are one of the only federal prisons in the nation that has implemented this technology. This has been the case for a full year now. I think, and my immediate boss confirmed, that a couple of the students believe it is easier to criticize from behind the projection screen in the classroom. Perhaps they think they can get away with saying things that they wouldn't say in person.

There are no grades for this class. There is a final project, which is the production of a creative writing journal called *4 P.M. Count*. If the students were receiving grades, I don't believe they would say a word. I made the mistake of giving one of these students time in class to teach us about story arc and screenwriting (his focus). He has jeopardized his future, so dreaming big may be his only option. He has writing chops and I enjoy his work. However, I am now realizing how much his bad attitude and whatever he's saying outside of class have affected the new students who want to be part of the thirteen-year tradition of publishing *4 P.M. Count*.

My specialty is nonfiction and poetry. As much as these guys (or at least two of them) want to write for the big screen, I have to keep delivering my class in the way that has worked. Families (including one of these guys' family members) have written to tell me how proud they are of the work we do. They say they can see positive change. They request free copies of the journal. Unfortunately, I can't respond to these family members or to former inmates. It's a rule. So when they reach out to me via email, I report it to authorities, send a journal to the family if they ask for one, and that's that.

I could sit here and complain or write an extensive response to this student—about how he knows my pedagogical approach and wants to change it to suit his own needs. He wants to argue. He's scared for his future. His impending release and now his anger have, in his eyes, a platform. This happens when men are getting released. All of a sudden, they become confrontational with me, someone who has been trying to help them use their voice in a positive manner. I could argue with the student and tell him he should get his PhD and then find a university and a prison where he can teach. In the meantime, I will continue to do what I do, acknowledging the students who are eager to learn. Some have writing experience, some have degrees, some just have a GED—the dynamics of this class are across the board.

The next week I tell these two and the entire class that they should respect their peers' comments—agree or disagree with their criticism. "At the end of the day," I say, "it's your writing and you can do with it what you choose. If you want to publish in the journal, we will go over guidelines and reiterate when we need to. You can respect the classroom or you can leave. Other people will fill your seat. I will not tolerate vulgarities or being laughed at or talked to disrespectfully. I'm the teacher and it's a privilege to be in my classroom—if you don't like the way I teach, go back to your unit and you won't be a part of the publication. Period."

I also add: "The goals for this class are for you to become better writers and communicators and for you to have something (hopefully a few things) ready to publish in *4 P.M. Count* by the end of August. Conducting class through a live video stream has made things more difficult. I'm not there in person. However, that does not mean you can be disruptive in class. One positive thing about the video classroom is that it has allowed me to show some online courses, which I purchased for you and will continue to present. My specialty—what I got my PhD in—was poetry. I am also a specialist in nonfiction. These courses I purchased will help us learn more about fiction, screenwriting, and graphic novels. I'm hoping you are sharing ideas within your units. I have a very eclectic pedagogical approach to this class because the students have varying levels of education. So, if you've been in class with me more than once and you aren't happy with the way class is going, you don't have to be in class any longer. Deviations will not be tolerated. You will adhere to the parameters of the class or be asked to leave. I will not tolerate vulgarities or profanities aimed at me or your classmates. We will offer each other constructive criticism, and it is up to you whether you want to accept suggestions for your work or not. I'm proud of what I am seeing so far from you guys. And your work will continue to become richer as you continue to read and write. One last reminder: Taking this class is a privilege."

The next week, both students are gone.

I'd like to tell you this was an isolated incident, but it's happened before. Years ago, a returning student who wanted a bigger platform—who wanted to teach—gave me a large envelope on the last day of class, when we had a guest author present. This was another man who had an education but made a wrong turn and was bottling up a lot of anger and giving it to me in the classroom. After we had left the prison and I was taking the guest author to a restaurant, I opened the envelope and read the first sentence: "I don't mean to be an arm chair quarterback, but . . ." I threw it in the trash can outside the restaurant.

Four years later, this student was back in my class. After he demonstrated months of good behavior, I gave him the floor a few times to present and direct lessons on certain topics. The entrepreneur in him began to shine.

Being an instructor behind bars is difficult. So many men want their freedom, of course, and they want to suck the life out of you. They want every ounce of information you can give them, and they want instruction on every genre that isn't your specialty. And then some have the nerve to tell you how you aren't doing anything right. Basically, they want an MFA in every genre. God bless them for wanting to learn, but some of them take the wrong approach. And the fact that they aren't receiving a grade changes the dynamics, especially when they are speaking through a computer monitor.

Blanket of Security

Men in my class frequently write tributes to someone they love—often their child's mother or an ex-wife, usually someone they've hurt. When writing these reflections, they use predictable metaphors and clichés. They believe rhyme is important because they have read rhymes in greeting cards and heard them in song lyrics. When I ask one student who his poem is about, he says his ex—his "baby mama." I ask him if he can recall an act of love, a specific moment he shared with this woman, something she might recall if he can invoke the right details, paint the right picture, something special that will touch her. He looks at me and asks, "You don't like my poem?"

"Not really. It's predictable."

He pauses and looks down at his notebook. He takes his time responding. These are the critical seconds when a student either explodes or hears me. He says, "When I write about specifics, I get embarrassed."

"Yeah, that's kinda the point. Your tough guy façade landed you here, didn't it?"

I tell him about a time about twenty years ago when I was on a road trip, driving back home from Red Lodge, Montana. It was a long and windy trip. I asked my wife and a van load of friends to describe one of their most memorable days with their significant other.

My wife took her time thinking about it. It drove me nuts.

"It was a day when we were raking leaves," she said. And I remembered that day. It was at the last house we rented. We didn't have that much money. I was in graduate school. We had raked these enormous piles of leaves. And we'd stuffed those brown recycle bags and lined them up on the curb like a chorus of fans—totems of the afternoon's accomplishments. And we had this loud basset hound named Doo Rite who would always bark and cause trouble. We had to buy one of those shock collars because the neighbors got so tired of the barking. The dog was ornery and just liked to play.

I tell the student what I recalled from that day.

"I remember the late afternoon—crisp but not cold. I had a glass of wine in a mason jar sitting on the ledge of the house trim. I was always drinking out of a box of wine back then. I remember we had one rake. Those bags. My glass of booze and piles of leaves. I don't remember any conversations or anything earth-shattering happening. We were just together—all our absolutes, failures, future, and hope. Ever since she told me that was a special day for her, I go back and think about it. Often our true love shows when we aren't trying. Does that sound cheesy?"

He didn't take long to respond.

"We used to love to get the kid down to sleep. Finally," he told me, "we'd pop in a VHS movie and just chill. It was our time. No one was trying to hustle. We could hold each other. Be with each other. Under this big quilted blanket. Those heavy ones, you know?"

"That's what you need to write to her," I tell the student, this man who is not much different from me. "Right there. Describe the colors of that blanket. Its history. Its weight and security."

Is This the Same as College?

One of the most hardened criminals I'd met, a repeat felony offender, was showing some real progress in our pilot class. One day he asked, "How much would this cost us if we were going to college? I mean, is this how you teach those students?"

I reassured him I didn't play favorites. This form of expressive writing is something I learned from some of my favorite mentors—especially

Maria Mazziotti Gillan. I said, "You may be in this prison, a fortified compound, but problems and prisons of all kinds exist outside these walls. People are so desperate to tell their stories. They want someone to truly listen to them."

And, I added, "It's free."

The guy honestly wanted to learn. "No. I mean, how much money would it cost right now if I was going to college to take this class? How many credits would it be worth?"

"If you were enrolled full-time at my private university, this three-credit class would cost you about three thousand dollars for the semester."

He turned to the classmate next to him and said, "See. We are going to college. Right here, right now. Same thing. Same teacher."

Rebuilding

In a 2017 *Yankton Press and Dakotan* article, "GED A New Start: Springfield Prison Inmates Rebuild Their Lives Through Education," journalist Randy Dockendorf writes:

> Most of his adult life has been spent inside prison walls and fences.
>
> "I've committed three felonies, and I've been in and out of prison for 28 years," [Rob] Apple said. . . .
>
> Apple wants to share his story with others. So do about a dozen other inmates who, like him, are part of the new "Writing for Re-Entry" program at the Springfield prison. . . .
>
> Through their writing, inmates open up about their past mistakes and the future direction of their lives. . . .
>
> By sharing his story, Apple wants to help others deal with their mistakes or avoid the wrong path. "I want to pass along my knowledge," he said."[10]

Shortly after this article ran in the newspaper, Apple received a call from his child, with whom he hadn't spoken in years. He told me all this in class. He had used his voice to make a difference.

As Rudyard Kipling said, "Words are, of course, the most powerful drug used by mankind."

5
Premeditation

Maybe the question isn't whether we can we define evil, but rather, who should be locked away for the rest of their life? Another one I keep wrestling with is this: Should I and could I forgive X, or is he justifiably beyond forgiveness? Underneath the abstraction of "evil" that I've seen in men and women are these personal questions of my own. Maybe if I can reach a firm conclusion—that X either is or is not evil—I can define him and be at peace with his actions. As a Christian, I have been taught to forgive. But when the crime cuts so close, it's not that simple.

There were guys at San Quentin and men and women in the South Dakota state prisons who murdered another human being and said they were out of their mind on drugs or booze—that I can understand but not condone. A crime committed because you're out of your mind is different from a premeditated crime. Who is more evil—the one who claims he can't help himself or the one who does it consciously and calculatedly? Is someone sitting behind a computer screen invading an innocent person's finances and life savings, and then stealing or intentionally mismanaging them for their own gain, a worse criminal than someone who kills a person in the heat of the moment or when they are out of their mind on drugs or alcohol? Can you imagine waking up in a holding cell—seeing blood on yourself—and asking a guard, "What did I do?" And then the guard perhaps saying, "I could tell you anything, and you would have to believe me. Why don't you just think on that for a spell?"

The men and women I've worked with who have murdered another human being were just people in a room writing, drawing, painting, or acting in the name of art and rehabilitation—in the name of "good time," which might equate to a reduction in their sentence. They weren't people in a room recommitting the atrocious acts that brought them to prison. Most weren't harassing me or trying to scare me. Some have been blatantly rude and disrespectful, but that's an easy fix—I just kick them out and they never get to come back. I can call a correctional officer (if one isn't with me) or sound the alarm that I wear. In fact, I've found dealing with disrespectful inmates easier than dealing with disrespectful students at a university. It takes weeks of discipline and paperwork to justify removing a student from class. In a prison it's pretty easy for me to separate myself from the people in the room and their crime, especially because I don't ask about what brought them there. But some staff members can't wait to tell me why certain people have been confined—even when I ask them not to. It's none of my business, and I try to remind the staff of that. I'm a professor, not a judge. But they do it anyway.

A lot of the men and women in class are very good at manipulating the system and me. I have worked with staff and had supervisors in prisons who didn't seem to believe in rehabilitation. One who had worked in high-security prisons said she needed to get back behind barbed wire, that the men in this particular prison were treated with too much respect—almost like humans—that identity thieves and corporate conmen were, in her opinion, worse than murderers. But conning others is something I see everywhere—in people at universities, in my neighborhood. It surrounds us. People will go to extreme measures and do very immature things to get immediate rewards. The conman lives in us all at times.

Bill Conroy, author of *Dispatches from the House of Death*, wrote me the following message after he read a draft of this book:

> As I read your work it jogs my memory and past experiences with crime, including international crime and players in it, and how national security and those with the power to define that hyperreality can easily blur the lines between the rule of law and crime. It's called foreign intelligence gathering, or spying, or covert ops, in the nation deploying it, and it's defined as a great crime by the nations targeted,

> including in our courts of law. Seems to me concepts like evil simply can't be defined by human law precisely because we are the "sinners" too. Only our history and an unconscious "collective conscience" can do that. That is a land of Jungian archetypes, which makes defining evil elusive.[1]

I realize there is no defining characteristic of people who commit heinous crimes. What exactly is the makeup of a serial killer? There is no clear classification for a malicious human. We are captivated by wickedness and the villains who seem to get away with it on the screen and in our favorite books, fascinated with a posh lifestyle that is above law and order. If these terms and labels—*heinous*, *wicked*, *evil*—could be defined very specifically, we could do more to understand and perhaps even help these kinds of immoral people and to comprehend our attraction to the grotesque.

Out of all the criminals I've known and worked with, and out of all the terrible things that some of them have done, the ones who premeditated their crimes, to me, are the worst. Child molesters, for example. I can't wrap my head around how somehow who does this, whatever their reasons, can be forgiven. I can't understand it. And as much as it disturbs me, I know I have helped students in my classes who have committed such heinous crimes. The state prisons where I taught imprisoned a high number of sex offenders.

X and his accomplice affected me personally, and I have every reason in the world to want to retaliate—to hate them. I have every right to have a host of emotions and feelings. I absolutely know that what happened to Christina was heinous and abhorrent—I don't have any disagreement within myself about this—no second guessing it—every nerve in my body knows it—but nevertheless, I can't pin down what evil is. Some argue that evil is a cultural construct—largely theological in origin. I ask a lot of questions and try to understand it the best I can. I have also realized that a heinous act can be committed by someone who maybe isn't evil, differentiating the act from the person.

With these uncertainties, I've chosen to immerse myself in this culture—into the world of prisons where some such people are contained. I have spent days, months, and years in rooms with men and women who have murdered. Were all of them wicked? Absolutely not. I remember talking with a correctional officer on death row at San Quentin, and he said, "There's some men here who have made some terrible, terrible decisions. But very few of them are evil."

There was a woman in my class at a state prison who seemed to look right through me and speak about murdering another person very matter-of-factly and without affect. She was short, thin, and innocent looking enough until she spoke of her premeditated crime, which was motivated by money and drugs. It was a cold-blooded act. She and one or two other women in the class wore red prison-issued shirts, which meant their crimes were more severe and they were more prone to violence than those wearing orange shirts. The prison's own hierarchy.

Society's attraction to the fictional world of crime seems to coincide with the onslaught of tape recordings and video footage surfacing in true-crime documentaries. The good thing about this trend is that we can see clearly—for example, in the police body-cam footage of Chris Watts arriving relatively calmly at his home hours after he dumped his children in oil vats and murdered his wife and unborn child—that there are no defining character traits of murderers. However, more often than not in these taped confessions, video footage, and reenactments, we see that these purportedly evil people were at one time law-abiding citizens who held jobs and did normal things, just like you and me—and that is stranger still. Like my classmate X in middle school, who leaned over our algebra assignment and said to me, "Listen dude, it ain't that hard. We want to isolate the variable. Get it all alone. We want to do the same thing to both sides. Whatever you do to one side you got to do to the other. You see?"

Fifteen Years Inside

"Having worked fifteen years in prisons, I can tell you that evil does exist. I've witnessed it," says Josh Klimek, former unit manager at Mike Durfee State Prison and winner of South Dakota's highest honor in corrections, the Santan Canary Award. He was nominated for the award by the South Dakota Corrections Association, a peer-reviewed selection process. "I 100 percent believe that there is evil or the devil and that there are evil people out there. It's small—a very small percentage of most adults who are incarcerated. They're probably not truly to-the-bone evil. But there are some individuals who are. There's only one way to keep society safe—you have to either lock them up or somewhat keep them isolated from the rest of society, because they're always going to pose a threat, and mitigate that risk for those select few," he says, as we walk the prison yard.

Like the federal prison where I work, this place is a former college campus. The yard is green and we are on a sidewalk. There are some flowers—mostly marigolds, which are resilient. Trees in a few places. It's desolate out here in Springfield, South Dakota. I can see why the college never made it. And if this prison weren't here, I doubt the town would be nearly as large or financially stable as it is.

"Now, the vast majority of people, even those incarcerated for pretty heinous crimes, are probably not inherently evil. There's crimes of passion and, you know, things just kind of happen sometimes. Whether those are accidents or whatever. But"—Josh pauses, looks up at the razor wire, then back at me—"there are some individuals who are just evil."

A Monster of a Question

How to define or describe evil seems like a monster of a question. It's impossible to pinpoint a simple definition or equation: If Criminal A killed his wife because the devil told him to do it, is he less evil than Criminal B, who did it because he was a brutal and controlling person and wanted to see his victim bleed?

I'm no theologian or philosopher, but that's not stopping me from digging. A few years after Josh was no longer working in corrections, I emailed him to see if he could give me some examples of inmates he encountered who he thought did truly unconscionable things and who should be locked up forever for the public's safety. Here is his response:

> At what point does some behavior go from a mental health issue (insanity defense) to an evil act? There are many examples of offenses

over the years. To summarize them into a few sentences will be tough, but I'll give you a few examples. . . .

We had a fairly well known offender (his crime was actually featured in an episode of Swamp Murders TV series). He and a few of his friends kidnapped, raped, tortured and murdered a young Native American woman. When they were done raping her, they dragged her behind their pickup, then dumped her in a creek leaving her to drown and die. In a case like this, how can anyone carry out such a long term torture?

I worked with one older inmate toward the end of his life who murdered his wife in front of a sheriff. She had filed for divorce. . . . When I was working with him his only comment regarding his offense was, "Bitch deserved it."

There was an inmate who was incarcerated for killing his parents; his mother made him a sandwich with the wrong flavor of jelly, so he stabbed them.

On the other side, you have those inmates who stood no chance. There was an inmate whose mother would give him meth so he would stay awake in school. . . . A similar story with a different inmate whose mother would put him in the windows of homes so he could run around and grab all the valuables and pass them out to her. . . .

There was the inmate who was incarcerated for sexual assault on his children. He and several of his friends would gather at an abandoned church and gang-rape his kids. He was a fairly compliant inmate and you wouldn't have guessed his past based on working with him after his conviction. But how could anyone let children, let alone his own kids, get gang-raped like that?[2]

Can We Define Wickedness?

In the article "The Effect of Prison Education Programs on Recidivism," in the *Journal of Correctional Education*, writer John Esperian notes that "undoubtedly, some individuals—murderers, rapists, child molesters—are either unwilling or unable to live and work as honest, hard-working brokers within the framework of society. These dangerous anti-social cases need to be kept in confinement permanently for the safety of the community."[3]

Charles Bowden stated that the sicario started as an acceptable person and then became a trained assassin—someone who murdered hundreds. It was a learned profession. He wasn't a wealthy man and he had little to lose. The drug business would allow him luxuries he'd never had before. Bowden writes that anyone—everyone—could become a torturer or murderer. Documentaries like *National Geographic*'s *Narco Wars—In Their Own Words* and articles like the Modern Language Association of America's "It's a Living: Hit Men in the Mexican Narco War" don't seem all that strange now. So many young men have turned to a life of murder—from rags to riches and mayhem. Although many articles have been published about these atrocities, they just continue. I don't think the United States and Mexico know how to deal with such malicious activity. Author Kent Meyers states that "with drugs, making them illegal makes them lucrative. Add that to poverty and economic injustice/inequality, and you give poor people a way to riches if they're willing to take the risk. Since they have little to lose, they take the risk. . . . The 'war on drugs' is simply an attempt to add more violence—by government—to fight the violence."

There's just too much money in the sicario and the cartel—on both sides of the U.S. border. Most publications and media outlets have run a story or news brief on the slaughter and carnage. It sure seems like whenever there's a crisis elsewhere in the world, the United States of America, with our self-assured hubris, is there to help restore peace. There have been nearly five hundred thousand murders in Mexico since 2007, when Felipe *Calderón*, the former president of Mexico, declared war on the cartels. His former public security minister was caught and convicted in early 2023 for working with and taking bribes from the Sinaloa Cartel—the evil enterprise he had sworn to protect innocent Mexican citizens from.

So you have to ask yourself, why is it allowed to continue? Because drugs are illegal. In criminalizing drugs, people have to weigh the reward against the risk. By decriminalizing drugs instead of sending all "drug criminals" to prison, we could fight addiction. We have to look at the root problems and fix them. That would be a humane thing to do and it would overhaul the way we run our justice and medical systems and the way we treat all people—the wealthy, the middle class, and the poor.

You know who understands that alcohol and drug addiction is an illness? The American Medical Association. Alcohol and drug addiction should be thought of in the same way that we think of cancer or diabetes. Both are illnesses. Neither is necessarily terminal. If you lock a person who has diabetes or cancer in a jail cell, they aren't going to get any better. But most people know that—it's common sense.

People who say they LOVE the United States of America and what it stands for should LOVE the citizens of the good ol' USA and should LOVE their neighbor as themselves. Is the United States a Christian nation? I know many people who stand behind the shield of Christianity, often preach it, and use it as a tool to gain power. I think Dave Barry said it best in his article "25 Things I Have Learned in 50 Years." He said, "People who want to share their religious views with you almost never want you to share yours with them."[4]

Incarcerating people with illnesses is unjust. So why do we do it? Because working to make things better is hard. And the people who control the money and in turn control people enjoy their control far more than they would enjoy rolling up their sleeves and getting to work to help people with addictions.

It's been reported that Charles Bowden's article "Sicario—A Juarez Hit Man Speaks" sat on President Obama's Oval Office desk for months after its publication in *Harper's*. No other president since has truly addressed these criminal enterprises. The atrocities and killings have become a living for so many adolescent young men, and no one seems to be doing a damn thing about it. It's no wonder everyone wants to flee. No living wages and fear for your life. All of it is a manifestation of evil enterprises. And these organizations of corruption—one could argue, of genocide—are allowed to continue because of the revenue the "war on drugs" is generating on both sides of our border. Who is benefiting besides the cartel? Those who are presumably fighting against the cartel—those seemingly in control of their countries and protecting their nations. These are the same people who oversee laws and the distribution of wealth in their respective countries.

The article "AP Report: Former DEA Agent Tells His Own Story of Corruption before Jail Time" quotes Jose Irizarry, now known as the most corrupt agent in U.S. Drug Enforcement Administration history: "'We had free access to do whatever we wanted,' the 48-year-old Irizarry told the AP in a series of interviews before beginning a 12-year federal prison sentence. 'We would generate money pick-ups in places we wanted to go. And once we got there it was about drinking and girls.'"[5]

President Obama, Charles Bowden, and I aren't theologians or philosophers—and we don't have time to turn ourselves into them, either. But surely those in power can try to combat this mayhem and these immense issues through the work they do. It's not difficult to figure out why it's happening and why no one is doing anything about it—and that is not only an atrocity, it's wicked.

Extremely Bad Decisions

"What Readers and Writers Can Learn from Cops and Criminals" is a presentation I give from time to time with *New York Times* best-selling author Marc Cameron. Cameron is a crime novelist, best known for his Jericho Quinn and Arliss Cutter series. He is also the author of the Jack Ryan series, which is part of the Tom Clancy universe. He knows how to write action. He knows a great deal about police work, too, having spent more than thirty years as a U.S. Marshal, retiring as chief. He's a certified scuba diver and a man tracker.

I saved some of our initial emails because it's such a pleasure reading, learning, and talking with him about his work. His writing is rich in character and detail because he is pulling from past experiences and he knows the work. He's not just researching—he has served and protected for over three decades.

"First of all—Yikes. I'm always nervous when learned folk read my stuff," Marc wrote in an email. "As rookie police officers we were assigned to a month rotation at the county jail—in the old days when they still had swinging cell doors with steel bars and female prisoners were around the corner from the males—out of sight but not sound. It was . . . raucous." He continued:

> As a deputy marshal I saw the inside of everything from tiny city jails to the federal supermax in Florence, Colorado.

During a Dixie Mafia trial in Mississippi in the early 90s, myself and another deputy lived in the Lamar County jail in Purvis, Mississippi, for two weeks, guarding separated in-custody witnesses, lifers from Angola state prison in Louisiana. It was an old jail with riveted flat-iron cages. The jailers who went home at night left the keys with the senior-most trustee so everyone could get out in case of a fire. I had a lot of time to talk to inmates—play cards, have push-up contests, and listen to their stories. I count that experience as one of the high points of my career, up there with my biggest fugitive cases.

I'd guess a third of my books have significant subplots involving incarcerated characters.[6]

During one of our first presentations together, he told the audience, "So you really get to know some of these people as individuals. People always ask me, 'You must meet a lot of evil people.' No. Over the course of 30 years, I could probably count the evil, and you know that's a judgement call, but what you'd call evil people—I could count on both hands and one foot. I've met a lot of people that have done evil things in the spur of the moment—heat of passion or whatever—very evil things, but very few people that are soul eating evil. Our prisons are just not filled with those kinds of people. They are there, make no mistake, but by and large we are just talking about people who have made bad, sometimes extremely bad decisions."[7]

The more sources I contact—friends and law enforcement professionals—the more I hear the same things about people who have committed evil acts in the heat of the moment or when they were out of their mind. Maybe people who do these bad things on the spur of the moment aren't truly bad people. All of us have had rage that seems to be pent up from all kinds of places—like Cameron says, "heat of passion or whatever." I can wrap my head around that—I seem to understand it. But I don't condone it. I also think there's a difference between acting out—in the spur of the moment, in a rage—and planning a crime and then executing it. That premeditation, planning, calculating, and following through on those actions is a much more extreme form of evil, if you ask me.

Random Act of Evil?

"He claimed that it was kind of a one-time deal," said Josh Klimek, as we walked the compound to class. "He was in med school, about twenty-five years old. And when I was talking to him, he was probably in his sixties. He'd been in prison literally his entire adult life. And he was still like, 'I have no idea why I did it. I have no idea.' I mean. You know. How does that happen? Comedian Jeff Foxworthy did a comedy skit once that went something like, 'Every criminal blames their parents. I just want to hear one criminal just once say, my momma was great! My daddy was great! I'm just a shit head.'

"This guy was the first inmate I spoke with that basically said this same line. He said that he grew up in a good household, his parents were good parents and provided for him and his siblings. They were all successful, good people. He hadn't really ever been in trouble before. He was in med school at the time of his crime. He described his crime being a random act, that he was driving around and saw a woman out jogging and just had this 'urge.' He pulled her into his car and raped her. He claimed to not have any idea why he did it. He expressed remorse but couldn't really describe a motive. He claimed he didn't know who she was.

"At some point in time you're an adult and you have to start taking responsibilities for your actions. Your life is not a smooth trajectory and you wouldn't want it to be because you wouldn't appreciate those good times if you didn't have challenges. So you need that yin and yang, you need the good and the bad, you need that dichotomy to kind of make it all work. I mean that wasn't the case for this guy.

"Perhaps this individual isn't necessarily pure evil, but I think there is definitely pure evil in the world where it's like, what would cause something like that to happen? What would cause someone who seemed to be doing well to all of a sudden snap? I mean this guy didn't have a motive. He had an urge."

When Josh described all of this, the act seemed evil. Yet it doesn't seem premeditated at all. An urge. What? And that demonstrates the impossibility of defining this monster of a word—"evil."

Josh continued, "One thing that I think is important when working with inmates is that while we may know what they did, we need to be aware of what they are capable of. There is also a need to kind of separate the individual from their act when discussing concepts like evil. I truly believe that generally good people can be capable of truly evil acts and truly evil people can be capable of generally good acts, depending on the situation. When I look at all the inmates I have worked with over the years, at all different custody levels and all stages of their incarceration, I have seen many individual inmates who have committed some truly evil acts. When you look at some of the worst acts that may have led to their first and only conviction, in general they lived what would be perceived as a law-abiding, productive life aside from committing one terrible act. Then you have some inmates who were in constant trouble—breaking laws all the time and in and out of prison constantly. Which individual is more 'evil'? Oftentimes people that are on the really high end of the intelligence scale are really borderline psychopaths, or at least sociopathic. There's that scale that we all have to some extent. A lot of times the highest intelligence is further towards that end."[8]

Although Josh Klimek is an expert in criminals and their behavior, statistical studies don't bear out the idea that sociopathy or psychopathy is necessarily related to intelligence. And here's where gonzo and immersion come into play for me. This is why I sometimes disagree with data. You can conduct all the studies you want, but I'm betting on the expert who has worked in the field for fifteen years. That kind of immersion—that kind of gonzo—trumps data, which can be subjective for a variety of reasons. Author and scholar Thomas Gannon states, "All data is 'subjective' because it is derived—and used—by an interested (and ergo biased) human."[9]

Did the data study over a thousand people a day in a prison? Either way, when intellectual people commit crimes, common sense says they may be and often are more calculated crimes committed by more wicked individuals. As a writer and an academic, I've always believed in experts with street cred, those who have rolled up their sleeves and worked in the field they speak and write about.

"Lay people tend to have a number of misconceptions about psychological disorders, and this seems to apply to their understanding of psychopathy as well," writes Scott McGrealin in *Psychology Today*. "Certainly, people of high intelligence have the potential to abuse their gifts for nefarious purposes: Evil geniuses do exist. Perhaps then it might be fair to say that highly intelligent people are not more likely than others to turn evil, but when they do, their potential for doing harm might be amplified due to greater mental ability."[10]

"You have no idea what would've possessed someone to do that. I mean it just seems bizarre to me, and it's essentially an unusual case," Klimek continued. "When you look at all the cases I've worked with while working with inmates, I can probably count on one hand the cases that are truly random. I mean, most of the time they were known to the victim. There's some connection, some tie. It was family, it was friends, you know.

"There was a friend who broke into his friend's parent's home. Okay, and so he's been to the house with a friend to a party or something, and then broke into that house later on. So there was a connection there in terms of, he'd been in the house. He knew the family, he knew where stuff was. Most of the time when those things happen, there's almost always somebody that has some prior connection. It's not just random.

"People are terrible assessors of risk. We frequently take undue precautions over very minor risks but don't take enough precaution against very high risk things. People in general are most afraid of the random act of violence, and while they do happen, most criminal activity is not that. Most crime is not violent. In most crime, whether violent or not, the perpetrator knows their victim."

Sunshine, Handcuffs, Plexiglas, Scars

I'm walking the prison yard when the student I'm walking with begins to tell me a story I'll never forget. "You know, one of the prisons they had me at, I could step into a corner of my cell and get a sliver of sunlight—it would hit me right here." He cranes his neck, closes his eyes, and traces a line down the side of his cheek and over a hard vein in his neck. "Right here for about a half an hour. That was the only sunlight I'd see. It's mental deprivation. It works.

"Hell, most guards don't know what you're in for. They don't care. We were loaded on a 747 one winter and we were standing on the tarmac without any jackets—bunch of us. Just a T-shirt and orange pants, no socks, no shoes. They had our legs chained at the ankles so tight I was bleeding all over my feet—freezing. Scars are still here." He stops, puts his leg on a bench and pulls down his sock to show me.

"See these flowers," he says. "They're closed at night, and in the morning they open. Stay like that most of the day. I don't know what they're called. I had the same ones by my front steps. The stems feel plastic, almost fake. They break easily. We aren't supposed to touch them here.

"You know, I'm no killer or sicko. I'm not an evil man. My whole stint that got me here lasted only five months. Meth will eat you up. Fifteen years I'll be down for an addiction I couldn't shake. Could have never imagined. When my daughter used to come visit me, I'd be behind those glass partitions. She'd tell me, 'Daddy, roll down this window.' I'd say, 'I can't, honey.' She'd ask, 'When you gonna come home?' 'Soon,' I'd tell her. Now she wants to know the date. She'll be graduated by then."

||||

For fourteen years I've walked this blacktop, a quarter-mile track, with my students at this prison camp. They are an eclectic mix of criminals, men with PhDs and GEDs. I ask them to write down five things they've never noticed outside while walking the track. Sometimes a student will say, "It's just the same old, same old. It's prison. Nothing's changing in here."

Today, in front of one of the housing units, the one with no AC, I see a miniature banana tree. It isn't blooming, but all the same, it's a bit out of place here in the Midwest. "Enjoy it while you can," one guy in the horticulture program says. "This is its last year."

When *Forbes* rated this prison camp as one of America's ten cushiest prisons, writer Asher Hawkins noted, "The winters are tough, and the nearest city of any size is at least an hour away, but this is a standalone minimum-security facility with a staff that's not too tough on prisoners. White-collar cons can take classes in accounting, business administration and business management."[11] I wonder how much time Asher Hawkins has spent at the prison camp.

I've visited Washington DC a few times. More than two million visitors pass through the Smithsonian Castle on the National Mall, where they have their exhibition gardens, each year. Maybe you have been there. This prison camp with its gothic style structure reminds me a lot of the gardens there; it's that nice. The lawn is perfectly mowed and trimmed, lined with petunias and perennials in an array of designs and a kaleidoscope of colors. On a busy day there might be twenty-five pruners and ten other men keeping the twenty-four acres mowed. Private wells owned by the Federal Bureau of Prisons supply the water that keeps the grass lush and greener than the surrounding neighborhood lawns.

As of November 6, 2024, the prison population was 464, with a maximum capacity of 850.[12] I've been here when it exceeded capacity. New laws, low-risk early releases due to COVID-19, and a reduction of mandatory minimums have cleared room.

I think of the smooth black track. One of my former students added up the miles he had walked over the past few years. "Enough to cross the country—twice." Barbed wire or not, how men spend their time in prison is a concern. Chances are really, really good you know someone who has been to jail or prison.

One of my students and I are walking quietly. I want to ask him something, but I hesitate. In the past I've kicked myself for not speaking up when I had a question, so I ask, "How many men do you think walk this path and contemplate really changing their lives for the better?" And I continue, "I walk around here and listen, and I can almost guarantee that some of these men will be back, just by the way they are talking to each other."

"It's where I come to clear my head," the student responds, "to get some peace. I know what you mean."

We published a piece in our prison literary journal by a father and son who were incarcerated together. The father was a nonviolent offender, and he was very upset with the way the criminal justice system had treated him. I agreed with him. There are probably other alternatives. However, men who are guilty and who are incarcerated need to own their mistakes. The copy editor of the journal *4 P.M. Count* and I were talking about the piece before we published it, and she said, "He might be 'defending himself' against the hurt and loss that family members might (rightly?) be upset with him for. . . . I'm sure all the difficulties he mentions are real—but who caused them?"

The copy editor is a nun, a person who has devoted her life to truly helping others. She's an excellent editor and writer. She taught scripture for decades and published the book *Beginning Biblical Studies* and some commentary for laypeople. As we collaborated on the piece via email, she continued: "It distresses me that Sessions says he wants to return to the longest sentence possible. If no one asks, 'What was leading this person to taking/making/selling drugs?' (or other criminal activity), there will be no viable alternatives to that 'throw 'em in jail and throw away the key' approach. Some rehab programs do work—but always the *catch* is that the offender needs to choose it and work at it. 'It's somebody else's fault' surely stands in the way of such a choice."[13]

So it's kind of an old-school means of discipline. If you broke the law when I was growing up as a juvenile, you got in trouble—community service or worse. We used to joke in Omaha, "Man, you're going to get yourself a one-way-ticket to Boy's Town." When I was doing ride-alongs in South Dakota, some juveniles who were caught defacing property or vandalizing were given a slap on the hand and were back out on the street within an hour of being questioned or ticketed. They weren't held at a jail for any length of time, if they had to go to jail at all.

A lot of juvenile detention centers have been shut down. Offenders usually aren't going to choose to help themselves until they have to, the same way a student won't stop cheating if they aren't held accountable. "Can I do the paper over?" is an expression that teachers hear frequently. And the answer should be, "Sure, but now you only have the chance to get 50 percent instead of 100 percent." Or the answer could be, "No. You cheated. You get a zero." If people aren't held accountable for cheating or breaking laws, they won't quit cheating or breaking laws.

Being Evil vs. Doing Evil

During one of my coeditor Sister Marielle Frigge's presentations at the prison, we discussed "being evil" and "doing evil" in class. Later, when I emailed her about that discussion, this is what she wrote in response:

> I think the discussion started with a student raising the question, noting that since he "got religion," some of his relatives were shunning or at least looking down on him somewhat. In the course of that, he suddenly asked, "Do you think there are people who are evil?" I said that I do believe that evil exists—not as a character with horns and a pitchfork, but as a power that can and sometimes does influence people.
>
> I mentioned the book, *People of the Lie* (subtitle: *Hope for Healing Human Evil*), by M. Scott Peck. Peck writes that his counseling experience convinced him beyond doubt that evil exists, and that he had witnessed it in action in several exorcisms. Then I referred to a clinical psychologist (she recommended the book to me—it was quite a few years ago), and she was the one who gave the example of people she had encountered in her practice who came to her "for help," yet seemed completely determined to act against any advice or guidance she would give. One of them had given a son a shotgun for a Christmas present, knowing the boy was suicidal. . . .
>
> . . . In light of Scripture and Catholic theology—no human being is "born evil," but is created in the image of God. The choices a person makes have a lot to do with whether one does "evil deeds," but of course, every human being's choices are limited to some degree by many, many factors—and that's where it gets messy. . . . Many people also don't make a distinction between BEING evil and DOING evil.[14]

The man who "got religion" and who started the discussion in class had been charged with multiple counts of identity theft, which landed him in prison. In fact, he was interviewed on the news. He said stealing people's identity was easy. He has since been transferred to a higher-level facility for breaking the rules at the federal prison camp—he was caught with a large number of cell phones. At least that's what the other guys in the class told me. I considered him one of my best students, thought that he was on the straight and narrow, that he was a changed man. I thought he had made the turn. He asked the right questions. He motivated others in class to be better men. He had a lot of us fooled.

When I think of him today, I am truly disappointed. So are his former classmates. He is a talented man. He had writing chops. But he was still conning inside—and getting religion was part of his con. Was he conning himself or trying to con others? Was he, like Mary Wollstonecraft stated, mistaking evil for his own happiness and the good that he was trying to seek? If so, that sure seems to me to be a "sincere" form of ignorance and manipulation.

This is the problem with dishonesty—no one can keep up the lies. Ever. What's he going to do when he is released if he never confronts his evildoing? Most times when I think of him I feel fooled for putting my faith in him. I feel a little naïve. And I'm pissed off because he lied to me. I don't have empathy for people who lie to my face. He knows the difference between doing evil and being evil. You want to believe as a school teacher that you can help everyone. But I've realized there are a few students I will never be able to connect with. I thought I had gotten to know him, but he proved to still be a stranger.

Basement Support Beam

If people are not born evil, then where does evil come from? There's a wide variety of literature on the topic of adverse childhood experiences. Evil seems to be passed down as a generational dysfunctionality. It surprises me—amazes me—when a student in the second row with thick bifocal glasses shares his story about being tied to a wooden support beam in the basement of his childhood home. "The beam in that musty room runs from the ceiling to floor."

He speaks very matter-of-factly. He is assertive and articulate. He provides enough detail to paint a picture for his readers. His reflection in response to an impromptu writing prompt seems to come so naturally, and this particular passage frightens us. It is evident that he experienced some serious trauma and abuse. Why, as a child, he was tied to a basement wooden support beam is not immediately clear. We can assume many things. I can't think of any rational reason that tying someone to anything is permissible.

He looks up at me as he is reading. His eyes appear bigger, magnified through his glasses. I keep staring straight at him, hoping that my undivided attention will give him some kind of assurance that someone is paying close attention to him. When he finishes, the students and I applaud his honesty and courage.

Months later, as I edit and prepare this student's piece for publication in a prison journal called *Off the Cuff*, one of the correctional administrators I report to tells me they are cutting the piece due to its graphic nature. I could have argued how wrong this was, but that would have jeopardized the whole project. This happens more than I would like to admit. It's a slap in the face to me as a teacher. Those in charge don't know the countless hours it takes to come to terms with emotional and physical wreckage. It's also a slap in the face to the man who wrote the piece. The prison had a public relations concern that overpowered an artistic one—reducing prison writing to a commodity. I doubt that the people making these decisions have the courage to look themselves in the eyes and come to terms with their failings the way my students do, let alone put pen to paper for the world to read. Considering the publisher, I understand they want "family-friendly" material. I'm sure this student, who had the courage to tell his story, wished for family-friendly once upon a time, too.

I can still see this student so clearly—his square glasses magnifying his eyes. He was looking to me for guidance—the others in class could see it—and I felt it in my goddam bones. He had survived adverse childhood experiences, which in turn may have made him do the things that landed him in prison. But here he was writing his wrongs—purging that evildoing. He had the courage to write about his abuse, its source—to try to reckon with his past and move forward. He wasn't hiding anything from anyone. There were mental health issues that seemed pretty clear to me; he was anxious and scared. But he was strong, and he had the audacity to lay it all out there on the page.

I'm no psychiatrist or judge, but to have that kind of bravery—to realize your past and own it—should be part of the rehabilitation we strive for. By refusing to publish his piece, the authorities stripped him of his right to use his voice; it seemed like they wanted to make him live in his past.

Slitting Throat

"I watched a man slit his own throat," said the correctional officer. "On both sides." He told me the number of the cell the guy was in and said he was taking the inmate to the segregated housing unit—per protocol—the day before he was to be transferred to another prison. The CO had a steady pace as we walked through the yard—walking and watching straight ahead through his mirrored sunglasses. "Instead of being sent to the other prison, he tried to kill himself. That shook me up pretty good. I spent two weeks sitting out in the parking lot before I came into work, drinking a fifth of vodka every morning. I grew up on the rez. I've been stabbed. Beaten. All kinds of things. Watching a guy look me in the eyes and slit his throat did something to me."

A Student Speaks of Her Sister's Murder

At the university a student is writing about her sister who was murdered. After she has written a brief introduction about the last time her sister and her family were all home together for the holidays, she doesn't know how to continue. The details of the introduction—the interior of the house, the piano music and cheer, the warm, welcome feeling of family—sing on the page. She is worried about the chronological order of things. She is also concerned that these details won't mean anything to the reader. When she finishes presenting her rough draft, she continues to tell us the story. She describes the random act of murder as it was told to her by authorities. She describes news accounts. Eventually, with my encouragement, she writes about it some more. The resulting in-class dialogue helps her to some extent, but I don't think anyone fully heals from a tragedy like this.

The student says she never found out if the killer was mentally ill, or why he did what he did. "Authorities gave him tests and concluded that he was . . ."—she can't think of the right words to say—"that something was wrong with the man. That they didn't know if he was on drugs at the time. He claimed he thought he was a hundred miles away in Oakland

and that he was stranded, and when he saw lights, he walked toward them, toward the restaurant and bar that my sister and friend had just left for the evening. When he demanded their keys, they wouldn't give them to him. He chased them back to the restaurant and bar, back to the front door they were running to, but the door was locked. That's when he killed her. Later, the police found him five miles away with her car. It was a done deal. The cops had him, the stolen vehicle, and the murder weapon."

She talks about the trial. Before they went into the courtroom, she says, they had a quick briefing with their lawyer. "I asked him if we could expect to see some of the murderer's family. The lawyer said no one had come to visit him the entire time he had been locked up."

She gives us a play-by-play of the court proceedings, with tears running down her face. She says the man who killed her sister sat silent as stone. Eventually her sister's friend who was with her that night read her victim's statement.

"I didn't take my eyes off the guy in court," she says. "I sat in the middle of my parents with both my arms around them. He just sat there staring blankly ahead. Cold. Lifeless. He wouldn't look at me. My sister's friend read her speech. She painted a picture of my sister—of her life—of how adventuresome and how funny she was. Her statement captured my sister's sense of humor. And for a few seconds I saw the man that murdered my sister almost grin at the funny, loving, and kind person that was being described. And then he must have remembered that he was the one on trial, the one that killed her. And his face again went blank."[15]

Does Everyone Deserve a Second Chance?

I think everybody, even cold-blooded killers, have emotions. Anger is surely one of them, jealousy another, and control seems to be a major theme in some horrendous crimes. So when I think of X, I realize how premeditated Christina's rape and murder was, how it went on for hours, how he was on the run for weeks. His accomplice turned himself in the next day. X ran.

I don't believe all people who premeditate and execute heinous crimes should be released from prison. Would it be easier for me to forgive or give a killer a second chance if I didn't know them? Of course. But again, it's not my choice. I don't want that burden.

Dr. Bill Miller, a criminologist and vice president and provost of Mount Marty University in Yankton, South Dakota, and I have talked on a few occasions about Christina's murder. He has studied and written about crime and its repercussions for more than two decades. In one of our conversations, he stated, "I had one experience, I think, that sheds light on you and why I think this is important. I never hid the fact that I was against the death penalty when I was teaching. For most people, that shut the conversation down. People who were with me weren't going to argue against me, and people who were against me were afraid to argue with me. But this one kid says to me, 'Let's just say, for the sake of argument, that someone kidnaps your wife and daughters, rapes them all, ties them up, slits their throats, and hangs them upside down so they bleed to death. What are you going to want to do?' I said, 'I'm going to want to find whoever did it and want to kill them.' He said, 'So you are for the death penalty.' I said, 'No.' You put your finger on exactly the issue here. This is why victims of crime are so passionate—whether they are primary victims or have been victimized [indirectly] by an event (which most people have been). This is why they [victims] don't make social policy. And this is why they shouldn't. Right. You want dispassionate people to make social policy. You don't want people who have either been victims or have been victimized by events that are associated, like yours. Of course, you feel that way about that guy—your friend's killer. And, of course, you can feel that way about that guy and not feel that way when you are in prisons. Because when you are in the prison, that is a set of organized criminals that haven't victimized you either directly or indirectly. This other person has victimized you indirectly, and therefore he triggers a very passionate personal response. Those are not people who should be making criminal justice policy."[16]

||||

We know imprisonment confines people for their worst actions—even if they are better people than their actions imply. These are the consequences of crime. If you commit crime and avoid prison, you get to go on—sit back and redefine yourself, maybe? Shouldn't people who commit premeditated and evil crimes have thought about their actions and weighed the consequences of such deeds before implementing them? Author Kent Meyers wrote the following to me in an email:

> What we have to do when considering crime and criminals is accept ambivalence. Perhaps that's the difficulty and paradox of the human condition—that the harder we look at other humans and their behaviors, the less certain we become about our judgements. Perhaps also, that's one of the ways that crime makes us victims and causes us trauma. And perhaps one of the reasons people get "tough on crime" is because they don't want to be feeling the uncertainty that you feel; they want to be able to say "that's evil" and quit thinking about it. You—and Bowden, too—seem to be saying something closer to "that's human," which is a way more disconcerting statement.[17]

Christina's story scares me still. But there's a reason I have chosen to write about it and not suppress it: to not forget her. We have to try to articulate our feelings. It helps deal with trauma. When Bowden said that if your writing doesn't scare you, doesn't put you in some sort of danger, it's not worth doing, he was right. At the heart of all of this are voices helping us to discover.

I'm unresolved. The more I try to reason, to define, to try to understand evil or its implied certainty, the more it slips away, shows another side of its ugly self, and my emotions don't align. However, I think there's a lot to be said about conscious crimes—identity theft, sex trafficking, the serial killer stalking neighborhoods, child molestation, premeditated murder. There are, no doubt, people who are and will continue to be harmful to society and who should be separated from the public.

Maybe I'll never know for certain if Christina's murderers were evil. The act in and of itself sure seems evil to me, however you choose to define it. And that brings us back to law and order, right and wrong, and the fact that we are not the judge or jury, no matter how much we want to be.

6

The Deputy and Imminent Danger

And it was the noblest act of courage that I have ever seen.

—TAYLOR MALI

Soon after the Thanksgiving pies have been violated and the Cool Whip containers scraped clean, some of the men and women who have prepped and cooked nod off in the living room and begin to snore.

"So do you wake up with your hair like that or does it take time?" a cousin asks. "You have a lot of product in there." There's something to be said about never outgrowing juvenile bullying, and you both embrace it.

A two-year tradition, one you hope continues, is that your family goes around the room and tells everyone what they are thankful for. Your free-spirited aunt says, "I have everything I need right here." On the drive over, you try to articulate your answer. We are so busy with our own small traumas—fears and anxieties. We are programmed to search for the next brighter and shinier thing, to forget what truly matters. When it's your turn, you emphasize the importance of empathy for others and kindness to ourselves. You stole the last part from Neal Brennan's new special, *Blocks*, on Netflix. At the end of it, he says something that sticks. Referring to himself, he says:

> Dude, how did you turn self-help into self-harm? I've been saying all night that something's wrong with me. And something is wrong with me. I won't show myself any kindness. I won't give myself any grace. Like I just grind and attack myself relentlessly like it's my job. I would love to stop. I like to believe that my ways of being, like my thoughts, my habits, my emotions, my beliefs . . . I'd like to believe

they're not defects. I'd like to believe that alchemy of a personality . . . my spirit . . . it's got to be enough. Please. Let that be enough.[1]

Your father added Kalamata olives to baby carrots and glazed them in butter, sugar, water, and chives. A simple dish that will stick with you a good long while. Your sister-in-law made her famous green bean casserole with cream and shredded cheese. Another cousin brought deviled eggs and you put the hurt on half a dozen. The turkey isn't dry—"It hasn't made anyone sick yet," your father says, smiling. There is gravy and homemade stuffing—stuffed mushrooms like your grandmother used to make. It is the bomb. For so many years you indulged in the holiday spirits—drinking and toasts—and paid little attention to the food. Now that's not the case. There is a lot to be thankful for. A crew has traveled thousands of miles collectively to be together.

On the way home, where 880 merges with I-29, you verge north toward Sioux City and on to South Dakota. It's dark. Strangely warm for November. De Soto National Wildlife Refuge just to the west, Missouri Valley to the east. Also to your east are the preserved Loess Hills—one of North America's environmental treasures. It's so dark that you have to remind yourself where the river is—how close you are to your home state. You have been traveling these borders all your life. I-80, 880, and I-29 are as common as Kraft mac and cheese.

It's 9:25 p.m. True North. Black. Glare of headlights. Your wife studying for another physician assistant exam behind you in the backseat. Your oldest daughter next to you with her music turned up too loud. Everyone on their earbuds and handheld devices.

You are listening to Dave Chappelle induct Richard Pryor into "The Hall," another Netflix special. The last thing you remember is Pryor's voice, "You ever hear of anyone blowing up? Why me? Ten million motherfuckers freebase, I got to blow up."

While you are laughing, you look into the rearview mirror, see flashing lights. You check the speedometer. You are cruising at seventy-seven—seven over the limit—in the interstate's left lane. The siren mingles with your laughter at Pryor's joke, and the two together create an odd ringing between your ears that seems to cancel the volume and scream of what's happening inside and outside the car. The lights throb against the dashboard and shoot off the hood. The cop flies by you in the right lane. *Jesus,* you think. Or say. Your heart pulsates. As it passes on your right, this cop cuts in front of you and suddenly brakes. You swerve, verge right. You begin to slow down. *Always pull over when you see first responders, like you have been taught. This is happening so fast. What is happening? Why are they hitting their brakes?* You see the red. You see a cache of colors and high beams in front of the cop. The interstate in front of you is lit up in a dark embrace.

Now you watch the cop play chicken with an oncoming truck that is on the wrong side of the interstate—in what was just your lane, this truck is dead set, heading straight into your entire family. As the cop is skidding to a halt on the interstate's left shoulder, you are approaching the right shoulder, slowing now to maybe forty miles per hour. You look over to your left and see the cop abruptly stop—dead set in front of a pickup—intercepting five thousand pounds of steel, ready to pulverize, head on. The front of the pickup is lit up, its headlights punctured by an arsenal of reds and blues. You see a white face leaning over the steering wheel. You see eyes squinting into the light. The person who just saved your life is an anonymous dark shape behind the wheel of a police cruiser. This happens in seconds.

Part of you wants to pull over and storm the man in the pickup . . . but that part doesn't come for a half-hour. That anger isn't present at first. What you are certain about is that lives have just been spared by this stranger, this cop who just risked their life to save yours.

Through your earbuds, you hear your wife yell, "Don't stop! Cars behind us!" This scares you. Pisses you off. Why isn't the traffic behind you stopped? Or slowing way down? Are they chasing this cop? Fascinated with lights? The macabre? Gruesome reality? *Must see. Must see.*

"What?" You scream. Pull out an earbud.

"Didn't you feel me tapping your shoulder?" Your wife screams again.

In a kind of clear bubble of thought, you wonder why you had your earbuds in. You know about situational awareness.

The entire interstate is a swamp of terror. In your mirrors, you see a car and a truck loom behind you. You know they watched this all unfold. The semi's too-bright headlights and red and orange running lights are framed in your rearview mirror. *Objects in mirror are closer than they appear*. The semi's getting closer. You speed up to sixty-two. You can't get past sixty-two. The dark is bearing down on you and your family—your wife and your daughters. You strangle the steering wheel with both hands. The trucker passes in the left lane. Driving has become a threat. You see another cop heading south—you assume, to assist.

You won't call 911 for another hour. You and your wife try to articulate what has happened. "What mile marker are we at? We just came out of Missouri Valley."

"Why do we have to talk about this? We almost just got killed! You are so annoying," your oldest daughter says.

"Because obviously we are pretty shook up," your wife says to your daughter, who turns up her earbuds.

Your younger daughter is asking, "Why was he driving down the wrong side of the road? Why was that person driving at us?"

"Most likely because they are drunk," you say. "Or lost. Or suicidal. Oh, my god," you say to the windshield. "Do you know how long that guy had to have been driving down the interstate for someone to call it in? Notify authorities? Dispatchers then to relay the message? Then this person respond? To save lives?"

Part of you wonders why you didn't immediately pull over and charge at this person who would have crashed into you head on. If this were in the city, you most certainly would have had some serious road rage.

In the moment, you had none of the feelings of rage you have had innumerable times in traffic. You had feelings of extreme anxiety, relief, and grace—is that the right word? Deep appreciation. Perhaps that's the feeling you are trying to articulate. Your family shouldn't even have been on the road. You should have been at the hotel fighting over who goes in the bathroom next—raising your voices, telling each other to get ready for bed and stop banging around. But you decided to drive home instead.

Hindsight.

Some people you know have been affected traumatically by oncoming traffic. Death ensued. They lost loved ones. You remember and relive the stories you've heard about those tragic accidents. A drunk driver and a head-on collision on a divided highway just east of Yankton. On that same stretch of road a former sergeant you know was in pursuit of two men in a car who flew through the city at over a hundred miles per hour, shut off their headlights, and drove straight into a family coming the other direction. Everyone died in the vehicles except one little girl. A peace officer held her and talked to her until the ambulance and paramedics arrived.

This act of bravery reinforces what you have seen time and again. You have to get this report right. What you want to do is paint a clear picture.

| | | |

You try to give students in your Crime, Literature, and Film class a play-by-play of the near-disaster on Thanksgiving night. When you say, "Never before have I experienced or seen an act of bravery like this," you feel your jaw begin to tremble. You turn your back to them and take some deep breaths. If you turn around and look at them, you know you will lose it. You're positive the near-fatal, head-on collision feels more monumental to your family than to any reader or observer. The reality is that you didn't die. No one was severely injured. The reality is that readers want gore and guts on the ground.

As you begin to blink back tears, you look at the smartboard you are facing. There's a picture of an ex-con cued up and ready to play—it's "A Drug Dealer Describes What It's Actually Like Being Arrested." Jesus, it's all entertainment, isn't it? The gore, the guts, the tell-alls. The fear and fascination. You are a part of it. Even right now.

You're certain that you and your family would have been seriously injured or your lives taken if it wasn't for the cop who made the split-second decision to keep you and the other motorists safe. This person, who took an oath to serve and protect, did exactly that. And you kept driving. You had to keep driving.

||||

You are still waiting to thank the cop who put your life and others' lives above their own on that stretch of interstate. You have not been able to get through to this cop. You and the director of criminal justice at the university have reached out to numerous locations. You have discovered which district would have been called to respond to that area of the interstate. The last correspondence you got was: "Lt. Borelli from Iowa State Patrol will research what trooper it was. He's aware that there was a collision in that area because he reviewed the report. He will call tomorrow or Friday once he has all the info."

No one is returning your calls. You do not know what collision has happened. You keep googling Thanksgiving night, I-29, Missouri Valley, collision. All you want to do is say thank you.

||||

On December 17, 2022, Lieutenant Borelli of the Iowa State Patrol identified the cop who saved our lives. He was Harrison County Sheriff's Department Deputy Justin McMurray. Also arriving on the scene were Harrison County Sheriff's Department Deputy Todd Denton and Deputy James Reynolds, Missouri Valley Police Department Officer Jacob Musfeldt, and members of the Iowa State Troopers.

On December 26, 2022, Deputy Justin McMurray wrote:

> Thank you for doing all you could to try to figure out who the officer was that night, as it sounds like you did a lot of leg work to find me! I have been in law enforcement since 2015 and have seen quite a bit of action even though our department is within a relatively small county. I would like to say that what I did was a huge act of bravery, but in reality I believe I did what any of my fellow brothers and sisters would do in the same circumstances to protect the public.
>
> I can't go into very much detail about the case, as I am set to go to court on the matter. However, I can tell you it was a mid 30's female who was very intoxicated that had left the bar and got lost trying to find where she lived. This female was unaware that she was even going the wrong way down the interstate. In the moment, I didn't even think

> about any injury that the driver could do to me in a head on collision. All I knew is that I needed to stop the threat before anyone was injured as there was so much traffic due to Thanksgiving. Thankfully, she stopped just short of the front of my squad car. It is very nice to hear the impacts we make on people's lives when most of us in law enforcement act on instincts when presented with imminent danger.[2]

I am certain Deputy Justin McMurray saved my family's lives and my own.

7

What They Do Not Tell You about Prison, Part 2

What-Ifs

Checking my rearview mirror for "what-ifs," I let the world and problems that haven't happened yet swallow me. I'm passing people in cars and trucks who are looking down—not ahead at the road—and I'm convinced that we are all distracted somehow. Good teachers tell me to enjoy the present, what's right in front of me. *Look forward*, I can hear them say. *Never look back*.

At the prison, I get buzzed in at control, and the heavy green military-grade gates slide open. I walk the yard with a correctional officer and pass through other giant barricades as hundreds of men in khakis, grey sweatshirts, and white T-shirts scatter on their way to jobs on the compound or to GED classes, to my Writing for Reentry class, to the pill line, to prayer groups, or to their bunks. I nod and say hello to as many men as I can. I hope my face says, *Smile*. I say, "Onward." I say, "We are living." I think, *Breathe*. I hear that little voice say, *You already have the answer*.

I'm in a real prison, with razor wire on fences already too tall to climb. No time to stop—no time to look back. One of the only places each week where I live in the present, always alert to my surroundings. I am alive and believe in these men. "Instead of what-ifs," a student in class says, "I'm assuming even-ifs. Then I can keep moving forward."

Flashback to Leaving the Q and the Limo in Jersey

A few months after I visited San Quentin, I was invited to read at the distinguished Poetry Center in Patterson, New Jersey, and to visit Eastside High to talk with students about writing and editing. You might remember the movie *Lean on Me* (released in 1989) if you came of age in the '80s like me. Joe Louis Clark was a principal of this inner-city school. Morgan Freeman portrayed Clark in the movie. Clark was known to carry a bullhorn or a baseball bat at school to intimidate students, and during his time as principal, he expelled hundreds of students for excessive absences and lateness. Clark's controversial practices may have contributed to slightly higher average test scores for Eastside High during the 1980s, but he was also roundly criticized for them. After his tenure as principal of Eastside High, Clark later served as director of the Essex County Detention House in Newark, New Jersey, a juvenile detention facility.

||||

In the limo ride to my hotel, I started talking to the driver. He was a retired New Jersey police officer. I told him about my recent visit to San Quentin and the work I was doing in prisons.

"There will be more cops at Eastside than you saw in San Quentin," he affirmed. I laughed at his comment, didn't really believe it. I remember looking at the crystal wine decanters on the tiny wet bar in the limo. They were empty. I really wanted a drink.

When I arrived at the school the next day, after I passed through the metal detectors, I noticed that the inner corridor of the school was surrounded by cops. I was escorted by an officer to a normal-looking classroom where students were busy talking. There was little to no control. I had brought copies of the university literary journal that I edit to hand out to students. The teacher and her students were looking at photos on a cell phone. I was not introduced, and I spent the beginning of class wondering what I had just walked into. I had never been in a classroom with such a deliberate disregard for education. After about ten minutes I decided to pass the books out to students who wanted them. And for a while I managed to talk to some of the students while the teacher (thank God I forgot her name) continued to look at her phone.

For the next period I went to another class, where I told the teacher (who had been assigned to escort me) that I would appreciate an introduction and that she and the students should stay seated, whether she chose to participate in class or not.

During another period, two classes were joined together to listen to me read some of my writing. The students seemed interested in what I had to say. At one point we all heard some commotion and a lot of screaming in the hallway. It sounded like people fighting. One of the teachers (a different one) jumped up from his seat and ran to the door to look out into the hallway. "Damn! Missed it," he said.

I did meet some nice teachers at Eastside High, and the fact that they were working with the Poetry Center in Patterson to bring writers to their school says a lot. Unfortunately, I wasn't able to work with many of the teachers who had control of their classroom. I'd like to go back now that I know what to expect.

A Ladder and Spaghetti Sauce

At San Quentin prison I had access to almost every part of the facility: the 4½ × 11 × 7 foot cells (the size of your typical walk-in closet); the kitchen where a man stood on a ladder stirring a cauldron full of spaghetti sauce with an oar; medieval rooms; a 164-year-old cavern in the exercise yard; even condemned row, where a longtime CO said, "The men sentenced to die aren't animals. They've made some horrible decisions. Some premeditated."

At a cocktail party one evening, I met a man who taught yoga to men on death row. "They are human beings," he said. It was odd to hear this. The feeling I had was different from the fear and anguish I still feel over my friend who was raped and killed, the tight knot in my heart that every parent has, the horrendous feeling of knowing what I might do if that happened to my child.

Jesus Christ Pose

In a theater practicum in the Arts in Corrections room, I watch you, a prisoner, standing in the center of the room. You raise your hands, palms up, head dangling down—your Jesus Christ *pose. You begin to stand on one foot. The room is quiet. People begin shifting in their seats. Minutes pass.*

You begin to lose your balance. "Every morning," you say, "after my foster father left for work, she made me stand in the corner like this." And when your desperate left foot hits the ground, you scream in the voice of a child being beaten.

Now I understand why some of you are here.

Vegetable Medley

My younger daughter Paige knows I work in a prison. People have told her, "Your daddy works at a prison. That's where they put mean, bad people."

Someday I will tell her what it is I do there. Today, when she asks for more chicken nuggets, I ask her if she has finished her vegetables. "Well, actually no. I am saving them," she says.

"'Actually' is such a big word, Paige. I'm so proud of you. But actually, you'll have to eat some vegetables first or you will have to go to prison."

I get up from the table, lower my head, and put my hands behind my back. I pretend to walk in shackles.

"They cuff you up and you'll have to eat your vegetables without any silverware." I keep pacing around the kitchen and stop to bob for my own vegetables from my plate. I come up for air and am a mess of lima beans and peas. "You'll never be able to use your hands again."

My daughter begins to cry. My older daughter tells me, "Stop—you are scaring her." Not only have I reinforced her fear of prison, I have ruined the vegetable medley.

Being a father isn't easy. Being funny isn't either.

Guard

"If you leave again, I have to report it."

"You are starting to sound like one of the guards," a student tells me in the hall as he leaves class again to use the phone in another unit. I want to defend myself and I wish I had said, "What's upsetting to me is that you are just here to use a computer. You don't even try. You won't allow yourself to actually knock some of your anger away. You are still feeling sorry for yourself. You keep making excuses to leave class to use the telephone—once a week, during my class." But I don't say anything. I get back to work. Once released, he'll be back.

Or shit, maybe I have it all wrong. Maybe he's all set up on the outside and this is all some big mistake.

Cow Capital of South Dakota

During a prisoner count, a little after noon in the education building, I was making copies of class handouts. Men were still filing in for duties and being accounted for. One man walked right up to the education director's desk with a shit-eating smile on his face. I just happened to turn away from the copy machine and look at the rest of the guys in line. I always try to keep an eye on things, to stay alert.

"Are you dipping?" The supervisor of education asked. "Is that tobacco in your mouth?"

The man smiled. "Yes." The SOE made him spit the tobacco onto a piece of paper (for proof) and made him stay put. "Now I have to do the paperwork again. You'll be sent away. For what? For chew."

I asked a student in class why men did this. He said, without hesitating, "The other prisons aren't in the middle of Nowhere, South Dakota, Doc. That's why. When I took the van here I passed a sign that said Cow Capital of South Dakota. My family isn't coming to visit me here. No one's coming."

Cat vs. Car

Recently, a student at the prison decided to stand up and interrupt his classmates because he wasn't happy about a typo—a mistake someone had made typing up one of his rough drafts. (I often ask a few Mount Marty students to type up the prisoners' works for them and help them with some initial editing.) He said, "It says *cat* here. It's supposed to say *car*. This changes everything." When I told him to sit down, that it was our mistake, that it was a typo that could be fixed, and that we could talk about it later, it made him furious. I also added, "You know, I've never had anyone type up work of mine—ever."

He glared at me and said, "I'm not even fucking listening to you now." That week he was sent to the segregated housing unit for anger issues.

Where I'm Going, Where I've Been

In the education building of the prison camp, you'll sometimes find a man tracing one of the large maps of the United States with his finger. Sometimes small groups of men huddle around the maps, talking about adventure, reminiscing about childhood birthplaces. One exclaims, "Here's where I'm gonna go once I'm outta here. Find me a job and do it up right. Gonna be a father this time 'round."

I stand at the map during the break. I trace the Missouri River south. Find its confluence, the Mississippi. Follow it down and down. An inmate walks by, says, "Anywhere but here. Anywhere but here." And I can't help myself—I laugh.

Onion Head

After class I have my usual brief conversations with the correctional officer who escorts me off the prison grounds. I am always interested to hear their points of view.

"It's kind of hard when you read a file about a guy who raped and then bound and dragged a woman behind his pickup. Then you read a little more of his file, find out he burned and drowned her after that. Now he's complaining about the food in the cafeteria," the CO says.

"What we know as basic life skills isn't the same for some," he continues. "Not long ago, a man came to prison and he constantly stunk. Finally, we had to ask him if he was showering. He said, 'Yes, every day.' When I pressed him about the issue, he did not know how to clean himself appropriately. He just stood under the water. He didn't know that he was supposed to use soap. We had to explain it to him. Show him how to apply soap to a wash cloth. No one ever taught him. Can you imagine?"

How do you become an adult without anyone showing you how to properly bathe? These things happen.

The conversation reminded me of another man at the state prison who would always ask me questions about writing after class. He was a talented storyteller and writer. However, he must not have brushed his teeth—for a long time. I had to turn away during our first encounter—my eyes started to water. I'm not kidding. By our third conversation, I kept moving so he didn't breathe on me or get too close. I still think about these incidents and wonder if I should have said something. I also often wonder if not brushing his teeth was a defense mechanism.

I have a cousin who used to eat raw onions like apples before his wrestling matches in high school. I saw him do it. Every once in a while, as a treat to himself, he'd sprinkle the onion with a little salt. It was a way for him to eat something while cutting weight and to ward off his opponent. His other tactic? He proudly exclaimed, "I never washed my jock strap!"

Big Money

An inmate who had the word *BIG* tattooed vertically in calligraphy on one side of his face, where sideburns normally grow, and a dollar sign on the other side leaned back in his chair. He always had a shit-eating grin on his face. He was a guy you knew would return to prison. He was the troubled student who didn't listen, who did the bare minimum, who would deflect and lie. As teachers, we always remember the bad students, seldom the good ones. When he was leaning back in his chair pretending to smoke his pen, which he had wrapped with a newspaper and scotch tape and which had the word *MONEY* imprinted on it, I asked, "What are you doing?"

"Just smoking money, PRO-fess-OR."

He'll Be Back

One student is being released soon and he has asked to leave the class for good. He'll go on his merry-go-round. And because some COVID restrictions are still in place, he will have to quarantine for two weeks before he leaves. He's a talented writer. I asked to talk to him once more before he leaves. I'd like him to stay as long as possible. Since COVID hit, so many men have been released. As soon as I make a connection with them in class—as soon as they seem to break through—they are gone.

We get to talking and he brings up the student in the class who got verbally abusive and told me, through the TV monitor, that pretty much everything I was doing was wrong. And this man leaving on his merry-go-round said, "You handled that well with him. He'll be back in prison. I know his type. Trust me, he'll be back. He's got some anger issues. Guys like him, they always come back."

Junk Food

After I enter the jail sally port and walk down the white cinder-block hallway, I come to my classroom, a white cinder-block room with bright poster board motivational collages of cut-outs from magazines. Among them are three with the sayings *Stay calm*, *Love yourself*, and *Be well* on them. Adjacent to the classroom are math GED classes. I'm going to miss this place. Back outside the sally port are the South Dakota Department of Corrections main administrative offices. The cabinet secretaries' office is just down this long hall of locked doors and passages.

The women's commissary is right outside my classroom. Most days the women line the hall; they are not quiet while they wait. They stand in line with see-through fishnet bags for their purchased items. This is a big deal. This is how things happen in prison—food as collateral, a bartering tool. The women get special permission to leave class to purchase items, and they return with what looks like large laundry bags full of chips, donuts, ramen noodles—an enormous amount of junk food. Food feeds the soul in here—and junk food reigns supreme. Women returning to the classroom with their bulging bags are often greeted with imperatives:

"You better start working on losing some of that weight if you are getting out soon, girl."

"Shut up, bitch."

Most prisons I've been in sound like sporting events, so the volume in the line outside the commissary is no surprise. What's astonishing is that when I am conducting class remotely via the computer, all I can hear is chatter, and I have to tell the women to shut the door. The GED instructor in the room with them reassures me that the door is already closed. "That's noise from the commissary line," they tell me. The staff does very little to quiet the noise in the hallway outside the education rooms. But if the women talk out of line in most other places in the facility, they are reprimanded.

Contractor for the Bureau of Prisons

DISCLAIMER: I do not speak on behalf of the Federal Bureau of Prisons (BOP). In fact, I don't even get a 1099 form from them anymore. I am a contractor, which means they treat me like a human being, but compassion and encouragement are pretty much nonexistent these last few years.

I am a writer-in-residence for the National Endowment for the Arts, for an interagency initiative with the Bureau of Prisons. I've had this position for fourteen years. It's a sweet title. And it is a good gig, especially when no one else bids for the job and I get the full amount of the contract. However, the program has shut down on three occasions—most recently when my five-year contract was advertised and granted to a company who bids on BOP jobs, gets them, and then finds subcontractors to do the work for them. When I was underbid, this company called me and asked if I would work for them the next day—doing the same job I had done for eleven years, but for less money. That's how government contracting works. They do not rehire someone who has experience running the program; they take the lowest bidder. I was featured in the BOP's book *Making Changes*—that did not matter. The lowest competent bid mattered. The expert did not.

This particular company had a bad track record. Articles written about them in the *Washington Post* and other credible newspapers stated that they were not fulfilling their contract obligations. The company did not have a storefront, and I was about to go to work for them. I had agreed to do it because I didn't want to lose the opportunity or have a program I'd sunk my heart into be sabotaged by a person who sat behind a computer screen and couldn't care less about recidivism or reentry. The BOP is a gold mine for contractors—this company knows that.

Long story short, my supervisor at the time was a meticulous micromanager. I explained that I had read about the company's seedy past, that it wasn't affiliated with a regional college or university (which was a requirement). The logistics of all of this were a nightmare. At the time, I was not only shortchanged but also scrambling to make money because I had turned down other freelance offers and had become dependent on this program, which the BOP glorified to every visitor who set foot on camp grounds. The BOP finally canceled the contract with the company that didn't meet its criteria. I had to start my own limited liability company, redo all my vendor and SAM (system awards for management) information to get my DUNS (data universal numbering system) number renewed, and then wait for the job to repost online at USA Jobs.

I bid again, for less money, and got it. So then, after all of that, when I was about to start my new contract—a year after COVID (during which I still managed to teach the class via WebEx and pick up and deliver paper copies of student work on the street outside the prison)—the program shut down because of the government's continuing resolutions. The government is always having continuing resolutions because they can't seem to ever be on the same page when it comes to budget issues. In the past, my program had continued during these negotiations. Not this time. All the writing programs under the National Endowment of the Arts umbrella stopped. My program was being rebranded—same program, but with a new name under the First Step Act, a 2018 prison reform bill.

It makes a guy wonder why on earth the BOP would do such a thing. If the government is truly interested in reducing recidivism rates and rehabilitating inmates so they can become law-abiding members of society when they are released, educational programs should never stop or be discontinued. Ninety-five percent of these men and women are coming to a neighborhood near you. Do you want them educated or not?

||||

At the federal prison, the official isn't sure when the writing program will continue—it's on hold because of internal issues—and as he points out the window of his office, he tells me, "As a contractor, you're no different from the guy over there putting shingles on that roof." The comment confirms a belief I've held for a while, which is that as long as the prison checks their boxes, they are happy. The goal of empathy and compassion for inmates and prison educators—of making prisons better—is diminished rather suddenly when comments like this are made. I want to ask the official, "If you don't care about rehabilitation, what are you doing in this line of work? What is it that gets you up in the morning? Power and control over prisoners? Being in authority doesn't make you a leader."

It's a shame to see all the men I've helped, all the good I've done, dissipate so quickly. Life is too short to waste time trying to climb walls that people systematically are building taller. I decide to start using my talents elsewhere—maybe my prison teaching days are coming to an end. I am hitting these walls at both the state and federal prisons where I teach. My friends and associates at prisons throughout the nation speak of the same resistance. How quickly the tides can change when different administrators enter a building. The fact is, education works. It's unfortunate that those who hold the reins know this but are more interested in power than purpose.

||||

Two months later, I learn that the state prisons where I have taught for the past three years won't renew my contract. My South Dakota State Prison writing program was funded by the Workforce Innovation Opportunity Act from the Job Corps, and the details are fuzzy. The new requirements mean that in order to continue teaching my writing class, I would also have to teach a GED class, that my class would have to coincide with the GED program. I am not a GED teacher. "We think it's a great program, but we don't have money in our budget to fund it this year. And if we wanted to consider it for next year, we'd have to weigh the pros and cons. I'm sorry to be the bearer of bad news," the official says.

I've never worked in another environment where there was so much negative energy—so much pride in control by those in positions of power. Most of the staff treat their work as a job. They do not believe in rehabilitation and making the world a better place. If you want to see some unhappy workers, go work in a prison. This is where, it can be argued, the bullies from high school, the ones who never quite grew up, go to further their careers.

I feel like I've wasted almost a decade and a half of my life working for the greater good, only to have it swept out from under me in an instant. I've changed lives for the better. There are families—hundreds of people—who have been helped by our services. It saddens me and frustrates me to see it all disappear. It's been stated before, and perhaps it is true—the system is set up exactly as intended. Corrections is a cash cow. And what is the war we are fighting now? A war on drugs (which is really a disease, according to the American Medical Association)? Is it a war on race? A war on poverty? All of it?

I've taught more than 350 men and women behind bars.

||||

So I'm starting my last classes in the state prisons. I have three months left in these medium-high and high-security facilities. The thing you hear over and over from staff, especially veteran staff who want to make a difference, is that prisons need more programming. It's frustrating, but I want to try to make this the best class ever and make it memorable for the men and women.

I'm driving away from Springfield. The fields are full of water, the snow melt in ditches. The flooding has been terrible here this late winter and early spring due to the storms—the trifecta of ice, snow, and rain. I can see the negative aspects of all this—the program closing, the cloudy day—but this has been a hell of an experience. I've gone inside these prisons and learned a lot about people.

It's always interesting, the writing prompts that work on the first day—how people are so eager to share their stories and be heard. Getting up the courage to speak in front of somebody for the first time takes a lot of nerve. In a prison, it takes courage and strength to speak out. Others in the class can use anything they hear against you once they walk out of the room. I always tell the students, "What goes on in the classroom stays in the classroom until we are ready to publish. If there are any discrepancies, you will be asked to leave class and forfeit your three-month early release."

In his introduction to the *Rain Shadow Review*, a literary journal for inmates of the Arizona state prisons, editor Erec Toso writes, "Inmates tend to be experience-rich and confidence-poor when they begin the workshops. Some of the men will sit quietly for months before bringing their first piece in for response, and if they are up to it, critique. That takes a courage that is not taught in the puffed up bravado of the yard. They have to reach deep, sometimes digging around in the guts of memory to bring something forth that a developing human will find worth giving his attention to."[1] For three years I had very few problems in the classroom, and when I did, they were quickly remedied. I suppose it helped that I took on the hardest criminals first, which set the stage for classes to come. Apparently, my reputation as a teacher behind bars stood up.

Even as the classes end at both the men's and the women's prisons, the passive-aggressiveness of the staff continues. Out of the blue, I get an email from one of the staff members who is helping me with the classes:

> *I took some time to look into the inmate's offenses in the current Writing for Reentry class . . .*
>
> > *Drugs: 6*
> >
> > *Sex offenders: 5*
> >
> > *Manslaughter: 1*
>
> *Have a Good Weekend!*

I made it clear to staff that I didn't need to know what crimes the men and women committed—that I am not the judge or the jury, I am a professor. But they still, almost always, feel compelled to tell me why my students are there.

| | | |

After class today the GED teachers and I talked about how all the good programming gets cut. When I mentioned that the grant for my program would not be renewed, the teachers expressed their displeasure. Their voices got louder—they were very unhappy. They said they've never worked for an organization that has more people micromanaging. One stated, "And then on top of all that, you have legislators who have no idea what they're talking about trying to make decisions for the budget and for programming." Another continued, "Obviously this program works. I'm disappointed that it won't continue." I offered a little bit of optimism, but to be honest, I don't have any faith that the program will continue. New tough-on-crime administrators are in place.

On the last day of class we presented a group reading via videoconference from two locations. The technology is available for everyone in corrections. All the teacher has to do is walk into a room and turn on the live webinar and voila! It would be very beneficial for taxpayers, families of those incarcerated, victims, and public safety. Wouldn't you like to know that when these men and women are released, they have learned some skills? That they can put pen to paper when they are frustrated and confused, instead of retaliating or turning to crime? Writing has been proven to help. It's a tool that men and women can use so they don't go back to using and abusing drugs. They can communicate their feelings on paper. It's why we writers sit here at our computers every day. If we didn't, we'd go mad. We understand the importance of voice, the power of words.

If you really want to make America great again, or even just a little bit better, you can't just don a red trucker hat—you have to have empathy; you have to keep trying to do the right thing. Tools. There are so many tools we could be using and we choose not to. To many people, chasing paper means far more than leaving a positive legacy—and that, to me, seems like a very lonely life to lead.

I believe everybody wants to do the right thing, to give to their communities the best way they know how. Sometimes people need help to learn how to do this. People on the outside assume that criminals have learned right from wrong when they are locked up, but a lot of them never have. There is ignorance and there are obstacles everywhere. How will people ever learn if you just leave them in a cage?

It's Just a Job

I'm talking to a crime reporter about my work in prisons. I tell him most of the time I feel like I'm fighting an uphill battle. About three-fourths of the staff don't like to see me enter the facility because I'm an English professor. I teach inmates how to come to terms with their emotional complexity through writing. I tell the reporter that I teach at two prisons within a fifty-mile radius of my house and that the prisons were colleges forty years ago.

"Most prisons are in small communities, and people see them as an employer. They don't care about rehabilitation," he says. "It's a job. That's it. They understand crime from what they see on TV and read in the paper."

I flash back to a job application I had to fill out at the state prison. There was a question at the end, and you had minimal space to write your answer. The question: What do you see your role as here at the prison? I wonder how many applicants write "to help rehabilitate."

Still and Silent as Stone

After dinner-count, I see you on the stairwell gazing out the large turn-of-the-century windows, each pane a looking glass into that world where you once belonged. I never say hello to you. You don't see me looking down these stairs at your back, your khaki shirt, your gray receding hair.

I climb the next flight, look out the window to see if I can decipher what it is you are fixed on. Parking lot? Midday traffic? Over the fence are homes. Families race about. A kid on a skateboard ollies over a manhole. Two speed walkers point and chatter as they chase the wind.

But shit, man, maybe I have it all wrong. I see the Chevys and Fords, hear the engines call, the glasspack's throaty cough. Maybe we're more alike than I thought, waiting patiently, considering that getaway car.

8

She Talks to Angels

She never mentions the word addiction
In certain company
—THE BLACK CROWES

I had anxiety in junior high and it got progressively worse in high school. I used to shake so much that my mom finally took me to the doctor to get drug-tested. She was concerned—and rightly so. I've always been hyper. Anxious. A highwire act.

In college, when I first met my future brother-in-law, I had kicked off my sandals and had curled my toes and was pressing them into the carpet. He kept looking at me and finally said, "What are you doing with your toes, there? You getting ready to go hang upside down and sleep in a tree?"

When I began dabbling in alcohol, the anxiety went away. It calmed my nerves. I didn't shake or get nervous around others. My social fears were gone. I thought I was a comedian. In fact, it made me feel invincible. And for a skinny guy, that added sense of strength and imaginary muscle was welcomed—it gave me power. More importantly, I drank because it was fun and I always equated fun with alcohol. Always. My kids' baptisms. Birthdays. Holidays. It all equated to booze. And I'm sure that philosophy is shared by hundreds of millions of people. We have been sold this idea of fun since we were old enough to watch TV and read—it's the single biggest marketing myth we have.

America is a junk food society, and alcohol is at the top of the shopping list. The "fun" for me replaced, momentarily, the stress of college, adulthood, and every dilemma that presented itself. Alcohol makes you numb. And it works pretty well until it doesn't and your body starts to depend on it. It was a deep discomfort I was inflicting on myself, and for a while I didn't even notice it—then I did, but I kept my blinders on.

And this prison I found myself in, was this what subconsciously drew me into work with prisoners to begin with? The idea that I could compare myself to them? That I could tell myself, *I'm functioning. I see you and I'm not you—yet*? Of course that was part of it. The money I received to teach in prisons was decent. The idea of the unknown. The danger. The fear and delusion I brought upon myself. How many staff or visitors have died in prisons in the last year? Not many—and there's no data to be found because it doesn't happen very often. The idea that prisons are a deadly place to work is another propagated fear that Americans have brought on themselves. Sure, it happens—the business of crime and punishment has more deadly incidents than, say, working at a grocery store—but it's not like what you see on TV. But I used working in prisons as an excuse for my drinking. Sometimes it was tough—sometimes I heard and saw things I couldn't forget. All of this madness was slowly creeping up on me as I continued to allow liquid to be my crutch and rule my life. As others reminded me to take it easy, I kept telling myself it would pass. I told myself I was fine. I was publishing and winning awards. But my body was shutting down.

Here it is again—the great gonzo fairytale. Like so many men and women, I bought into the myth that the crazier the exploits, the better the story. The wreckage that occurred along the way would be minor collisions, with pieces spread here and there. I could eventually pick them up—no sweat. The story was out there—somewhere—underneath some empty bottle. This was how all the great artists did it, I thought. Perhaps Hunter S. Thompson had fallen for his own myth, too. But he had helped mastermind the term *gonzo*, and I'm guessing he felt trapped. Thompson's role models all practiced and believed the same philosophy, that alcohol fuels great art. The trap—the reality—is that liquid eventually ruled all of our lives, and it continues to dominate our culture. There's not a single mile you can walk in most places where you won't see at least two empty beer cans.

Reading Harry Potter to My Daughters

I am excited when my ten-and-a-half-year-old daughter asks me if we can read the Harry Potter books out loud to each other, alternating pages. "A chapter a night," she proclaims. My older daughter, who is fourteen and a half and driving with a restricted license, has outgrown bedtime stories, but I remember tearing through *The Sorcerer's Stone* with her and am happy to pick up the series again.

On the pages, we empathize with Harry. "'Happy birthday to me . . . happy birthday to me . . .' No cards, no presents, and he would be spending the evening pretending not to exist." And we feel sorry but not so bad when we laugh at Dudley, "who was so large his bottom drooped over either side of the kitchen chair," saying "Pass the frying pan." And don't forget Moaning Myrtle, the ghost who lives in her out-of-order bathroom. All these years, the strange noises coming from bathrooms—the moaning has always been suspect, but I've never seen a Myrtle.

When I met Megan McDonald, author of the Judy Moody series, at the South Dakota Festival of Books, I introduced myself and told her I couldn't leave until I had her signature and a selfie with her. "Daughter's orders. She knew both of us would be here." She laughed and told me that she'd been at a grade school in California recently and asked all the students to bring a book from home the next day. She would be visiting with them again and was curious to see what they were reading. A large majority of the students showed up the next day and were hesitant to share; a lot of them had brought magazines with the covers ripped off. She showed me a statistic from the Children's Literacy Network that shocked me: "Children from middle-income homes have on average 13 books per child. There is only 1 book for every 300 children in low-income neighborhoods."[1]

It's a delight listening to my daughter articulate some brilliant sentences, reading confidently, so excited to enter this made-up world and the magic of black words on white paper, both of us laughing together. When we are done with our fifteen pages, I tell Paige, "Thanks for reading with me."

"Can we read again tomorrow night?" she asks.

"You bet. We are going to read all of them."

"Yay!"

Joey Hollywood

When our kids were young, we once had a family gathering at a large lake, and my Uncle Joey, also known as "Joey Hollywood," and his kids were along. Uncle Joey was my best man in my wedding, and I was his. At night, when all our kids piled in to their bunkbeds, my wife read a story to them. One little cousin was very attentive and asked my wife to keep reading. She said, "No one reads me bedtime stories much." I was shocked to hear this. Uncle Joey and his wife had recently gotten a divorce, so I thought maybe that was to blame. How could my best man not read books to his kids? Here was a guy who always encouraged my creativity—"You're doing it, man!" he'd say to me throughout my life. "You're a motherfucking rock star!"

That same bedtime-story-less cousin is a TV producer now. From what I can tell, she has an inimitable drive. I'm excited for her future. Her father, Joey Hollywood, is dead. A heart attack. He died too early—fifty-five years old. He drank too much. He partied too much. For the last five years of his life, I separated myself from him. I stopped answering the phone when he called me late at night or at four o'clock in the morning, drunk. I had found myself at the end of my road; I had hit bottom and started to change my ways, and I believed that by leading by example, I might get him to change his ways, too.

||||

When my father was attending Drake University in his hometown of Des Moines, my parents moved in with my father's parents so my mom and dad could afford the tuition and living expenses while there was only one income coming in. I was elated. I would be sharing a room with Uncle Joey! I admired and loved my uncle. He was a big brother to me. We shared a bedroom together for a few years; he was seven years older than me. We all lived in a big house together on campus—all eight of us—mom, dad, grandparents, aunts, uncles—with one bathroom. The house is now demolished and has been replaced with decorative grass and a courtyard just south of the fieldhouse on the Drake campus.

My uncle Joe put a line down the middle of the room with masking tape. The walls on his side of the room were adorned with KISS and Kristy McNichol posters. On my side I had a few stickers that I'd gotten on my daycare assignments and had peeled off and stuck to the wall. After my father's graduation, my mom, dad, and I moved to Nebraska, where my father began working as an actuary at Mutual of Omaha. He was twenty-nine, and they were a young couple on the road to success.

A few years later, Joe was selected as North High School's Mr. Polar Bear, an award given to the best and most popular athlete. He was the center on the football team—snapping the ball—and he was a leader. We drove back to Des Moines to see the award ceremony. I must have been eleven years old. On the night Joe went to midfield to receive his honor, my father held me up above the crowd and I waved a poster I'd made for him. After the game, he came out of the locker room, said hello, and was off to party with his friends like most teenagers do. I was disappointed that he didn't want to celebrate with us; any kid would be. We've all experienced that feeling when we are almost invited to the party. I didn't quite make the cut when I was a kid; that's how I felt my whole life with Joe. I was always playing second fiddle—to his friends, to the bands he toured with, and later, to his addictions. I taped the poster to his bedroom door that night after the game. The next day I knocked on his door to see if he was around. No one answered.

Joe would later visit Omaha for extended periods of time—a weekend or a week—and stay with us when he was off the road on breaks from doing sound and lights for a touring band. The band, Made Ya Look, had made Omaha their home base. They rocked virtually every night—an average of 250 shows a year—playing bars and clubs throughout the Midwest. They were recording and producing their own music, too. Joe was a sought-after roadie who was very good at mixing sound, and his size gave him an added advantage. He played protector—and sometimes bodyguard—for a lot of bandmates. To say I was excited to have Joey Hollywood and the band back in Omaha from time to time would be an understatement.

Most mornings when he was visiting us there would be empty tallboy Budweiser cans upside down in the kitchen sink and an empty frozen pizza board in the trash. A rebranded yellow tour bus—and later a blue tour bus with black windows—would be parked at the end of our block. He would always proclaim, "I'm Joey Motherfucking Hollywood, man." I think he could have achieved his goal of becoming famous as a stand-up comedian, actor, or musician if he had worked harder for it and reined in the partying. "You know, all these rock stars want to go home with the skinny girls after the show," he joked. "Not me. I want to find a Midwest girl with a little meat on her bones. She's got food in her fridge."

After I turned sixteen, I spent many nights tagging along, sneaking into bars (when he'd let me), watching bands while he mixed various acts and ran lights. He was the guy behind the scenes who made thousands of musicians sound good. From touring around the Midwest with Made Ya Look to the endless hard rock and punk acts at Hairy Mary's in Des Moines, then going back on the road with Fat Tuesday and House of Large Sizes, and even working with Slipknot, he worked with and introduced me to an eclectic mix of some of the best music the Midwest had to offer. He worked with all kinds of artists and played his own songs, too.

One of the first bands he ever let me run lights for was Made Ya Look, at Creighton University's prom. "Just don't go crazy," he said. "Keep a beat with the floor tom. Not the kick." This was about the time I started home-perming my hair, singing out of tune, and playing rhythm guitar in bands. I was there, man—circa 1990. This is where it began.

Joe was always a champion for the bands he worked for. Starting when I was five years old, he had encouraged me to be my own "rock star." That idea was ingrained in me, although no one really knew how you became a rock star—another great myth that millions of men ponder as they learn the first few chords of Deep Purple's "Smoke on the Water" and Led Zeppelin's "Stairway to Heaven." Joe would see me playing my guitar and say, "You're doing it man! Motherfucking rock star."

The first time I ever went out of town—and out of state—to play at Mr. Tunes in Sioux City, Iowa, I came home with my guitar in hand and Joe happened to be in Omaha for the weekend. I felt like it was all coming together—being seventeen, walking up the few steps of our split-level house with a guitar case covered in a million stickers. I looked the part, sang out of tune, and knew how to play rhythm guitar okay. It was a small moment in time I'll never forget.

When he was on the road, he was disciplined, at least from what I could tell. He acted different, didn't seem to party as much, and couldn't, because often the band relied on him to drive the bus or van. He also knew how to fix things—mixing boards, speakers, busses.

When I was in college, Joe was working with Fat Tuesday and House of Large Sizes. Both were national acts. When he was off the road at home in Des Moines and doing house sound at Hairy Mary's, he partied too much. He knew how to mix a show and drink at the same time, and he did it quite well. He knew the room, no matter the act. On the nights when I was back in Des Moines, I'd always follow him to the club, meet the bands, party with everyone. It seemed to be a good night when he would look at his plastic cup of Budweiser and say, "You're the only one who understands me." Then he'd ask me to refill the pitcher of beer, and I would, because I was drinking for free, too. There were many weekends when even though I had little money in my pocket, I drove from Wayne, Nebraska, to Des Moines and partied all weekend. I loved the loud music and the drink.

Many people tried to help my uncle in the last twenty years of his life. After his death, many musicians and people he worked with told me the same story. He was good at putting up a wall and he seldom let anyone in. "I could always see a deep but meticulously veiled insecurity in Joey Hollywood," wrote Michael D., the drummer for Made Ya Look. "Joe Reese was a sensitive and really great guy; Joey Hollywood was a bold and blustery character that many people were drawn to. It took some work to see through all that and anyone who didn't know him well never saw it."

I often think of the characters that populate *A River Runs Through It*. Norman Maclean was seventy-four when that book, a semi-autobiographical novella based on his family, was published. Maclean writes, "For it is true we can seldom help those closest to us. Either we don't know what part of ourselves to give or, more often than not, the part we have to give is not wanted."

Joe Reese was my hero for the better part of forty years. He acted as my big brother. I had to reevaluate my idol and my own addiction issues before it was too late. Some nights when I am awake late at night and unable to sleep, I wonder if I could have done more to save him from his demons. Some of his brothers and sisters have expressed the same anguish. And a lot of the nights I'm still very angry with him, and with myself for following in his footsteps for so many years. "The road goes on forever and the party never ends." That's fiction. It's just a song.

Alcoholism and addictions make people do unpredictable things. I've been one of those people. I have learned that people have to want to help themselves before they can conquer these afflictions—a tired expression but one that is true. You can't help someone who doesn't want to be helped. I knew for quite a long time that I needed help, and I believed for a long time that I could get my act under control. I was lying to myself. And I was believing those lies. I didn't know how I could have fun without something to drink. I had depended on it for so long that it scared the hell out of me to live without it. But I had to come to terms with it. My family knew. The guys in my prison classes knew. I wasn't fooling anyone. How could I preach immersion—to write from the gut—if I wasn't doing it myself? My gig was up.

||||

I think how quickly time flies by. My daughters are teenagers now. Instead of bedtime stories, I try to recommend enticing books for them to read. I remember nights when I wanted to hurry through a book—I had stuff to do, and they needed to get to bed.

I have learned it helps to talk about our trauma, whatever it may be. What is the alternative? Bottle it up. Pretend it doesn't exist. By sharing our collective stories we can help each other heal. Whoever still believes it's macho to suppress their feelings—this toxic masculinity—will live a sad and painful life.

I talk to my cousin, Joe's daughter. We share stories. Good and bad. She has read what I've written about her father. She has told me more stories and I have a more complete picture of this person I admired and will always hold close to my heart. We have projects we are working on that we will share with the world.

The weird thing about addiction is that it sneaks up on you and starts talking in your head. Often there are snapshots—drunken bursts of excitement—all *good times*—followed by a face plant, something you feel sorry for saying or doing. I can still remember almost all of these moments—unfortunately, I never blacked out. A stronger person might call these my alcoholic memories.

I never liked the word *alcoholic*. Everyone wants to put a label on things, though. Then they can send you to the right meeting. I'm a guy who liked to drink. I've always equated the word *alcoholic* with verbal and physical abuse. That's the Hollywood version, isn't it? Most domestic abuse involves alcohol. The World Health Organization estimates that roughly 55 percent of domestic abuse perpetrators were drinking alcohol prior to their assault. Women who are abused are fifteen times more likely to abuse alcohol.[2] If I am being honest, I have screamed at those closest to me too many times. Pushed them away. For years it was always someone else's fault—surely not mine.

I drank, I suspect, like most people, because it was fun. It gave me a powerful, almost invincible feeling that I chased long into the night and many early mornings. It was my own self-righteousness. I had, like a prisoner in my class used to joke, "gotten right with the world," and in turn, the world was now, finally and at long last, the way it was supposed to be. All of this clarity came first from drinking and later from slamming vodka and waiting about twenty minutes for it to kick in. How could liquid give me power? It's an absurd question now as I type it but one that many people can relate to. Most of us have heard expressions such as, "When you drink you say exactly what you mean." Alcohol gives people confidence to speak their mind. And that may be the disillusioned power so many men and women search for. It's part of the gonzo cliché.

We carry many voices within ourselves, and in the moment, that alcohol-induced singing might seem urgent and necessary. Speaking from experience, that boisterous voice usually got me into trouble.

When the buzz wore off, I would be second-guessing the words that had come out of my mouth. Booze gave me opinions, even ideas—often jumbled and incoherent. I remember the comedian Chelsey Handler in one of her shows saying something like, when we are drinking, we spend the whole time trying to pretend we aren't drunk. This is the same comedian whose book is titled, *Are You There, Vodka? It's Me, Chelsea*.

Sometimes when these snapshots show their faces, they aren't very kind—they remind me what a fool I was for not listening to those closest to me. When Bill Kloefkorn, State Poet of Nebraska, was a guest lecturer for my class, he showed me and the whole class his five-year coin. He joked, "There's nothing better than bourbon on ice." He continued, "I've drank swimming pools of booze. Oh, well, that's in the past now." He was a very intelligent man and good friend, and I knew he was sharing this information about his sobriety and his funny anecdotes for a reason.

I remember what a friend told me when I asked him what his daughter did for a living. He said very matter-of-factly and assertively (while I was still drinking), "She's an alcoholic." He wasn't just talking about his daughter. There were innumerable times friends told me to stop. Guys in the band in college told me to take it easy and practice. There's nothing more dangerous than ignoring those closest to you, those who see right through your disguise.

After I had declared a major and minor in the great social quest for more—I was entering what some might call the first stages of a major problem—I remember performing a face plant on concrete outside some apartments by campus. I have no idea what we were doing there, and it was still daylight outside. I saw the incident coming, and there was no way my motor skills could keep me from falling. Fortunately, I did not black out. It took me some time to get on my feet. That was one of a lot of embarrassing moments. But within an hour I was drinking again. I had made up some bullshit story to leave band practice early to get to that moment. I was chasing a scream—and I knew better, but I didn't stop for another twenty years.

During some of those years, I did seem to have it more under control. Was I lying to myself? Was I wearing out the people who were closest to me, and had they given up hope? Or were there times when I actually had made strides to rid myself of this addiction? Because I continued to be successful professionally, I stopped asking myself these questions. I built more walls around myself, blamed my increased anxiety on my growing responsibilities. It surely wasn't the booze's fault. Teaching in prisons was a real fear in the beginning and very stressful, and I added that to the growing list of reasons why I drank. But it wasn't a matter of why at that point—it seemed to be a necessity.

||||

Sometimes these stories help other readers who have experienced similar episodes and would like to take back a decade or two. I suppose the only difference between me and millions of other people who abuse alcohol is that I stopped. I had to. Apparently, I couldn't cut back. I ran away from everyone until I couldn't hold a fork in my hand to cut a waffle. I was shaking too much.

What I found is that life is just as fun without booze in it. That was a terrible fear of mine. Could I really have fun without certain liquids in my life? Now I wake feeling good and I have very little regret. I can do a lot of things that I ran out of breath for before. I have rediscovered how competitive I am. I play soccer—play it well—with guys twenty-five years younger than me. I'm a striker. And when I set my mind to most goals, I achieve them. I'll never play football, but hey, I was a college mascot and have been on more turf than most Americans.

I told a guy I work with that I wish I could get back some of that time. I always managed to work and I got a PhD and I wrote and published three books before I got sober. I still have to say that—it gives me some satisfaction that I wasn't a complete loser. And this guy I work with said, "There's no need to regret that time. That's what makes you—you." That was a nice thing for him to say.

When I write about addiction and talk about how frustrated, confused, and angry I was, it's important that I explain that I know I was no saint. I spent a lot of time in car washes slamming vodka I had mixed with juice. I could drink a lot all by myself in five minutes. And then I drove. It was a criminal act, and I did it consciously. That not only was childish but it put other people in danger.

My cousin David, whom I also thought of as my older brother, said to me when I told him I stopped drinking, "Good. You are too creative to drink." Those words carried me through many temptations and difficult situations. They still do. And that advice was the opposite of what I had believed since I was younger. Gonzo says, *You're creative so you must drink*. Reality is, that's not true.

"Go big or go home!" is an expression I hear a lot both in prisons and in the free world. I decided to ask some very talented musicians to talk about themes of addiction and music. I reached out to some musicians I admired when I was growing up—the same ones who shaped me and inspired me. Here's what Michael D., the drummer from Made Ya Look, had to say on the subject:

> Hi Jim, I spent a lot of time this weekend writing my thoughts on addiction and my life in music. 90% of it is unreadable, but it was a valuable lesson in self-awareness. Maybe it will evolve into a book someday. Thanks for the assignment. Here's what it boils down to:
>
> It's hard to say whether my desire to be a rock star came from the love of music my Dad instilled in me at a very young age (I could sing every word of Folsom Prison Blues phonetically, before I understood what they meant) or my own need of acceptance, the admiration that he clearly had for his favorite musicians at that time—Johnny Cash and Hank Williams. Dad was a major influence on me. Not surprisingly, he was also an alcoholic; a handsome, James Dean-style rebel with a Norton motorcycle and a pack of Salems rolled up in his white t-shirt sleeve.
>
> When I saw The Beatles on Ed Sullivan in 1964 that was it. It was that reaction of the audience, the utter pandemonium that made such an impression on four-year-old me. Young women were filled with such emotion I didn't know what to do with it, but I knew I wanted to be the object of that excitement. I decided then and there that I wanted to be a musician and the one who stood out to me was Ringo, towering above the others on that absurd drum riser. I would be a drummer, driving the car and electrifying audiences.
>
> But don't underestimate the power music has held over me. It is the most important thing in my life that's not a person, and it has

always been so. The number of hours I spent in my youth absorbing Led Zeppelin songs, taking acid and studying Pink Floyd music, or dissecting every note of Return to Forever albums is incalculable. I started formally studying as a classical percussionist at age 10 and have played ever since, but without exception, the most pleasure I've gotten from music has been sharing it with an audience and seeing people moved by it.

> At the same time, I've also fancied myself an informal student of promotion. That's pretty much the antithesis of the art of music . . . the science of publicity and persuasion. In fact, it brings us right back to the need for acceptance. It's not lost on me that that is also a primary reason many people start drinking and using other substances. My love of music is a chicken while insecurity and the need for adoration is an egg. Or is it the other way around? Does it even matter? Six decades in, I'm still trying to sort it out. The only thing I know for sure is that alcohol addiction hampered my progress at times and utterly roadblocked it at others.[3]

When I read this letter, I am also reminded of how alcohol gave me a sense of security. I felt much more accepted when I was drinking. Just like in the TV show *Cheers*—everyone seemed to know my name. That popular sitcom was fiction, too.

Gambling

His voice comes to me in a nightmare. I don't remember his name, but his prison, his addiction, seemed so unusual to me the first time I heard him speak. I was with a group of men—sitting in a circle—talking. This is what I did in rehab before I decided it wasn't for me. I had too much work to do and I dropped out a week into treatment.

Not all the men were there for drinking or drugs. The speaker seemed to be successful. Seemed bright. Could articulate his thoughts and feelings well. He said that when he was on the road for business trips, his coworkers always asked him to join them for dinner and drinks. He couldn't. He'd spent all of his money at the local convenience stores buying scratch tickets. He'd be broke by the first night of his business trip. He'd leave town and blow through all the money he had. Go hungry.

Eat the freebie bananas and fruit in the lobby. "I have to win. I always have to win. When I lose, I gamble more. That's why I am here."

Garden Hose

The garden hose is where the man hid his vodka from his wife. He'd pour about a liter into the end, tighten the nozzle to make sure it was closed. When he went to take a drink, he'd turn the hose on just a squirt—enough to give it some pressure. "I got used to shot-gunning a liter in seconds," he told a group of us, still laughing about the cleverness of his hiding spot.

Sing Backwards

I was talking with a local musician about the book *Sing Backwards and Weep*, by Mark Lanegan. He was the lead singer for Screaming Trees and a member of Queens of the Stone Age. I've read a lot of addiction memoirs. They act as therapy, much like meetings do for others. I'm a former mediocre musician from the grunge era, and the memoirs of Lanegan, who was one of Kurt Cobain's only friends at the height of his *Nirvana* superstardom, are engaging. I'm not sure Lanegan could have gotten any deeper in the horrendous hole he had dug for himself—shooting heroin everywhere, including a vein in his penis—arms covered in scabs and sores—selling crack to the homeless outside his apartment in Seattle to feed his addiction.

Luckily, he lived to tell the tales, finally taking Courtney Love's advice and money, checking himself into rehab. It's an enthralling and exhausting account of drug use and how far down he went—penniless in another country while on tour, banging on Screaming Trees T-shirt vendors' hotel doors for an advance from their sales, for his cut of his royalties so he could score more brown. The drug is like no other and it baffles me. I used to love to get bent, but I knew I'd never shoot anything into my arm—ever. And perhaps out of pure luck, I never got too close to anyone who was smoking it.

"Well, Jim, have you ever done any drugs?" a musician asked me.

"Why? Do you have some?" I laughed. "I've never done heroin."

"Well, I have," he said. "I smoked it. And let me tell you, it was the best feeling I've ever had. I knew right after, I could never do it again. I was lucky I could tell myself that."

Mommy's Medicine

A colleague recently told me about a university student's visit to a grade school, where she observed the teacher and helped in class to complete the student teaching hours she needed for her degree. The student reported that one of the second graders was playing with chalk dust and had brought some erasers and chalk over to the table where her friends were playing. She took her time collecting the chalk dust in a pile and then moved it into perfectly thin lines. She then bent her head down close to the lines, inhaled deeply, and said, "This is how my mommy takes her medicine."

Talking Tom Petty at the Women's Prison

Today at the women's prison I read a statement that I copied from Tom Petty's website about his accidental opioid overdose and death. It starts a discussion about drugs in my class—one we've had before, but not this intensely. I read the class my poem "Full Moon Fever." I tell them it is more than just a poem about a father-son road trip. It's about love's inability to always stand on two feet, how life can shift, and how we learn from all of it. There are some subtle hints in the poem—perhaps things I wished I'd described more specifically and bluntly—but the haze is all part of it. E. L. Doctorow said, "Writing is like driving at night in the fog. You can only see as far as your headlights, but you can make the whole trip that way." Isn't that a lot like life? Our lives often are like walking through a smoke machine or fog at night. We can't see the destination, but we know where we want to be.

M raises her hand immediately after I finish the poem. She begins talking about being a heroin addict for over fourteen years. She is privileged, went to a prestigious university, played DI sports, and is very aware that coming from a well-to-do family didn't stop her from using when she was only fifteen. She says, "That's almost half my life. I don't want to continue to live this way. I am that girl—that 'American Girl' in the song. Or I was." She looks around the room briefly and continues, "Things will be goin' good and then I think I need to start using again. I feel this urge to risk everything. So I do. One time, I was just bored. So I went looking. I can't be at peace. I can't even be quiet in this class."

M has natural writing chops. I don't want her to be quiet. Her work has rhythm, and she has a voice filled with power and angst, which I can relate to—not to the heroin, but to the addiction. We can all probably admit to addiction to something. I understand what she's talking about with the boredom, and it's frustrating to be a creative person and not feel like you have an outlet. Or to be bored because you aren't utilizing your talents. I spent years talking about being a writer instead of writing. I encourage her to try to get things down on paper during these moments of unrest.

"I remember a counselor telling me a craving only lasts for three to five minutes," I tell the class. "It seems to work well for me." I tell M to get busy. "If you're bored, then do something. It's your own fault if you aren't pushing yourself." Maybe that's not the nicest thing to say, but it's the truth.

Someone like M, with her kind of talent, who is well read—if she learns to work and discipline herself, her story is a gold mine. Maybe next week I'll encourage her to make a list of important moments in her life, starting fourteen years ago, and see how that might serve as a template for a memoir.

I end class with a prompt: Why do we hurt the people that we love? Valentine's Day is coming soon, so I'm trying to find unique ways for my students to express their feelings, to write about love, but not in the traditional, cheesy, Hallmark card or movie sense. Poetry that has end rhyme is predictable—it becomes singsongy. And more importantly, the message is lost because the writer is usually too focused on making words match.

I share two of Kim Addonizio's poems, "You Don't Know What Love Is" and "Forms of Love." I ask the students to write a letter to a loved one. I read the poem "Splitting an Order," by Ted Kooser. I tell them about the Valentine's Day poem Kooser wrote each year—for more than two decades—and sent as a postcard to thousands of women on his growing list, over twenty-five hundred. "Splitting an Order" is one of the best love poems I've ever read; it's about an older couple sharing a sandwich in a café. What brings it to life is the ceremony of cutting the sandwich, placing the napkins in their laps, and the man's two "old hands" passing half the sandwich to his wife.

Splitting an Order

I like to watch an old man cutting a sandwich in half,
maybe an ordinary cold roast beef on whole wheat bread,
no pickles or onion, keeping his shaky hands steady
by placing his forearms firm on the edge of the table
and using both hands, the left to hold the sandwich in place,
and the right to cut it surely, corner to corner,
observing his progress through glasses that moments before
he wiped with his napkin, and then to see him lift half
onto the extra plate that he asked the server to bring,
and then to wait, offering the plate to his wife
while she slowly unrolls her napkin and places her spoon,
her knife, and her fork in their proper places,
then smooths the starched white napkin over her knees
and meets his eyes and holds out both old hands to him.[4]

||||

It's not quite a blizzard out yet, but it looks like it's going to get ugly. I leave the women's prison slowly. As I dictate notes about class into my iPhone, I remind myself to show M how she can piece together the six short prose pieces she's written already. She has the start to a great chapter with all kinds of hooks about an all-American California girl. If she played DI, she knows how to discipline herself. I really hope she does this, that she doesn't fall back in the trap.

I recommend books like *The Glass Castle* and *Liar's Club*, and all of David Sedaris's work. More than a few of them have read these authors, M included, which is surprising, but it makes sense. Did she read these when she was locked up or before? I keep telling my students they need to write memoirs, and a few of them have the talent to do it. M certainly does.

The students discuss early release. A lot of the women are getting ankle monitors and are being sent home—some up to six months early. Three out of the six women in my class are being released due to overcrowding. This always happens. I've never had a consistent set of students, especially in the last five years, in any prison where I've taught. Almost all of the women here are incarcerated because of drugs, crimes associated with drugs, or being high when they broke the law. Our drug laws are bogus. They are intended to make criminals out of regular citizens. Just tonight I was reiterating a tired story I heard from students in my prison classes. They were trying to make ends meet and they turned to meth to pull the double shifts at work. The drug kept them awake. It's as simple as that.

The war on drugs never worked. We should be careful with what we make illegal. How is locking up someone with an addiction—with a disease—going to help them heal or get to the root cause of their problem? It's one thing if you want to rehabilitate people who are incarcerated, but after fourteen years working in prisons, I know that's not the main focus of incarceration—and it should be. And what are these people being punished for? Getting hooked on drugs? In what ways is simply using a drug worthy of punishment? America is addicted to alcohol—but that's legal. Is it really safer than all the drugs that are illegal? No.

I've always asked officials in charge this question: Would you rather get in a car with someone who has been drinking or with someone who has smoked some marijuana? Most of the time their answer is that they'd go with the person who has smoked pot. Or they say they don't know because they have never smoked marijuana. Well, if that's the case, they shouldn't be making or enforcing such laws. Marijuana is not a gateway drug, but alcohol is. I can justify this statement because I have used both substances. Marijuana has never made me feel invincible—it never made me combative or argumentative—I never spoke absolutes that I might not have otherwise. In fact, marijuana made me talk less and laugh more. Marijuana never gave me the feeling that I was above the law, but alcohol gave me beer muscles. It made me aggressive, argumentative, and loud, and it made common-sense decisions seem irrational and unimportant—like getting behind the wheel of a car. Millions of people do it every day and tell themselves they are okay. Have you ever driven a car after drinking when you knew you shouldn't?

I remember the first class I taught at the state prison. I passed around a blank piece of paper and asked the students to write yes or no in response to the following question: Were you under the influence of drugs or alcohol when you committed your crime? All of them wrote yes.

||||

The main focus of prison is controlling the individual. What time to wake. What time to pee. What to eat. What mail you can read. How long you can talk to someone on the phone and how ungodly expensive that phone call is going to be. And while you're on that phone call, there will be a recording that plays—a voice that reminds listeners that they are on the phone with an incarcerated individual: *Hello, this is Global TelLink, you have a call from Jim Reese from San Quentin Prison, in San Quentin, California. This call and your number will be monitored and recorded. Facebook is listening too and will try to sell you a phone card after the call. Press 5 to continue.*

Prison correctional officers have said to me time and time again that they are just adult babysitters. Well, that's a real problem. People become addicted for various reasons. Meth will keep you up so you can work more, which in turn gives you money to pay bills. Alcohol gives some people the feeling of acceptance and power. And alcohol and drug use are fun. But one is legal and one is not.

It's rewarding to see these students open up and talk about real concerns. None of them seems overjoyed to leave. I was shocked when I first started experiencing this, seeing it for myself. It's like the college senior who just stops coming to class. The real world is approaching and they have decided to check out instead of facing life's challenges. A lot of the students are anxious and nervous, and a lot are afraid of using again once released. What does that tell us about drug rehabilitation behind bars?

Ajax Bottles

I still think about you, after all these years. Probably because you were younger than me when you were in class my first year in prisons. I had so much to learn. I was so eager to talk about what I knew and me, me. I was very interested in bragging to people, especially other writers who were more experienced. I could hold my own. I was writing poems about prisoners, by god. And most of those writers were eager to listen—I had information they could use. We steal from the best, one writer friend likes to always remind people.

What I remember about you is not your crime but your story. How counting the years was too hard, so you measured your time behind bars in Ajax liquid dish soap bottles. The Bureau of Prisons gives you months—not years—120.

You were halfway through bottle two. You had counted cinder blocks. Check. Tested your ego. Check. Were enrolled in every class you could be in. Check. You wore your shame—that's probably what scared me the most, since I was trying so desperately to hide mine. Check. Check. You also worked hard. You were the first man I believed would really turn his life around.

Someone in your family lived nearby and stopped me one night at a local gas station to thank me for helping you. That was one of the first awakenings I had. It wasn't me on a radio interview or bragging about training in San Quentin to some magazine; it was your family who stopped me and said, "Thank you," and told me what I was doing was helping. In all my frustration with the systems of our lives—those in charge who will always want to be just in charge and never more—I still carry you with me.

Last I heard, you had kids and were doing well. I hope you have stopped counting Ajax bottles.

Hydraulics

One day in prison, a student told me a story about one of his greatest regrets. What I began to discover was that addiction, in all of its gross immaturity, will make people go to extreme measures. The student, an inmate in his late twenties, was built, as we say here on the plains, like a brick shithouse. He and I talked briefly at the back of the class.

"My grandfather had a Farmall 300. You had a need for hoses for your tractor so you could raise the lift cylinders and tilt bucket with the hydraulics. When the hose went missing, I'm sure he was shocked. When he asked me if I'd seen it, I lied. He said, 'I've had that tractor I don't know how long. No one's ever taken a hose off it.' What he didn't know was that I used the hose to cook meth. I can't keep feeling guilty about my past. I'm done paying that bill. But I tell you, I wish I'd never took that hose."

Tragedy on the Reservation

One of the toughest men in my class wore sunglasses throughout the entire class, but he wasn't a punk. He sat right in front and shared honest reflections, and when he did, everyone stopped to listen. The other guys knew not to interrupt him.

After the third week of class, the unit manager told me, "We wanted to see how you'd fare with these guys. They're some of the worst troublemakers we have here. We try hard to keep them in line."

I hadn't done anything differently than I normally would. Hotheads, mean motherfuckers, whatever you want to call troubled men—there's a trick to getting their attention. It's the oldest trick in the book. As a teacher, you must go into every class and listen. You must command authority but also create an environment where people will share their most personal stories. And the only way I've ever figured out how to do that is to be completely honest. I too have to admit my fears, failures, uncertainties. I have to let these men speak when they finally get the courage to do so. I have to prove to them that I am listening and offer constructive criticism and encouragement.

During the last class the sunglasses-wearing student broke down and told his story. He said, "My brothers and I were all out in the front yard playing. We were getting ready to go somewhere. Adults were in the house yelling at us to get everyone ready and in the car. We were just kids. Someone had strapped our baby brother in the carry-along seat and set it down by the back passenger car tire so he would be there ready to go. One of my older brothers backed up the car. Backed over my baby brother. The adults stumbled out of the house—could barely walk, screaming at us once someone told them what had happened. They blamed us for the accident. They still do. This accident ruined our family."

He finished his story. He removed those dark Ray-Ban knock-off, prison-issued sunglasses. He looked up at me, tears coming down his face, and said, "I haven't cried in over ten years. I don't know what you are doing, but keep doing it."

Coming to Terms with Myself

Often when I was in the prisons, I felt like I had pulled the wool over the staff's eyes, like I was getting away with something. My addiction was a legal one. I might be hungover—like millions of others in the country and other staff at the same prison—or wishing work would be over sooner so I could get a drink (like so many millions of people, some of whom partake at their desk toward the end of the day if their establishment allows such things—and many do!). What would have happened to my life if alcohol was illegal? I can tell you it wouldn't have prevented me from drinking. I'd have done the same thing and convinced myself it was okay in the privacy of my own house or wherever I partook, which in turn could have turned me into a criminal. The difference between me and my incarcerated students was as thin as a legal definition.

My gonzo became the dark substitute for creative discipline. I was writing, but I lacked control. What I first believed to be artistic expression—mainly partying and talking about being creative—turned into a problem. I was making a lot of bad decisions instead of getting to work. When those bad decisions became harmful decisions, that's when I crossed the line in my life from right to wrong. And I kept crossing it, because I was lying to myself and believing I was only harming myself. Eventually I had to take responsibility. In the end, I was vulnerable and scared. I was weak.

If you have to drink to steady a fork in your hand, there's a real problem. I had to go from what I thought was my artistic expression to some real thinking and doing. I had to accept who I was and the harm I was causing to myself and those who cared about me. And this led to rehabilitation—to LOVE to WORK.

9

Coda

Coming to a Neighborhood near You

I have been influenced on this journey by murder and other criminal activity. I never wanted to admit it, but if I look deep, it's always been there. I've spent over thirty years thinking about the serial killer John Joubert and about my friend Christina's murder. I assumed—maybe I was even conditioned to believe—that it's best to suppress certain memories. But what I discovered in writing this book is that our personal dilemmas—some might call them demons—are neither a strength nor a weakness but trauma that is present for a host of reasons: One, we live in a society that takes crime for granted. Two, we don't recognize and try to help secondary victims and the people and communities that crime invisibly influences and inevitably affects. Three, locking someone up in a cage is the response. Four, although we know that this is not a humane solution to our problems, we continue to do the same thing decade after decade for billions and billions of dollars a year because the business of punishment is a fucking cash cow. It doesn't matter if you live in a big city or a small town—these "systems" that we have created are sending those we have branded "criminals" to a neighborhood near you.

Research shows that two-thirds of these "criminals" will reoffend within the first three years after their release.[1] So, like warden Jordan Hollingsworth used to say, "These men are coming to a neighborhood near you. Do you want them educated or not?" After I heard him say this, I told him that one day I was going to write a book called "Coming to a Neighborhood near You." He smiled and said, "Good. Do it."

When I discuss the power of voice and really get going about the awakenings some men and women have in my prison classes—when my students feel like for once they are being heard and they realize that they can turn their lives around for the better—I am astonished at some of the responses I get from others who teach or work in prisons, too. I have heard teachers say, "It's not like the work we are doing is missionary work" and "It's just a job."

I disagree. We should be trying to make prisoners better, more fulfilled people. We should be challenging them to find the best parts of themselves. Punishment in prison is isolation from society and loved ones. What is our obligation as a just and fair society once people are locked up? I feel we are indebted to help these men, women, and juvenile offenders turn their lives around. This isn't a black-and-white movie. This isn't chain-gang mentality. We are beyond that. I want to believe that most decent and caring human beings understand that locking someone in a box and letting them out after an extended period of time doesn't rehabilitate them. It doesn't sedate an animal and it doesn't begin to fix a troubled person. Putting a dog in a cage doesn't make it stop barking. You have to teach it to behave and you also have to love it—and in the process, the dog learns. I don't expect everyone to jump up and down and get excited about rehabilitating criminals, but I do expect people, at the very least, to understand that rehabilitation is necessary. Most offenders are going to get out of prison, whether we like it or not.

The gonzo slogan has always been, "When the going gets weird, the weird turn pro." God, I wish that were so. The author of that statement killed himself. And suicide, unfortunately, in this warped society of ours, has been normalized, too.

We have, for over fifty years, concentrated on a war on drugs and gotten "tough on crime," when all along we should have been putting our efforts into rehabilitation. What is the war on drugs, really? It's a war on race—a war on the poor—a war on the disenfranchised. Words like *gentrification—mass shooting—cracking down—control—socialism—freedom—addiction* (not *illness*)—*military tactics*—these words began to rear their ugly heads after peace and love and on the cusp of cocaine, when everyone began living faster and meaner in our society. I'd like to ask every boomer-aged policymaker if they feel safer now than they did in the late sixties. Even former president Bill Clinton, who got tough on crime, later admitted he got it wrong and has since changed his tune. Tough on crime seems like the right answer until it affects us personally and we realize that it is human beings we are warehousing. And why? I never knew the truth until I started working in the system and opened my eyes.

We have a world full of addicted people. Everyone is abusing something, and most are addicted to social media—to little screens—willingly getting behind the wheel of thousands of pounds of steel and treating vehicles as mobile telephone booths, rarely looking up, taking their sweet time staring into their laps, checking their texts and posts, playing, swiping left or right. They are ready to be blown away by the next machine of interest—the next "like"—looking down for salvation to see whatever it is they think they've missed. We have created a culture so disconnected from reality that human decency and kindness get overlooked. Hold the door open for someone and a lot of the time they don't even look up from their phone. On more than a few occasions I've seen grown men riding motorcycles and texting. I thought that was a circus act, but apparently it's legal in my state.

We live in places—in virtual spaces—so engrossed with the next shinier thing that we forget to stop. To listen to one another.

To live in the moment.

What has happened to human appetite, to discovery, to drive? Four on the floor used to mean something. Now a gear shift just gets in the way of electronics or infotainment centers across the dashboard. People throw around words like *freedom* but are so locked into their ideologies that they couldn't claw their way out of the razor wire they've built around themselves if they had to. Some even call it doomsday prepping. And speaking of survival—who knows how to make a fire these days? Grit is turning into a lost art. Ask yourself this: what is the one thing everyone on earth craves and seldom gets? To be listened to. To be heard. I'll stop now.

||||

I've spent fourteen years working behind bars with men and women who have committed an assortment of crimes. Like my wife has said, "Crime has affected your life more than a lot of other people's." It has become a deep psychic element and an influential aspect of how I have formed my thoughts, words, and endeavors, whether I asked for it or not. And crime and its consequences seem to affect more and more Americans these days. That's nothing to celebrate in the land of the free and home of the brave.

I have discovered that speaking up and discussing our trauma and our concerns and our fears is okay. Kendra Horsley, a triple major at Mount Marty (psychology, human services, and English writing), said to me after a class in which we discussed anxiety, depression, and the repercussions of trauma, "It's like we finally have permission to feel pain." And I agreed. And then she joked, "But who is actually policing us—the pain police?" Maybe what we both realized was that we were the ones throwing up walls in our own lives. We both have come to understand that by speaking about trauma, we help one another and others. I hope that writing what I've learned—about the shadows and concerns I've carried and the things I've discovered about crime and punishment—has helped to elucidate Christina's murder and give voice to all victims, even if it's a small whisper from afar.

Time and time again we learn that "criminals" have been victims themselves and that that is what drove them to commit their crime. Being a victim *does not* excuse committing crimes. My uncertainty, my conundrum about X, Christina's murderer, is beside the point. What I have learned is that I am speaking for *all* victims—even "criminals"—because they are all human beings and all deserve mercy. And deserving mercy doesn't necessarily mean that everyone should go free. But everyone can be treated humanely and with empathy.

I'm not sure I'll arrive at a neat conclusion. Some questions are beyond answers. Who really can define or tell us what evil is? No one. There are no data. Evil is always, to an extent, subjective.

Why? Because.

I've learned more about myself and my feelings, confusions—that's what makes me who I am today. As former LAPD sergeant and professor Dr. Stephen Bell said to me, "You aren't creating with this book as much as you might be realizing." And he's right. I am realizing and uncovering something that has always been there—a part of me. And in this creation I have found an epiphany—perhaps even a manifestation of something divine—a way to give voice to the life of someone who had it stolen forever.

||||

Public safety should always be our number one concern. We could talk about an eye for an eye. We could talk about the death penalty. I know that most prisoners aren't heinous—they aren't wicked. Locking people up and disregarding them is not an answer. The death penalty—not an answer. Understanding and education are. Maybe some people should never leave prison, but that doesn't mean that we can't provide them with tools to make their own life and other people's lives better while they are behind bars.

We have disregarded, failed to see, and pretended not to see the larger effects crime has on society. Crime doesn't just mark the victim and the criminal—it touches all of the families involved and their friends, acquaintances, and employees. The circle is far-reaching. If we are focused solely on punishment, what have we solved? How are we making things better for everyone involved—for society?

After fourteen years of working in prisons, the best solution I have come up with is that if a person is incarcerated, they should have to prove that they have done something about restoration for the victim and themselves—they should have to prove they are rehabilitated. If educational assessments of inmates prove they are able and they don't have any kind of developmental disability, a high school diploma or GED should be mandatory for them. As Literacy Mid-South notes on its website,

> A low level of literacy is not a direct determinant of a person's probability to be convicted on criminal charges, but correctional and judicial professionals have long recognized a connection between poor literacy, dropout rates, and crime. Individuals with below-average levels of education are overrepresented among people in prison compared to the general population. According to the National Adult Literacy Survey, 70% of all incarcerated adults cannot read at a fourth-grade level, "meaning they lack the reading skills to navigate many everyday

> tasks or hold down anything but lower (paying) jobs." Data supports that those without sufficient income earned by work are the most prone to crime.[2]

Also, if a person in jail or prison doesn't have any form of higher education, they should be required to earn at least an associate's degree before being released. Studies show the more education a person receives behind bars, the less likely they are to return to prison. That's common sense.

If someone is behind bars, they should have to learn to make their life better. And they should have to pay back child support if they owe money. Somewhere along the line they (corrections and inmates) need to fix this problem. Inmates should be able to earn enough money to pay back restitutions instead of being free labor for the department of corrections. They can't just sit around—play cards—shoot the shit—easy time. There are far too many people in jails and prisons doing very little for themselves or society.

Some people drop out of school because it's a challenge, and they turn to a life of crime because it's easier to hustle and steal. Prison becomes a rite of passage, and once they are in the cycle, the cycle seldom ends for them or their family. Let's eliminate that cycle. If someone chooses a life of crime—drops out of school—it should be made very clear to them that they don't get to be locked up and do easy time. Hard time is holding these men and women accountable. Hard time is making them learn before consideration for release is even brought to the table.

And we need to stop the cycle before it starts in the perpetrator's family, by making criminals right their wrongs with the victim and their own people, so their family members (most importantly, siblings, daughters, and sons) don't see crime as some glorified rite of passage and decide to pick up the reins. The cycle of crime can end. It can stop. We can provide tools and programming to help with this. Kent Meyers wrote, "Crime matters in ways people don't consider—and it has a double edge. 1) If criminals aren't rehabbed, they return to those very communities as further threats to emotional stability. 2) Communities themselves need rehab far beyond the extent we usually think."[3]

||||

I want to believe, at my core, that X is better than the worst act he committed. However, his reconciliation with his victims and his accountability for his crime are on him. At first I felt strange writing about Christina's murder and how it affected our community, but not anymore. I arrived here for a reason. My work in prisons may have been happenstance (or perhaps it was karma), but I know my voice is not. We need to speak to crime and how it controls us. Otherwise, nothing changes. I suspect I'm not the only one who never knew how to deal with Christina's murder—my feelings, my rage and fear. Our idea of safety was lost forever. Or so I thought. I am hypervigilant, and maybe that's not such a bad thing. I am always on the lookout. I am prepared. I am also willing to help—and have helped—some killers.

If we don't find ways to rehabilitate those who victimize all of us, both primary and secondary victims, we're going to continue to live with these atrocities. We will continue to bring criminals back to our neighborhoods and communities, where they will continue to infect us with victimhood, with their misplaced guilt—with their misplaced regrets, distress, undigested life material, and all of the other mysteries that we can't solve.

||||

Netflix's eighth-ranked TV show in early 2023 was *My Lover, My Killer*, a docuseries examining "murder cases in which the victims meet tragic ends because of relationships that go very wrong."

Over a two-year period I did more than 250 hours of ride-alongs with police to investigate the front end of the cycle of crime. Innumerable welfare checks were conducted. Unless you show up with handcuffs, you aren't stopping anything. But handcuffs are a Band-Aid—a very temporary fix. Victims of domestic violence are scared to death to talk. More than once I heard, "If I say anything, he will kill me when he gets out" and "He'll be out in twenty-four hours. Then what?"

What I witnessed on most occasions after arrests were made and comprehensive reports were written was that the cases were dismissed—reduced to lesser charges or plea bargains where the victim, inevitably, suffered the most. How many beatings does it take to ask for help, and what kind of recourse does this leave for victims? The police are the public figures who take much of the blame. You won't see victims showing up at a district or state attorney's office asking why the case was dismissed. The victims of domestic abuse and intimate partner violence are confused and scared for their lives. They most likely don't know what happens after a peace officer does their job or why their case has been dismissed. Who tells the victim? Who?

Your typical criminal is after power and control. And the need for power is far-reaching—it's everywhere, including in the criminal justice and carceral system. This is a prime example of how our justice system is criminal-focused instead of victim-focused. If you are going to dismiss a case or dismiss charges, there must be mandatory follow-up, and it must be for an extended period of time so that victims of domestic abuse (or worse) can think clearly and be provided with the resources they need. Everyone in America should know that there is a safe place to go—for however long it takes. It feels ludicrous to write this. How can safety for victims of domestic violence not already be available everywhere? Ensuring safety would be a start. It most likely would fall to the police (or perhaps some kind good-faith officer), which in turn could show that policing is more than just restraining or stopping a crime momentarily.

||||

I'm starting to see a pattern with men and women in prisons, a lot of whom have dropped out of school and don't have GEDs. In 1989 you only needed to be sixteen years old to drop out of high school in Nebraska. Do you think X would have committed the crimes he did if he hadn't been allowed to quit school, if his parents and the state had made him stay in school whether he wanted to or not? How can states even consider letting teenagers quit school when they know teens' brains aren't fully developed? The fact that kids can drop out says a lot about the emotional intelligence of some of our policymakers and the parents of those kids who are allowed to give up. According to CNN, in 2012 (six years into my tenure as a teacher in prisons), "high school dropouts committed about 75 percent of crimes in the U.S."[4]

According to a 2022 Prison Policy Initiative report, "The State Prison Experience: Too Much Drudgery, Not Enough Opportunity," "an underutilized government dataset goes deep into daily life in state prisons—including work assignments, programming, and discipline—revealing lost opportunities for rehabilitation, education, and hope." The report's author, Leah Wang, writes the following:

> Offering education in prisons has a known return on investment, leading to well-documented reductions in recidivism and providing the credentials that lead to better jobs. People tend to enter prison with lower-than-average education levels, and were often under-supported and over-disciplined while in school. Yet instead of being able to make up for lost time by enrolling in educational programs, the *Survey* data reveal that only 43% of people in state prisons have participated in educational programming (even though 62% had not completed high school upon admission). Participation rates in education are similar among men and women and across age groups, though incarcerated women are more likely to have a high school education than incarcerated men.[5]

||||

I have spent almost a decade and a half doing my own time, working with and reading the writing of many prisoners. I acted as a counselor for many years. I bought into the myth that those in the government and in corrections truly care about rehabilitation, that the main reason they get up in the morning is to help others. Dr. Bill Miller, a criminologist, asked me very matter-of-factly, "What makes you think the department of corrections cares about rehabilitation?" A valid question. Then he asked me another question: "Why is nothing being written or done about corporate crimes that take place every single day?" It is easier to throw blame at one individual instead of entire companies and the systems that betray us daily. And really, doesn't that seem to be the American way? Find a patsy and convict? America doesn't seem as concerned with reducing crime as it is with assigning blame. Assigning blame ends that crime. Doing something about it takes WORK.

My colleague on campus at the federal prison, author Jamie Sullivan, said, "What makes your perspective special is not just the crime that haunts you, but the fact that you have worked with and read the writing of many prisoners." Then he asked, "What does our awareness of crime do to our sense of what is human? Maybe that's what the book is about."

We are all human beings who have made mistakes. Most of our mistakes won't land us behind bars, but we never truly know what the future holds. The vast majority of men and women I have worked with in jails and prisons have made some misdirected decisions, but they aren't any different from most people I know in the free world. Sullivan's words have helped guide me to all sorts of realizations.

||||

Media coverage of crime in our bizarrely real world has the effect of normalizing it rather than sensitizing us and making us more aware of its horrifying effects. You can open up a newspaper anywhere in America, from small-town USA to large urban cities, and find a series of regional and national stories—all about crime and criminals. If it bleeds, it leads—it runs above the fold. Turn on the TV, radio—it's the breaking news that networks rely on for ratings. Corruption and chaos are so much a part of our country—a country I love but am losing hope in. An insurrection in the U.S. Capitol, which is now denied—really? President Donald Trump "was found guilty on May 30 of 34 counts of falsifying business records after more than nine hours of deliberations, making him the first former American president to be convicted of felony crimes."[6] He's the only president ever to face criminal charges by the U.S. Department of Justice. According to *Politico*, "For the first 234 years of the nation's history, no American president or former president had ever been indicted. That changed in 2023."[7]

What is true and what is not true?

It's really hard not to get political in these times, not to question the foundation of the U.S. Constitution, our way of life, and our future. When you are fed lies through a multitude of media platforms, those stories become normalized. Has our culture changed since 2006 or so? Maybe social media has affected our communities both for good and bad; it definitely plays a role in all of this chaos. Behind our tiny screens, we have created cultures that express and promote ideologies that we can't seem to live without. We can just keep scrolling, suppress what we need to, stay in our silos, and call the "others" the "evil" ones.

If I was wrong about our relationship with social media, I don't think our society would embrace guns the way it does. Most countries don't allow citizens to conceal and carry, and most countries don't have nearly the number of gun crimes we do. We can celebrate all of this, and we do. This is our liberty and freedom and individuality—to buy and own whatever we choose (except "those one things") and to be whom we want to be (well, sometimes). If you live out in the country, away from police, owning your own gun is a necessity. Cops can't get there in time. Nor can they protect livestock from predators. Seeing a gun in the country—on a ranch or farm—is not the same as discovering a gun inside an apartment or home in the city. Where I grew up, if you saw a gun in a drawer—or worse yet, out in the open—it usually wasn't a good thing.

I'm a crime and mystery genre junkie. I love the suspense. But with our increasing exposure to crime and our cultivated culture of fear, I think we may be mixing up real crime with fictional crime. According to the president of Mount Marty University, my Crime, Literature, and Film class is the most popular elective on campus. I am intrigued by true-crime documentaries—I enjoy being scared by films—but I know that, for the most part, this isn't reality. And if we get too spooked, we can always turn off the television or put the book away.

When I asked students to describe their definition of and feelings about evil, one student, Paige Raker, wrote about a senseless mass shooting in 2007 at an Omaha mall where her aunt was gunned down and lost her life.

> As I got older, I heard more and more stories similar to the one that happened to my family and over time we became "used to it" and they all blend into one story. We tend to lose our sympathy and compassion because it's such a common occurrence, especially in America where we have an astronomically high incidence rate of mass casualties. Many people think this is a gun problem and that regulating and cracking down on gun control will fix this problem but, in all reality, this is not a gun problem it's a people problem. Evil lives in these individuals, whether they were "born that way" or a childhood of trauma is to

blame. I will end with a powerful quote by Ray Bradbury that fits this idea of mine, "Evil only has the power that we give it."[8]

Whether fact or fiction—news or Netflix—media coverage usually concentrates on the villain and the police, seldom the victim of crime. In the news, on shows, in documentaries and books, we hear partial stories. But what happens after the blood is dry? Who cleans up the crime scene? This is not *Pulp Fiction*—Harvey Keitel does not magically appear as the Wolf and clean the scene. Families are the ones who pick up the pieces, who scrub the blood from the carpet. There are no crime scene cleaners to call—not in real life. We don't hear about the victim's fear and dread.

If the villain is prosperous, they are seen as a success in the story—remember *Breaking Bad*? If they are caught, the police become the heroes. The victims are seldom successful protagonists. And what are we learning from this formula of storytelling? We are usually fed one side (either the detective or the criminal), not both sides. Telling a partial story is a version of fiction, too.

||||

As I tried to wrap my head around the notion of evil and as I interviewed and spoke about Christina's murder, I realized that I'd like to see as many people rehabilitated as possible. Like most advocates, I believe that looking into the eyes of criminals—to see who they are or could be—is more useful and important than the other option—an eye for an eye.

There will never be a decisive test to determine what true evil is. My personal feelings about X don't matter. When questioned about the topic now, I can simply say that this is why people like me, who have been affected by crimes like murder, don't make sentencing decisions.

I've learned a lot about trauma, how it affected me, and how much it must have affected others who were in my high school. What a crime like Christina's murder has done to Beth Ann and to Christina's family is indescribable. When things like this happen to us in our lives, we are told to talk with a counselor, talk with friends and family, and then move on. As a person who has spent some time in counselors', therapists', psychologists', and psychiatrists' offices, I can tell you that you don't have to move on. But do try to learn. Take that knowledge, apply it in the world, and help others. And let's stay with the criminals and rehabilitate all of them, whether or not all of them deserve to be released. We must stay with the victims—we must, for all of our communities that exist on both sides of razor wire. This is key. I didn't know that when I started this journey, but by helping others, I have discovered some peace and purpose.

||||

I knew there was a bigger story in the central essay—"Never Talk to Strangers—12 Years in Prisons and What Criminals Teach Me"—of my book *Bone Chalk*. (Passages from that essay appear throughout this book.) I am still glad there was something on record—snapshots and anecdotes, a testament to my teaching behind bars, and more importantly, the truth I was uncovering about our criminal justice system as I helped men and women find their voices and bear witness to what put them in a cage.

But to be honest, I didn't know how to summarize my fourteen years in the prisons and all the years before, when crime was having an effect on me. Maybe I could present it chronologically like the essay in the book. It was obvious that critics and fans wanted more. One journalist, perhaps in her own gonzo approach, went straight to the million-dollar question while interviewing me about the essay, asking, "Can we talk about this line . . . 'Is there a killer in me?'"

I was speechless. *That didn't happen*, I thought. It felt weird. What I wanted to say was that as a father, husband, and son, if anyone ever hurt my family, I'd want revenge. I suspect most people would. And if push ever came to shove, who knows what I, or any of us, would be capable of. But that wasn't the whole answer, either. I stumbled over responses to the journalist's question. Later, I realized that although I was frustrated by the question at the time, I would have led with that question, too. But taking my line—"Is there a killer in me?"—out of the context for the interview right out of the gate wasn't the best approach. I made mistakes early in my journalism career. I didn't heed the advice of my advisor and couldn't let a call and response go in interviews or editorial sections—I felt like I always needed the last word. And often the last word is a far cry from the original idea or argument. In my essay, "Is there a killer in me?" represents an awareness that a simple answer to the questions I was trying to answer wasn't possible.

And how do you summarize revenge? Hurt? Fear? Wickedness? Of course, like any father, I'd want retribution for my child's murder. But I also knew this was unreasonable thinking and that there was a deeper philosophical element behind these complex feelings. So I kept digging, kept listening and asking questions. I was starting to discover what the answers might and might not be—and my ambiguity and ambivalence were justified.

Bill Keller, Pulitzer Prize–winning journalist, former executive editor at the *New York Times*, and founding editor-in-chief of the Marshall Project, a nonprofit news organization that covers criminal justice in the United States, wrote the following in a 2022 report:

> Some newly galvanized critics rejected the very idea of humane prisons in favor of more radical alternatives to incarceration. One is "restorative justice," a protocol that—with the blessing of a judge—invites accused individuals and victims into a moderated discussion about the harm done and the best way to make amends. As Danielle Sered has pointed out, decades of studies identify four main conditions that foretell violent behavior: "shame, isolation, exposure to violence, and a diminished ability to meet one's economic needs." Those, she notes, are defining characteristics of life in American prisons. Sered, founder of the group Common Justice, works with district attorneys to deal with violent crime (excluding murder and rape) outside the traditional courts-and-corrections system. "One of the problems with prison," she said, "is that there is never a time in the prisoner's incarceration where they are required to actually grapple with the impact their choices had on other people's lives. . . . We've ended up with a country that is very rich in punishment and very poor in accountability."[9]

I think most people can agree that positive reinforcement from those closest to us helps us make positive changes. Change ultimately does come from within, but without external forces pointing you in the right direction, you are almost destined to fail. A lot of offenders don't have anyone to turn to. Don't we have a moral obligation to try to rehabilitate? To encourage growth? The problem is that there is a shortage of people and funding to do this work. As my friend Brian Daldorph, a twenty-year veteran of teaching at the Douglas County Jail in Kansas, said, "So many facilities are cutting programs because they're chronically short staffed. Everyone's struggling to get corrections workers."

You have to believe not only in helping your neighbor but even in helping the neighbor who has done wrong. That's a hard pill to swallow, especially when the person has done something heinous. An expression I've heard over and over is, "Jails and prisons are adult babysitting facilities." And the babysitters aren't getting paid nearly enough—they put their lives in danger by just going to work, all for less than you can make at many other places. In 1982 the average life expectancy of a correctional officer was fifty-nine years, as opposed to the average of seventy-five among the general population—this was eleven years into the war on drugs.[10] And frankly, the staff in most prisons where I've worked don't much care about helping incarcerated individuals. It is just a job—maybe the only one around for miles, besides the one at the Dollar General. There's very little talk about a mission or goal of rehabilitation. And it's really hard to rally workers to rehabilitate sex offenders and criminals guilty of rape and murder. I completely understand that.

Maybe corrections is set up to work exactly as intended. The real problem now is that states can't afford to keep incarcerating individuals. They are running out of manpower, space, and money to feed the machine. If you are just starting at Walmart in South Dakota, you can make $18.50 an hour working the night shift. All you have to do is stock shelves—and you don't have to risk your life.

||||

There are spiritual elements at play all around us; you can see them if you are listening and watching. I believe that something happens after all of this—that our time here on earth is not only a gift but a test, and that people who live an honorable life and help others will transcend into another life with their spirits and what they learned in this life.

Call me crazy, but I have to believe this. It's what keeps me hungry, grounded, and optimistic. I feel that, given my experience, I should be helping to inform and change our dialogue around incarceration. When trauma affects us, we should not turn the other way or try to suppress it. We need to listen to each other and learn.

For fourteen years I've helped men and women dig deep to tell their stories. I have listened and encouraged them to share their feelings, and that has made a difference to them and the others in class. I can't guarantee that they are going to be changed people when they are released, but for a time they have written their wrongs—their fears, their failures—and their hopes for a better life. It's the first step of many.

||||

I've never written anything as hard as this in my life. It's late, like most nights, when I sit in front of the screen—I carry this manuscript into the wee hours of the morning. I hammer it out because if I don't, I might let some people down, myself included. No one is holding a gun to my head, but I have goals. It would be foolish not to share what I'm learning by writing and what I've learned from working in prisons and from two years of ride-alongs and from almost becoming a reserve officer. What I have picked up along the way keeps pushing me toward new realizations. I hope that this book will help us remember Christina and other victims like her. I hope that we use our voices to make things better. This alchemy—this magical transformation during creation and realization—is my unrestrained rhapsody.

I didn't set out to write in great detail about Christina's murder. I didn't think I had the authority to. I was wrong. I didn't know I'd write about my own past the way I have. I had walked in a prison of my own making for far too many years. I've been telling everyone who has asked about my GONZO tattoo since I began my gonzo crusade that I am not happy at all that Hunter S. Thompson killed himself—with his grown son and grandkid in the house. What kind of fear and loathing is that? I see it as a sadness and pain that I hope I never experience.

I still believe in immersing myself in the story, however long it takes. I am fortunate to have a host of friends who have supported me and answered questions about criminals and what they believe evil could be. I remind myself of what Michael D. wrote—that rock and roll and marketing and promotion are antithetical—however, great leaders seem to embody both. Discipline. Like Ted Kooser has said time and again. Discipline. There's no easy button. You sit in your chair and write.

I think Chuck Bowden would want me to remind everyone of what he wrote on that casino voucher on the first day we met: "Appetite is the road to life and culture."

||||

Have I ever been an insider? No. With my freedom, I will never be "one of them"—a prisoner behind bars. But I am human and so are they. We are all family. Perhaps I can only help them realize that through my classes and by helping them write their memories.

"Never talk to strangers"—words drilled into us since we were children. But who really is alien in our culture? Could the stranger be the prison staff? The prison professor? How can anyone stand in judgment? Petty or not, we are all guilty. We exist within physical and sociological entrapments—concepts of freedom and staunch viewpoints—but these are all ideals we can free ourselves from if we are willing to learn.

||||

I daydream that maybe I'll spot some of you—holding your children's hands, running your tattoo parlors, catfishing in your favorite holler holes, facing your demons the best you know how.

Imagine a greeting from an aging mother who still relentlessly milks the Holsteins, imprisoned on her own farm, the smell of rotten silage and the overwhelming burden of not having enough time. She, though, will be waiting at her threshold, doors wide open for you.

Imagine the toy brontosaurus on laminate flooring pointing its head to your childhood bedroom—you will be welcomed again. When you board that Greyhound to the halfway house, keep your head high. With smart time, you'll have only two months to go.[11]

Perhaps I played a part in some of this healing, here in this place any of us could have landed after a few misdirected decisions.

Acknowledgments

I never thought I had the authority to talk about Christina's murder. But when I first mentioned her murder, and how it affected my classmates and me, in my book *Bone Chalk*, critics wanted to hear more about it. Critics and journalists also talked about serial killer John Joubert who had abducted kids and then murdered them for no apparent reason. I felt we needed to try to understand more, but I never thought this would result in a book. I didn't think I would search for years—learning about and understanding trauma and what crime does to families, communities, and secondary victims.

This book started as a chronological collection of anecdotes and lessons from working in prisons for fourteen years and turned into something I never would have imagined. Writing it has allowed me to explore something much larger than myself, something spiritual—an investigation and interrogation of my beliefs and ideas.

Inimitable content and developmental editors have acted as spiritual guides during my writing journey. The author Kent Meyers's guidance and suggestions are omnipresent throughout. Since we first became friends, Kent has pushed me to think hard—deeply—and to explore every possibility. He was the first person to introduce me to Chuck Bowden's work, and he was the first person who wasn't family who looked me in the eyes and showed a genuine concern for my well-being, who questioned certain decisions I was making. It made a difference. I am forever grateful for his help and advice.

My father, Mike Reese, helped me clean up my chaos—in life and in this book. He read through every section I had organized alphabetically—every anecdote that related to crime, punishment, addiction, and my own shame. After reading the section "She Talks to Angels," he told me not to change a word. That message gave me strength to believe in myself, even though I was writing about the time when I was at my worst. A writer faces self-doubt and delusion daily, and to lay it all out there on the page and then decide to share it with the world—it can be dehumanizing. But it can also be exactly what some people need to help themselves. My father, more than once, told me to stop beating myself up and second-guessing, and he always encouraged me to keep going. He has a knack for helping me edit and use my voice without telling me what to do, a skill I am trying to master with my own kids.

Thanks to my mother, Linda Reese, whose encouragement has never faltered and who sent me some crucial totems during the writing of this book.

Josh Klimek believed in my writing program in prisons when I first proposed it to him at the Yankton Mall, when he and his wife were selling ballet tickets. His wife was a deputy warden at the state prison at the time and had the program on its feet in two months. It was a prime example of music producer Rick Rubin's observation in his book *The Creative Act* that "if a piece of work, a fragment of consciousness, or an element of nature is somehow allowing us to access something bigger, that is its spiritual component made manifest. It awards us a glimpse of the unseen." Josh's voice is present throughout the book; we are all richer for his insight.

Chuck Bowden's spirit is always lurking. I hope my words about his amazing career make him proud, wherever he is flying. I am glad we became friends. He had made some big changes in his life and habits right before we met. He taught me that being a gonzo writer didn't have to mean killing yourself with booze. *You follow?* He said he didn't like teaching, but he's been one of the best mentors I've had.

Thank you to Potomac Books acquisitions editor Taylor Gilreath for believing in the manuscript. She understood the book's rehabilitative message and call to social activism, and she kept me moving forward with the pages and passages I doubted. Thank you for the close readings, constructive criticism, and insightful ideas. Thanks to Sandy Crump for her inimitable editing assistance. Thanks to the University of Nebraska Press and Potomac Books staff.

Thanks to warden Jordan R. Hollingsworth, who used to say, "These men are coming to a neighborhood near you. Do you want them educated or not?" After I heard him say this in 2009, I told him I was going to write a book one day and call it "Coming to a Neighborhood near You." He smiled and said, "Good. Do it."

Thanks to Patrick Hicks for the manuscript review that allowed me to move forward and the critique that made the manuscript better.

Thanks to J. Ryan Stradal for the constructive criticism and praise that really boosted my spirits right before a crucial editing phase.

Thanks to investigative journalist Bill Conroy for his steadfast drive, advice, and honest voice.

Thanks to Sophie and C. J. Reese for letting me tell some of their dad's stories.

Thanks to Michael D. Moore for encouraging me and for his part in this book.

Thanks to the Lammers and Reese families for their love and patience, and for letting me tell my stories.

Thanks to David Sedaris for the advice, encouragement, and opportunity to share the stage. That encouragement gave me strength as I was shopping this book to agents and publishers. And it continues to fuel the fire.

Thanks to Kimberly Verhines of Stephen F. Austin State University Press for letting me reprint parts of the essay "Never Talk to Strangers—12 Years in Prisons and What Criminals Teach Me" in this book.

Thanks to *Journal of the Southwest* editors Jeffrey Banister and Emma Pérez for first publishing "Redefining Gonzo: Tattoos, Prisons, and My Friend Charles Bowden."

Thanks to border and Latin America specialist Molly Molloy for her steadfast work at Frontera List and for her advice.

Thanks to the Charles Clyde Bowden Literary Trust.

Ted Kooser once said to me after a poetry reading, "Jim, that last poem was an entire Willa Cather novel." Thank you, Ted, for always pushing me to write nonfiction and for being a critical reader and friend.

Thank you to Daryl Farmer for always encouraging the early nonfiction work and for our lifelong friendship—Where(ever) We Land.

Thank you to Maria Mazziotti Gillan for your inimitable heart and giving a young poet a chance to travel east and perform when no other editor would.

To Ray Hammond at *New York Quarterly* and NYQ Books for the years of faith in my work and for believing in me—thanks for letting me reprint some of the poems that now appear as prose in this book.

Thanks to Tom Gannon, line and content editor extraordinaire. Thanks for offering new perspectives.

Thank you to Marc Cameron for our crime presentations and for your insight and wisdom.

Thank you to Dr. Kyle Roberson, Stephen Bell, Captain Samantha Bruening, Joe Weil, Neil Harrison, George Bilgere, Jim Daniels, Kevin Clark, Keith Lesmeister, Don Welch, Bill Kloefkorn, Jonis Agee, Marielle Frigge, Stephanie Schultz, Fran Streff, Christine Stewart, Kathy Magorian, Marilyn Johnson, Jamie Sullivan, Dana DeWitt, Cynthia Binder, Dante DiStefano, Kevin Carey, Paul Smith, Matt Mason, Dan Jenkins, Bret Gottschall (www.gotty.com), Lori Walsh, and South Dakota Public Radio; Bernie and Katie Hunhoff and *South Dakota Magazine*; Pete Dexter who encouraged me early on and told me what to work on; Jennifer Widman, Sherry DeBoer and the South Dakota Humanities Council; Grace Cavalieri and *The Poet and the Poem* at the Library of Congress; David Cremean, John Price, and Susan Maher, and Lauren Tuzzolino; and Beth Bienvenu at the National Endowment for the Arts.

Thanks to Shanna Ibarolle, Jerod Ibarolle, and Sarah Nizzi for letting me tell a bit of your stories. Thanks to Marc Long, Bill Miller, and Nick Shudak at Mount Marty. Thanks to Jerold Ryken, Danny Flahie, Ross Den Herder, and Dave "His poetry doesn't even rhyme!" Dannenbring for our friendship and for listening to me talk shop.

Thanks to Javier Murguia, special agent at the South Dakota Division of Criminal Investigation, for the two hundred hours of ride-alongs and for encouraging my true-crime writing.

To my past and present students at Mount Marty and the various prisons where I taught—thanks for pushing me to practice what I preach.

Linda, thank you for seeing me through and for your continued belief in me. And, of course, for Willow and Paige. My hope as a husband and father is that I make you proud and that we continue to use our voices for positive change.

Notes

1. The Shadows We Carry

1. For the purposes of this book, I have not used the killer's name in the text or in quoted material.
2. Katherine Ramsland, "John Joubert, Nebraska Boy Snatcher," Crime Library: Criminal Minds and Methods, n.d., https://www.crimelibrary.org/serial_killers/predators/john_joubert/index.html.
3. State v. Joubert, 399 N.W.2d 237 (Neb. 1986), Justia, US Law, https://law.justia.com/cases/nebraska/supreme-court/1986/843-8.html.
4. Marco Margaritoff, "Inside the Chilling Crimes of John Joubert, the Eagle Scout Who Became a Serial Killer," All That's Interesting, January 10, 2022, https://allthatsinteresting.com/john-joubert.
5. Joe Chiodo, "Killer Faces Resentencing in 1990 Murder . . . ," WOWT 6 News, n.d., accessed December 19, 2019, https://www.wowt.com/home/headlines/Killer-faces-resentencing-in-1990-murder-368620461.html. The killer's name has been changed to X throughout the quote.
6. Samantha Enslen, "What's It Called When You Refer to Yourself By Name?," Quick and Dirty Tips, March 30, 2018, https://www.quickanddirtytips.com/articles/whats-it-called-when-you-refer-to-yourself-by-name/.
7. Christopher Turner, "20 Things You Didn't Know about *The Silence of the Lambs*," AmongMen, 2021, https://www.amongmen.com/entertainment/20-things-you-didnt-know-about-the-silence-of-the-lambs/.
8. Tracy Moore, "'Jonathan, Are You Crazy?': The Making and Meaning of *The Silence of the Lambs*," *Vanity Fair*, February 16, 2021, https://www.vanityfair.com/hollywood/2021/02/the-abiding-complicated-legacy-of-the-silence-of-the-lambs.
9. Moore, "Jonathan, Are You Crazy?"

10. "Transcript: Donald Trump's Taped Comments about Women," *New York Times*, October 8, 2016, https://www.nytimes.com/2016/10/08/us/donald-trump-tape-transcript.html.
11. "Man Caught Peeking in Outhouse," *Santa Maria Times*, August 4, 1987, https://www.newspapers.com/image/446810890/.
12. Greg Howard, "Why 'Transcending Race' Is a Lie," *New York Times Magazine*, June 17, 2016, https://www.nytimes.com/2016/06/17/magazine/why-transcending-race-is-a-lie.html.
13. David Doody, review of *ghost on 3rd*, by Jim Reese, *American Poetry Journal* 10 (2011), http://jimreese.org/wp-content/uploads/2011/02/ghost_on_3rd_review_American_Poetry_Journal.pdf.
14. Kent Meyers, email message to author, May 1, 2023.
15. Erin Grace, "Grace: She Listened as Baby Sitter Was Murdered, and She Wants Killer to Never Walk Free," *Omaha World-Herald*, February 12, 2016, https://www.omaha.com/columnists/grace/grace-she-listened-as-baby-sitter-was-murdered-and-she/article_6ed32a35-44a6-5f0b-8647-ce68f280e55f.html.
16. The Santan Canary Award is South Dakota's highest honor in corrections. Klimek was nominated for the award by the South Dakota Corrections Association in a peer-reviewed selection process.
17. Josh Klimek, interview with author, June 26, 2021.
18. Krista Tippett, host, *On Being with Krista Tippett*, podcast, "Mary Karr—Astonished by the Human Comedy," October 13, 2016, https://onbeing.org/programs/mary-karr-astonished-by-the-human-comedy-jan2018/.
19. Rui Costa, Stephen Machin, and Brian Bell, "Why Education Reduces Crime," VoxEU, October 14, 2018, https://cepr.org/voxeu/columns/why-education-reduces-crime.
20. Jim Reese, "Never Talk to Strangers—12 Years in Prisons and What Criminals Teach Me," in *Bone Chalk* (Stephen F. Austin State University Press, 2020), 63.
21. Reese, "Never Talk to Strangers," 63.
22. State v. Garza, 492 N.W.2d 32 (Neb. 1992), Justia, US Law, https://law.justia.com/cases/nebraska/supreme-court/1992/283-1.html.
23. "How Sociopaths and Psychopaths Are Different," WebMD, March 16, 2023, https://www.webmd.com/mental-health/features/sociopath-psychopath-difference.
24. "Man Loses Appeal of 90-Year Prison Sentence in 1990 Killing," Associated Press, December 30, 2016, https://apnews.com/article/85cab160584540288

a112ae3d9be5430. The killer's name has been changed to X throughout the quote.

25. Comments made on the *Omaha World-Herald* article posted on Facebook. Paul Hammel, "Convicted Murderer Christopher Garza Has Lost Another Appeal of His New Sentence for the Gruesome Slaying of a Teenage Baby Sitter," *Omaha World-Herald,* April 10, 2018, https://www.facebook.com/WorldHerald/posts/convicted-murderer-christopher-garza-has-lost-another-appeal-of-his-new-sentence/10156340858309630/.
26. State v. Garza, 888 N.W.2d 526 (Neb. 2016), Leagle, https://www.leagle.com/decision/inneco20161230206. The killer's name has been changed to X throughout the quote.
27. Paul Hammel, "Man Resentenced for 1990 Murder of Teen Loses High Court Appeal," *Omaha World-Herald,* December 30, 2016, https://omaha.com/news/crime/man-resentenced-for-1990-murder-of-teen-loses-high-court-appeal/article_1cee05d0-ceb8-11e6-ba13-b3d5b536457a.html. The killer's name has been changed to X throughout the quote.
28. Joe Chiodo, "High Court Rejects Killer's Appeal That 96-Year Sentence Was Excessive," WOWT 6 News, February 12, 2016, https://www.wowt.com/content/news/Nebraska-Supreme-Court-rejects-killers-appeal-408834585.html.
29. Grace, "Grace: She Listened as Baby Sitter Was Murdered."
30. Fritzi Horstman, email message to author, September 20, 2021.

2. Redefining Gonzo

1. U.S. Attorney's Office, Eastern District of New York, "Ex-Mexican Secretary of Public Security Genaro Garcia Luna Convicted of Engaging in a Continuing Criminal Enterprise and Taking Millions in Cash Bribes from the Sinaloa Cartel," news release, February 21, 2023, https://www.justice.gov/usao-edny/pr/ex-mexican-secretary-public-security-genaro-garcia-luna-convicted-engaging-continuing.
2. "More Than 29,000 Homicide Victims in Mexico in 2017," Frontera List, January 24, 2018, accessed September 13, 2018, https://fronteralist.org/2018/01/24/more-than-29000-homicide-victims-in-mexico-in-2017/.
3. Executive Secretary of the National Public Security System, Government of Mexico, "Víctimas y unidades robadas, nueva metodología," https://www.gob.mx/sesnsp/acciones-y-programas/victimas-nueva-metodologia?state=published.

4. International Commission on Missing Persons, "Mexico," https://icmp.int/what-we-do/geographic-programs/mexico/.
5. Jim Reese, "WSC Students Volunteer for Kerrey—NORML Helps Senator, Imparts Ideas on Legalizing Marijuana," *Wayne Stater* 82, no. 7 (October 12, 1994): 1.
6. Patrick Doyle, "How Hunter S. Thompson Became a Legend," *Rolling Stone*, July 18, 2019, https://www.rollingstone.com/culture/culture-news/rolling-stone-at-50-how-hunter-s-thompson-became-a-legend-115371/.
7. Nikki Finke, "The New Hunter S. Thompson: A Doctor of Gonzo Journalism Turns Political Man," *LA Times*, October 18, 1987, https://www.latimes.com/archives/la-xpm-1987-10-18-vw-15236-story.html.
8. Christopher Ingraham, "The U.S. Has More Jails than Colleges. Here's a Map of Where Those Prisoners Live," *Washington Post*, January 6, 2015, https://www.washingtonpost.com/news/wonk/wp/2015/01/06/the-u-s-has-more-jails-than-colleges-heres-a-map-of-where-those-prisoners-live/.
9. Jim Reese, "Never Talk to Strangers—12 Years in Prisons and What Criminals Teach Me," in *Bone Chalk* (Stephen F. Austin State University Press, 2020), 59–60.
10. Charles Bowden, "The Sicario: A Juárez Hit Man Speaks," *Harper's Magazine*, September 8, 2014, https://harpers.org/archive/2009/05/the-sicario/. Permission to reprint granted by the Charles Clyde Bowden Literary Trust.
11. Charles Bowden, *Red Line* (University of Texas Press, 2018 [1989]), 10.
12. Douglas Brinkley, "Football Season Is Over: Hunter S. Thompson, 1937–2005," *Rolling Stone*, June 22, 2005, https://www.rollingstone.com/culture/culture-news/football-season-is-over-hunter-s-thompson-1937-2005-171034/.
13. Henry David Thoreau, *The Essays of Henry David Thoreau*, ed. Richard Dillman (Rowman & Littlefield, 1992), 80.
14. "Directory of U.S. Free or Low-Cost Tattoo Removal Programs," Jails to Jobs, https://jailstojobs.org/resources/tattoo-removal-programs/. "Prison Tattoos" originally appeared in Jim Reese, "Redefining Gonzo: Tattoos, Prisons, and My Friend Charles Bowden," *Journal of the Southwest* 65, no. 1 (Spring 2023), 122–23. Reprinted here by permission.
15. Bill Conroy, *Dispatches from the House of Death* (Moonshine Cove Publishing, 2023), 290.
16. Publisher's summary for *El Sicario: The Autobiography of a Mexican Assassin*, ed. Molly Molloy and Charles Bowden. New York: Nation Books, 2011.

17. Cover copy for Celeste González de Bustamente and Jeannine E. Relly, *Surviving Mexico: Resistance and Resilience among Journalists in the Twenty-First Century* (University of Texas Press, 2021).
18. Neil Harrison, email to author, March 29, 2024.
19. Chuck Bowden and Molly Molloy, "A Letter for MMC Students from Charles Bowden and Molly Molloy," *Paddlefish* (2014–15): 43. Permission to reprint granted by the Charles Clyde Bowden Literary Trust.
20. "Frontera List," Google Groups, https://groups.google.com/g/frontera-list.
21. Molly Molloy, "Give Us This Day Our Daily Massacre . . . ," *Paddlefish* (2010): 126.
22. The White House, Office of the Press Secretary, "Fact Sheet: White House Launches the Fair Chance Business Pledge," news release, April 11, 2016, https://obamawhitehouse.archives.gov/the-press-office/2016/04/11/fact-sheet-white-house-launches-fair-chance-business-pledge.
23. "Policy Impact," RAND, https://www.rand.org/well-being/justice-policy/portfolios/correctional-education/policy-impact.html.
24. Charles Bowden, email messages to author, May 4, 2010, and July 10, 2013. Permission to reprint granted courtesy of the Charles Clyde Bowden Literary Trust.
25. Bernie Hunhoff, email message to author, 2012.
26. James Jones, *From Here to Eternity* (Charles Scribner's Sons, 1951; repr., Dell Publishing, 1998), 216. Citations refer to the Dell Publishing edition.
27. Kent Meyers, email message to author, March 2, 2023.
28. Kent Meyers, email message to author, March 2, 2023.
29. Charles Bowden, "Investigative Reporting," unpublished manuscript, 2011. Permission to reprint granted by the Charles Clyde Bowden Literary Trust.

3. Crime as Entertainment

1. California Department of Corrections and Rehabilitation, *Adult Institutions, Programs, and Parole Operations Manual* (2021), https://www.cdcr.ca.gov/wp-content/uploads/sites/186/2019/06/article-44-prea-policy-may-15-2018.pdf.
2. Jim Reese, "Never Talk to Strangers—12 Years in Prisons and What Criminals Teach Me," in *Bone Chalk* (Stephen F. Austin State University Press, 2020), 48.
3. This excerpt originally appeared in Reese, "Never Talk to Strangers," 48-49. Reprinted with permission.

4. Graeme Wood, "How Gangs Took Over Prisons," *The Atlantic*, October 2014, https://www.theatlantic.com/magazine/archive/2014/10/how-gangs-took-over-prisons/379330/.
5. "San Quentin Receives 'the Ophir Prison Marching KazooBand and Temperance Society,'" *San Quentin News*, December 1, 2008, https://sanquentinnews.com/san-quentin-receives-the-ophir-prison-marching-kazooband-temperance-society/.
6. "About Us," *San Quentin News*, https://sanquentinnews.com/about-us/.
7. Bill "Woody" Woodward, "Working with the Incarcerated: San Quentin, California," University of Pennsylvania alumni newsletter, n.d., https://www.alumni.upenn.edu/s/1587/images/gid2/editor_documents/classes_and_reunions-non_reunion_docs/1968/1968_woody_woodward_for_may_3_class_email.pdf.
8. "About," *Ear Hustle*, https://www.earhustlesq.com/about.
9. "Our Story," Mount Tamalpais College, https://www.mttamcollege.edu/about/our-story/.
10. Juan Haines, "Newsom: Major Changes Ahead for San Quentin," *San Quentin News*, April 27, 2023, https://sanquentinnews.com/newsom-major-changes-ahead-for-san-quentin/.
11. Wendy Corr, "Author Craig Johnson Says No Immediate Plans to Bring Back 'Longmire' Series," *Cowboy State Daily*, April 21, 2022, https://cowboystatedaily.com/2022/04/21/author-craig-johnson-says-no-immediate-plans-to-bring-back-longmire/.
12. Tayler Stephenson, "Craig Johnson's Personal Take on *Longmire* Days and His New Book," *Oil City News*, August 28, 2021, https://oilcity.news/community/2021/08/28/craig-johnsons-personal-take-on-the-the-upcoming-events-and-his-new-book/.
13. Kieran Nicholson, "Christopher Watts Documentary on Murdered Colorado Family Has Netflix Premiere," *Denver Post*, September 30, 2020, https://www.denverpost.com/2020/09/30/christopher-watts-documentary-premiere-netflix/.
14. Nicholson, "Christopher Watts Documentary."
15. "O.J.: I Did Not, Could Not and Would Not Have Committed This Crime," *The Record*, September 23, 1995, https://www.recordnet.com/story/news/1995/09/23/o-j-i-did-not/50861708007/.
16. Rick Rubin, *The Creative Act: A Way of Being* (Penguin Press, 2023), 179.
17. Rubin, *The Creative Act*, 33.

18. Adrienne Tyler, "Every Stephen King Story Inspired by His Own Life," Screen Rant, July 13, 2022, https://screenrant.com/stephen-king-books-true-story-real-life-inspirations/.
19. This story originally appeared as "The Snorers" in *Oakwood 2024* (South Dakota State University), 174–76.
20. *Inside the Labyrinth: The Making of "The Silence of the Lambs,"* directed by Jeffrey Schwarz (Automat Pictures, 2001).
21. Christopher Turner, "20 Things You Didn't Know about *The Silence of the Lambs*," AmongMen, 2021, https://www.amongmen.com/entertainment/20-things-you-didnt-know-about-the-silence-of-the lambs/.
22. Jim Harter, "In New Workplace, U.S. Employee Engagement Stagnates," Gallup, January 23, 2024, https://www.gallup.com/workplace/608675/new-workplace-employee-engagement-stagnates.aspx.
23. Kevin Mims, "High White Notes: The Rise and Fall of Gonzo Journalism—A Review," Quillette, November 11, 2021, https://quillette.com/2021/11/11/high-white-notes-a-review/.

4. What They Do Not Tell You, Part 1

1. "South Dakota Profile," Prison Policy Initiative, https://www.prisonpolicy.org/profiles/SD.html.
2. "Recidivism Rates by State 2024," World Population Review, https://worldpopulationreview.com/state-rankings/recidivism-rates-by-state.
3. Chris Bowling, "A Day in the Life (and Death) of Whiteclay," *Nebraska Quarterly* (Fall 2017): 40.
4. Fred Knapp, "Views of Whiteclay Mixed, a Year after the Beer Stores Closed," Nebraska Public Media, May 18, 2018, https://nebraskapublicmedia.org/en/news/news-articles/views-of-whiteclay-mixed-a-year-after-the-beer-stores-closed/.
5. Morgan Voigt, "10 Facts You Probably Didn't Know about the Library of Congress," DCist, February 12, 2020, https://dcist.com/story/20/02/12/10-facts-you-probably-didnt-know-about-the-library-of-congress/.
6. Jim Reese, *Dancing Room Only—New and Selected Poems* (New York: NYQ Books, 2024), 120.
7. Rita Pierson, "Every Kid Needs a Champion," TED Talk, New York, April 2013, 7 min., 34 sec., https://www.ted.com/talks/rita_pierson_every_kid_needs_a_champion.

8. AP News, "Iowa Man Sentenced to Prison for Killing Girlfriend's Father," https://apnews.com/994b8c7c2d2f4debbe312daa0ca130c5.
9. "Educational Programs," Allegheny County Jail, Allegheny County, PA, https://www.alleghenycounty.us/Government/County-Jail/Programs-and-Services/Educational-Programs.
10. Randy Dockendorf, "GED a New Start: Springfield Prison Inmates Rebuild Their Lives through Education," *Yankton Daily Press and Dakotan*, November 9, 2017, https://www.yankton.net/community/article_e3f00f3a-c5ce-11e7-a565-5fb24a87723f.html.

5. Premeditation

1. Bill Conroy, email message to author, April 8, 2024.
2. Josh Klimek, email message to author, April 26, 2023.
3. John H. Esperian, "The Effect of Prison Education Programs on Recidivism," *Journal of Correctional Education* 61, no. 4 (December 2010): 316–34, https://www.jstor.org/stable/23282764.
4. Dave Barry, *Dave Barry Turns 50* (Crown, 1998), 182.
5. Jim Mustian and Joshua Goodman, "AP Report: Former DEA Agent Tells His Own Story of Corruption before Jail Time," PBS News, November 14, 2022, https://www.pbs.org/newshour/politics/the-drug-war-is-a-game-collaborating-with-cartels-money-laundering-how-a-dea-agent-became-the-agencys-most-corrupt.
6. Marc Cameron, email message to author, March 2, 2022.
7. Marc Cameron and Jim Reese, "What Writers Can Learn from Cops and Criminals," presentation at the South Dakota Humanities Council Festival of Books, September 2021.
8. Josh Klimek, interview with author, June 26, 2021.
9. Thomas Gannon, email message to author, July 30, 2023.
10. Scott A. McGreal, "Are Psychopaths Really Smarter than the Rest of Us?," *Psychology Today*, December 11, 2016, https://www.psychologytoday.com/intl/blog/unique-everybody-else/201612/are-psychopaths-really-smarter-the-rest-us.
11. Asher Hawkins, "In Pictures: America's 10 Cushiest Prisons," *Forbes*, July 11, 2012, https://www.forbes.com/2009/07/13/best-prisons-cushiest-madoff-personal-finance-lockups_slide.html#30b2b2f3fb6f.
12. U.S. Federal Bureau of Prisons, "Population Statistics," updated October 31, 2024, https://www.bop.gov/about/statistics/population_statistics.jsp.

13. Marielle Frigge, email message to author, quoted in Jim Reese, "Never Talk to Strangers—12 Years in Prisons and What Criminals Teach Me," in *Bone Chalk* (Stephen F. Austin State University Press, 2020), 55.
14. Marielle Frigge, email message to author, quoted in Reese, "Never Talk to Strangers," 61–62.
15. The section "A Student Talk of Her Sister's Murder" originally appeared in Reese, "Never Talk to Strangers," 60. Reprinted with permission.
16. Bill Miller, interview with author, March 28, 2023.
17. Kent Meyers, email message to author, April 12, 2023.

6. The Deputy and Imminent Danger

1. *Blocks*, directed by Derek DelGaudio, written by Neal Brennan, aired in 2022, on Netflix.
2. Justin McMurray, email message to author, December 31, 2022.

7. What They Do Not Tell You, Part 2

1. Erec Toso, "Composing Humanity in Prison Writing Workshops," *Rain Shadow Review* 5, (2015): 1.

8. She Talks to Angels

1. Jordan Langs, "Poverty Impedes Children's Education Long Before They Enter the Classroom—Here's How We Can Change That," *Forbes*, April 12, 2022, https://www.forbes.com/sites/forbeseq/2022/04/04/poverty-impedes-childrens-education-long-before-they-enter-the-classroom---heres-how-we-can-change-that/.
2. "Violence against Women," World Health Organization, March 25, 2024, https://www.who.int/news-room/fact-sheets/detail/violence-against-women.
3. Michael D. Moore, interview with author, 2021.
4. Ted Kooser, *Splitting an Order* (University of Nebraska Press, 2008), 4. Used with permission.

9. Coda

1. M. Alper, M. R. Duros, and J. Markman, "2018 Update on Prisoner Recidivism: A 9-Year Follow-Up Period (2005–2014)," Special Report NCJ 250975 (Washington DC: U.S. Department of Justice, Office of Justice Programs, Bureau of Justice Statistics, May 2018), https://www.bjs.gov/content/pub/pdf/18upr9yfup0514.pdf.

2. “The Relationship between Incarceration and Low Literacy,” Literacy Mid-South, https://www.literacymidsouth.org/news/the-relationship-between-incarceration-and-low-literacy.
3. Kent Meyers, email message to author, 2022.
4. Donna Krache, “By the Numbers: High School Dropouts,” CNN, June 20, 2012, https://www.cnn.com/2012/06/20/us/by-the-numbers-high-school-dropouts/index.html.
5. Leah Wang, “The State Prison Experience: Too Much Drudgery, Not Enough Opportunity,” Prison Policy Initiative, September 2, 2022, https://www.prisonpolicy.org/blog/2022/09/02/prison_opportunities/.
6. Michael R. Sisak, “New York Hush Money Case,” AP News, updated September 7, 2024, https://apnews.com/projects/trump-investigations-civil-criminal-tracker/.
7. “Tracking the Trump Criminal Cases,” *Politico*, updated November 6, 2024, https://www.politico.com/interactives/2023/trump-criminal-investigations-cases-tracker-list/.
8. Paige Raker, email message to author, July 9, 2023.
9. Bill Keller, *What's Prison For? Punishment and Rehabilitation in the Age of Mass Incarceration* (Columbia Global Reports, 2022).
10. F. Cheek and M. D. S. Miller, “Reducing Staff and Inmate Stress,” *Corrections Today* 44, no. 5 (October 1982): 72–76, 78.
11. Jim Reese, “Never Talk to Strangers—12 Years in Prisons and What Criminals Teach Me,” in *Bone Chalk* (Stephen F. Austin State University Press, 2020), 66.

www.ingramcontent.com/pod-product-compliance
Lightning Source LLC
Chambersburg PA
CBHW030816110725
29381CB00003B/3
* 9 7 8 1 6 4 0 1 2 6 6 7 1 *